Mr Jelly's Business

Other Titles by Arthur W. Upfield:

1 The Barrakee Mystery

2 The Sands of Windee

3 Wings Above the Diamantina

4 Mr Jelly's Business

5 Winds of Evil

6 The Bone is Pointed

7 The Mystery of Swordfish Reef

8 Bushranger of the Skies

9 Death of a Swagman

10 The Devil's Steps

11 An Author Bites the Dust

12 The Mountains Have a Secret

13 The Widows of Broome

14 The Bachelors of Broken Hill

15 The New Shoe

16 Venom House

17 Murder Must Wait

18 Death of a Lake

19 The Cake in the Hat Box

20 The Battling Prophet

21 Man of Two Tribes

22 Bony Buys a Woman

23 Bony and the Mouse

24 Bony and the Black Virgin

25 Bony and the Kelly Gang

26 Bony and the White Savage

27 The Will of the Tribe

28 Madman's Bend

29 The Lake Frome Monster

ARTHUR W. UPFIELD

Mr Jelly's Business

ETT IMPRINT
Exile Bay

This edition published in 2018 by ETT IMPRINT, Exile Bay

ETT IMPRINT & *www.arthurupfield.com*

PO Box R1906,
Royal Exchange
NSW 1225 Australia

First published 1937
This ett edition published 2018

Copyright William Upfield 1937, 2018

ISBN 978-1-925416-96-1 (pb)

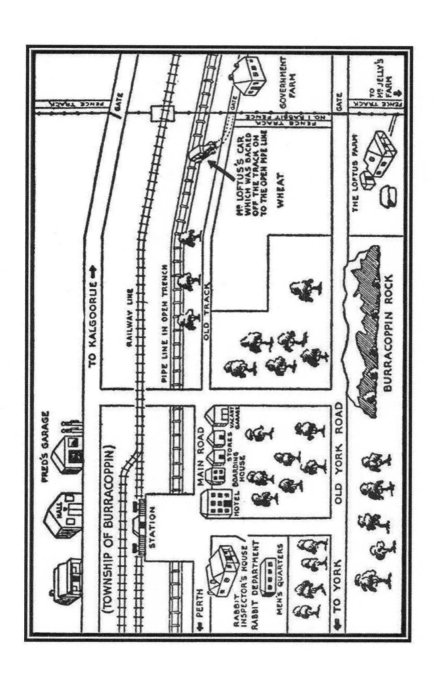

Chapter One

Napoleon Bonaparte's Holiday

If it had not rained! If only the night of 2nd November had been fine! Raining thirty points that most important night was sheer cursed bad luck.

John Muir sauntered along the south side of Hay Street, Perth, heedless of the roaring traffic and of the crowd. To him the life and movement of the capital city of Western Australia was then of blank unconcern; of greater moment was the heavy shadow of failure resting on his career. To the average ambitious man temporary failure may mean little, and that little but the spur to the posts of achievement; failure now and then interposed among marked successes to one of Muir's profession merely delays advancement; but failure repeated twice, one treading on the heels of the other, raised the bogey of supersession.

Detective-Sergeant Muir was not a big man as policemen go. There was no hint of the bulldog about his chin, or of the bull about his neck. Although he walked as walks every officer in the Police Force, having attended that school of the beat in which every constable is enrolled, John Muir in appearance looked far less a policeman than a smart cavalryman. Not much over forty years old, red of hair and complexion, he did not seem cut out to be a victim of worry: worry crowned him with peculiar incongruity. So deep were his cogitations about the weather that it was not the hand placed firmly on his left shoulder, nor the words spoken, but the soft drawling voice which said:

"Come! Take a little walk with me."

It was a phrase he himself had often used, and the fact that other lips close to his ear now uttered it produced less surprise than did the well-remembered voice. The drabness of his mood gave instant place to the lights of the world about him. He swung towards the kerb, caught the arm of the man whose hand was upon his shoulder, and gazed with wonder and delight into a pair of beaming blue eyes set in a ruddy brown face.

"Bony! By the Great Wind, it's Bony!"

"I at first thought you were the ghost of the Earl of Strafford on his way to the block," Detective-Inspector Napoleon Bonaparte said gravely. "Then I was reminded of poor Sinbad the Sailor, wearied by the old fellow who so loved him. Why the mantle of gloom this bright Australian morning?"

"Where were you the night of the second of November?" demanded John Muir, his grey eyes twinkling with leaping happiness.

"November the second! Let me think. Ah! I was at home at Banyo, near Brisbane, with Marie, my wife, and Charles, and little Ed. I was reading to them Maeterlinck's ——"

"Did it rain that night?" Muir cut in as though he were the prosecuting counsel at a major trial.

His mind being taken back to the night of importance by Muir's first question, Bony was able to answer the second without hesitation.

"No. It was fine and cool."

"Then why the dickens couldn't it have been fine and cool at Burracoppin, Western Australia?"

"The answer is quite beyond me."

Detective-Sergeant Muir, of the Western Australian Police, slipped an arm through that of Detective-Inspector Napoleon Bonaparte, of the Queensland Police, and urged his superior across the street. The delight this chance meeting gave him, resulting in this impulsive act, suggested to the constable just behind them that the quietly dressed half-caste aboriginal was indeed taking officially a little walk with the detective- sergeant. He became puzzled when the two entered a teashop on the opposite side of the street.

They were fortunate to secure a table in a corner.

"The fact that it rained a certain night at a particular place seems to perturb you," Bony remarked, with his inimitable blandness, after tea and cakes had been set before them.

"What are you doing here?" Muir asked with a trace of anxiety.

"Waiting for you to pour out my tea." Bony's deep blue eyes shone quizzingly. Perfect teeth gleamed between his lips when he spoke. His fine black hair, well brushed, had the lustre of polished ebony.

"Well, what are you doing here in the West?"

"Impulsive as ever, John. Your head is full of questions as uncontrollable as the tides. After all my interest taken in your career, despite my careful coaching extending over a period of eight years, in spite of your appearance, which is less like that of a policeman than any policeman I know, you flagrantly give away to even the most unsuspecting person your precise profession through your excessive questionings."

John Muir laughed.

"By the Great Wind, Bony, old chump, I'm glad you are with me in this teashop," he exclaimed with dancing eyes. "I've been wanting one man in all the world to get me out of a thunderin' deep hole, and lo! that man whispers into my ear'ole: 'Come, take a little walk with me.' But tell us the story. How is it you're in Perth just when I needed you?"

Muir was like a youth in the presence of a generously tipping uncle.

Softly Bony murmured, "I am here because you wanted me."

"You knew it? How did you know?"

"You made a tangle of the Gascoyne affair, didn't you?" Bony countered accusingly.

"Ye-es, I am afraid I did."

When next he spoke Bony's gaze was centered upon his plate.

"After all my tuition you took a creek without first ascertaining the depth of the water. You accepted a conclusion not based on logical deduction. You ignored science, our greatest ally after Father Time. It was unfortunate that you arrested Greggs, wasn't it?"

John Muir mentally groaned. Bony, looking up swiftly into his grey eyes, saw once again the shadow.

"You see, John, I have been following your career closely," he went on in his calm, pleasant manner. "Because a man's trousers are bloodstained, it does not follow that the blood on them is human blood. Granted that at the time you did not know Greggs was a sheep-stealer supplying the local butcher with cheap meat, you should, however, have walked slowly, making sure that the stains of blood were human or animal, and making equally sure Greggs did not get away whilst you were walking. Jumping thus to a most unscientific conclusion, which that great mathematician, Euclid, would have bitingly termed absurd, you permitted Andrews to get clear away."

"I know, I know! What a fool I was!"

"Hardly a fool, John, but too impetuous. And now, why your worry regarding the weather during the night of November the second?"

Again sunlight chased away the shadows. From an inside pocket John Muir produced a wallet, and from the wallet a roughly drawn plan, which he laid before Bony.

"Here's a drawing of a wheat town and locality named Burracoppin, one hundred and eighty miles east of Perth on the goldfields' line," the sergeant explained. "For eight days prior to the second of November a farmer named George Loftus was down here in Perth on business and pleasure. The licensee of the Burracoppin Hotel, Leonard Wallace, met Loftus in Perth during the afternoon of November the first, and Loftus, having unexpectedly completed his business, offered Wallace a lift to Burracoppin the next day.

"They left Perth at ten o'clock, and, as Loftus's car is a light one, it was ten o'clock that night when they arrived at Wallace's pub. After supper they went to the bar and stayed there drinking until one o'clock. By that time, according to Wallace, they were both well down by the stern. He says that when they went out to the car it was raining, and he urged Loftus to stay the night. But Loftus appears to be a pigheaded man in drink, and, drunk as he was, determined to drive home. Wallace, deciding to go with him, induced Loftus to wait while he informed Mrs Wallace. She heard them set off at ten minutes past one."

With a stub of pencil Muir indicated the plan.

"When they left the hotel Loftus drove along the main road eastward. At the garage he should have turned south to the old York Road, a mile farther on, which would have brought him to the Number One Rabbit Fence in about another mile. This night, however, Loftus drove straight on east, following the railway, and Wallace expostulated, as this road was in bad condition. They had proceeded a quarter of a mile, still arguing, when Loftus stopped the car and ordered Wallace to get out. He then drove on alone, according to Wallace. He had about one mile to travel before reaching the rabbit fence, where he would turn south, traverse it for another mile, cross the old York Road, and after covering a third mile would arrive opposite his farm gate.

"But he never reached home. He crashed into the rabbit fence gate, and, when backing his car, backed the car into the State water-supply pipeline, which at that place runs along a deeply excavated trench. The car was smashed badly, of course. It was impossible for Loftus to get its back wheels up out of the trench. His hat was found beside the car, and Wallace's hat was found on the back seat. Close by were two newly opened beer bottles.

"Of Loftus there had been no sign since Wallace, as he alleges, parted from him about one-twenty A.M. A search lasting twelve days has produced no result. If only it hadn't rained thirty points the black tracker, brought from Merredin, would have picked out Loftus's tracks, and have found him dead or alive."

Muir ceased talking.

"Well?" urged Bony.

"The funny part about the affair is the time Wallace reached home. When he alighted from the car they were less than half a mile from the hotel. They left the hotel, remember, at one-ten. It would be one-twenty, no later, when they parted company, yet it was two-fifteen when he entered his bedroom, according to Mrs Wallace. He states that when Loftus drove away he walked back as far as the garage turning; there, feeling the effects of too much grog, he turned up along the south road for a walk.

"I think he did nothing of the sort: it doesn't sound reasonable. Yet what did he do during those fifty-five minutes? He wouldn't require fifty-five minutes to walk back to his home, a distance of less than half a mile. But if the two were together at the time of the smash, if they fought and Wallace killed Loftus, there was time to hide the body and get back home at the time Mrs Wallace said he did."

"You have not found a body?" interposed Bony.

"No."

"Then until a body is discovered we must assume that Loftus is still living. Has Wallace a record?"

"Nothing against him."

"You are sure that Loftus did not reach his home?"

"Quite. Mrs Loftus is frantic about him."

"Is the car still wedged above the pipeline?"

"Yes."

"Why not arrest Wallace on suspicion?"

"Not on your life. Greggs was enough," John Muir said fervently. "In future I'm creeping that slow and sure that a turtle will be a racehorse against me."

"Overcautiousness is as big a fault as impetuosity," Bony said with sudden twinkling eyes. "Your Burracoppin case captures my interest."

"Will you lend a hand?"

Bony sighed.

"Alas, my dear John! You will have to go to Queensland."

"To Queensland! Why?"

"If you go to Myall Station, out from Winton," Bony said slowly, "if you proceed circumspectly, you will there find your lost friend, Andrew Andrews, whom you let slip away because you were so sure of Greggs. As the delightful Americans say, 'Go get him, John!' "

"But why didn't you have him arrested or arrest him yourself?" demanded Muir, so much astonished that he swayed back in his chair.

"Not being an ordinary policeman, but a crime investigator, I seldom make an arrest, as you well know. Arresting people is your particular job, John. We will tell a tale to your commissioner. We will persuade him that getting Andrews is of greater importance than finding Loftus, who, after all, may be playing a game of his own. I have still three weeks of my leave remaining, and, while you are away in Queensland, I will look after your interests in Burracoppin."

"Bony, old man, how can I— —"

"Don't," Bony urged with upraised hand. "I often enjoy a busman's holiday. Between us we will make them promote you to an inspectorship. But curb your desire to question. It is your greatest fault. Curiosity has harmed other living things besides cats. Read Bunting's 'Letters to my Son'. He says— —"

Chapter Two

An Ordinary Wheat Town

In the investigation of crime Napoleon Bonaparte was as great a man as was Lord Northcliffe in the profession of journalism. Like the late Lord Northcliffe, Bony, as he insisted upon being called, interested himself in the careers of several young men of promise. John Muir was one of Bony's young men, having learned the rudiments of crime detection by valuable association with the little-known but brilliant half-caste. Yet of his several young men the Western Australian detective-sergeant was the slowest to learn Bony's philosophy of crime detection. Although he knew it by heart he often failed to act on it, and consequently Bony's advice was often repeated: "Never race Time. Make Time an ally, for Time is the greatest detective that ever was or ever will be."

Together they gained an interview with the Western Australian Commissioner of Police. By previous agreement Bony was permitted to do most of the talking. He melted Major Reeves's reserve, which his duality of race had created, with his cultured voice, his winning smile, and his vast store of knowledge that now and then was revealed beyond opened doors. He charmed John Muir's chief as he charmed everyone after five minutes of conversation.

The interview resulted in Major Reeves believing that John Muir had traced the murderer, Andrew Andrews, with the slight assistance rendered by the Queenslander. He consented to send his own man to Queensland and permit Bony to interest himself in the Burracoppin disappearance. It thus came about that Bony and Muir left Perth together by the Kalgoorlie express, the former alighting at the wheat town at five o'clock in the morning, and John Muir going on to the goldfields' terminus where he would board the transcontinental train.

Day was breaking when the express pulled out of Burracoppin, leaving Bony on the small platform with a grip in one hand and a rolled swag of blankets and necessaries slung over a shoulder. No longer existed the tastefully dressed man who had accosted Detective-Sergeant Muir in Hay

Street. In appearance now Bony was a workman wearing his second-best suit.

At this hour of the morning Burracoppin slept. The roar of the eastward-rushing train came humming back from the yellowing dawn. A dozen roosters were greeting the new day. Two cows meandered along the main road, cunningly putting as great a distance as possible between themselves and their milking places when milking time came. A party of goats gazed after them with satanic good humour.

When Bony emerged from the small station he faced southward. Opposite was the Burracoppin Hotel, a structure of brick against the older building of weatherboard which now was given up to bedrooms. To the left was a line of shops divided by vacant allotments. To the right the three trim whitewashed cottages, with the men's quarters and trade shops beyond, owned by the State Rabbit Department. Behind Bony, beyond the railway, were other houses, the hall, a motor garage, and the school, for the railway halved this town; and running parallel with the railway, but below the surface of the ground, was the three-hundred-miles-long Mundaring-Kalgoorlie pipeline conveying water to the goldfields, and, through subsidiary pipes, over great areas of the vast wheat belts. Thus is Burracoppin, a replica of five hundred Australian wheat towns, clean and neat, brilliant in its whitewash and paint and its green bordering gum-trees.

Till seven o'clock Bony wandered about the place filling in time by smoking innumerable cigarettes and pondering on the many points of the disappearance of George Loftus contained in the sixteen statements gathered by John Muir. The case interested him at the outset, because there was no apparent reason why Loftus should voluntarily disappear.

A man directed him to a boarding-house run by a Mrs Poole. At that hour the shop in front of the long corrugated- iron building was still closed, but he found the owner in the kitchen at the rear, where she was busy cooking breakfast. Mrs Poole was about forty years old, tall and still handsome; a brunette without a grey hair; a well-preserved woman of character. Into her brown eyes flashed suspicion at sight of the half-caste, at which he was amused, as he always was when the almost universal distrust of his colour was raised in the minds of white women—instinctive distrust which invariably he set himself to dispel.

"Well!" Mrs Poole demanded severely.

"I arrived this morning by the train," he explained courteously. "A townsman tells me this is the best place in town at which to get breakfast."

"It'll cost you two shillings," the woman stated in a manner denoting doubt of his ability to pay.

"I have a little money, madam."

Sight of the pound note Bony produced changed Mrs Poole's expression. The change he hoped was caused by his accent. Mrs Poole produced cup and saucer and seized the teapot.

"Thank you," he said, gratefully accepting the cup of tea. Offering the treasury note, he added, "It might be as well for you to take that on account. I may be in Burracoppin for some time. As a matter of fact, I have got a job with the Rabbit Department."

"You have!" Obviously Mrs Poole was pleased. "Then you will be boarding here, I hope?"

"For my meals, yes. I understand, however, that sleeping quarters are provided by the department at the depot."

"Yes, that's so." Quick steps sounded from without. "Oh my! Here's Eric."

A man entered as might a small whirlwind from the plains of Central Australia.

"Ah, late again, Mrs Poole! Quarter past seven, and breakfast not ready. When is that husband of yours coming back? Every time he's away you hug that bed, don't you? You'll die in it one of these days. Now, don't argue. Get on — get on. No burgoo for me. There's no time to eat. I'll be getting the sack for being always late."

The whirlwind was dressed in dungaree overalls. Keen hazel eyes examined Bony humorously.

"Good morning," Bony said.

"Going to work for the Rabbits," interposed Mrs Poole.

"Oh! Well, I'd advise you not to board here. Better stop at the pub. Mrs Poole's husband is a Water Rat, and sometimes he's away for weeks on end. When he is away Mrs Poole hardly ever leaves her bed, she loves it so. You only get one minute ten seconds to gollop your breakfast, but you do get plenty of indigestion. I'm half dead already."

"I'm not as bad as all that, Eric," pleaded Mrs Poole in a way which decided Bony that he was going to like his landlady. To him she added:

"Don't you believe him, Mr— what is your name?"

"Bony."

"Sometimes I'm late, Mr Bony, but not always. Will you take porridge?"

"Please."

"You married?" inquired the subsided whirlwind.

"Yes."

"Then you'll be Mr Bony henceforth. All married men here are called misters, and single men are called by their Christian monikers. I'm Eric Hurley, unmarried, and, therefore, plain Eric. What's yours?"

"Xavier," replied Bony blandly. "But everyone calls me Bony without the mister. I prefer it."

"Just as well. Xavier! Hell! Bony will do me. Come on, we've only got forty seconds. Shoot in that tucker, Mrs Poole. Come on. Get going."

In the dining-room between kitchen and shop the two men ate rapidly. Hurley, Bony observed, was not much beyond thirty years old. He liked his open face, lined and tanned by the sun and lit with the optimism of youth.

"I'm the boundary rider on this section of the rabbit fence," Hurley explained between bursts of rapid mastication. "I've got two hundred miles of it to attend to—a hundred miles north and south of Burracoppin. When the depression crash came all hands bar ex-soldiers were sacked. Hell-uv-a job. For each Sunday on the job I get a day off here. But I'm workin' today, as the farm push are short-handed, and there's a chaff order to be sent away. Hey, Mrs Poole, my lunch ready?"

"I'm cuttin' it now."

"Make it big. I haven't time to eat a decent breakfast." From the railway yard came the sound of a petrol engine. Through the window they saw the motor-propelled trolley sliding away loaded with permanent-way workers. "Hurry! Hurry! The Snake Charmers have gone. If I'm sacked for being late I'll murder your husband and take his place. And I won't get up and light the fire for you. I'll kick you out of bed."

A tin rattled. The whirlwind rushed out. There was silence. Then Mrs Poole's voice was raised urging someone to get up and fetch the cows before Mrs Black got them and "sneaked" the milk. She came to the door.

"Don't you hurry, Mr Bony. The inspector isn't so sharp as Eric makes out. You see, my other boarders all work about the town and never come to breakfast till a quarter to eight. This place is easier when Joe's at home, what with the woodcutting and the cows, an' that Mrs Black who always tries to milk them first. And I've been busy lately. I've had two policemen staying here ever since poor Mr Loftus disappeared. They are gone now, back to Perth."

"Oh!"

"It's funny, that affair," she went on. "I'm sure he's been murdered. Eric was camped half a mile from his house that night. Although it was raining, it was quiet, and he could hear the dogs howling about two in the morning. When my sister had her husband killed on the railway, down near Northam, her dog howled awful for more than an hour. Dogs know when their friends die—don't you think so?"

Fifteen minutes after Bony left Mrs Poole's boarding-house he was watching the changing expressions on the face of the Rabbit Fence Inspector while that official read the letter written by the chief of his department and delivered by the detective.

"You are a member of the Queensland police Force?"

Bony inclined his head.

"I am instructed to assist you in every way. What can I do?"

"Permit me to explain. I am a detective-inspector, at present on leave. My friend, Detective-Sergeant Muir, has been obliged to go into another matter, and, as the disappearance of George Loftus interests me, I have decided, with the sanction of the Western Australian Police Commissioner, to look into it. Outside police circles, your chief and yourself are the only people in this State who know I am a police officer. I rely upon you to keep my secret. People talk and act naturally before Bony, but are as close as oysters in the presence of Detective-Inspector Napoleon Bonaparte. I want you to give me employment on the rabbit fence, preferably near where Loftus's wrecked car was discovered. I would like you to take me to see that car this morning."

"All right. We'll go now."

Seated in the department's truck beside the Fence Inspector, Bony said:

"Please proceed direct along the route taken by Loftus the night he disappeared."

Bony was driven round the hotel into the main street, then eastward past the shops and the boarding-house and the bank, on past the garage at the extremity of the town.

"Loftus should have taken this right-hand road, but despite Wallace's objection kept straight on," explained his companion, whose name was Gray.

"Ah! Has that garage been long vacant?"

"Yes, about a year. The garage on the other side of the railway does all the business now."

Once past the garage and the wide, good road running up a long, low hill south, they abruptly left the town, the road becoming narrow when it began to wind through whipstick mallee and gimlet trees. Now and then to his left Bony could see the rampart of mullock excavated from the great pipeline trench, with the railway beyond it.

"By the way," he said, smiling, "I understand that Mrs Poole's husband is a Water Rat. Precisely in what manner is such an epithet applicable to a woman's husband?"

Inspector Gray chuckled.

"The men employed along the pipeline are called Water Rats because often they have to work deep in water when a pipe bursts."

"Thank you. And what are the Snake Charmers?"

"They are the permanent-way men. Now that you are a Rabbit Department employee you are a Rabbitoh."

It became Bony's turn to chuckle.

"What are the road repairers called?"

"Well, not being a blasphemous man, I am unable to tell you."

"Then I must invent names for them myself. Did you know George Loftus well?"

"Moderately well. He was never a friend of mine, although he has been here five years."

"Tell me all you know about him, please. What he looked like, everything."

The Fence Inspector hesitated, and Bony saw that he was weighing carefully the words he would use to a police officer when there would have been no hesitation had Bony been an ordinary acquaintance. Why men and women should be so reserved in the presence of members of the police, who were their paid and organized protectors, was a point in human psychology which baffled him. At last Gray said:

"I suppose Loftus would be about twelve stone in weight, and of medium height. He was a rather popular kind of man, a good cricketer for all his forty-one years, would always oblige with a song, and was a keen member of the local lodge. For the first three years he worked hard on his farm, but he slacked a bit this last year. He left most of the farm work to his man."

"Did he drink much?"

"A little too much."

"His wife on the farm, still?"

"Yes. She is a good-looking woman, and, I think, a good wife."

"Any children?"

"No."

"The farm hand? What kind of a man is he?"

"He'd be about thirty. A good man, too. Loftus was lucky in getting him. Mick Landon his name is. Born in Australia. Fairly well educated. Is the secretary of several local committees and is the M.C. at all our dances."

"Do you know, or have you heard, what Mrs Loftus intends doing if her husband cannot be found?"

"Well, my wife was talking to her the other day, and Mrs Loftus told her she didn't believe her husband dead and that she was going to run the farm with Landon's help until he came back."

"I suppose his strange disappearance has upset her?"

"Yes, but there is more anger than sorrow, I think. Of course, he might come back at any time. There's old Jelly, now. He disappears three or four times every year, sometimes oftener, and no one knows where he goes or what he does."

"Indeed! You interest me. A woman, perhaps?"

"Knowing Bob Jelly, I can think so. Here we are at the fence."

Chapter Three

The Wheat Belt

A wide tubular and netted gate in a netted fence four feet nine inches high, and topped with barbed wire, halted further progress. Climbing from the truck. Bony made a swift survey of the surrounding country.

The fence ran north and south in a straight line, to the summit of a northern rise and to the belt of big timber to the south. Elaborate precautions had been taken in its construction to keep it rabbit-proof where it crossed the pipeline, whilst the single-track railway line passed over a sunken pit. The fence gate had been repaired, but the wrecked car was still lying partly down on the massive pipeline. The half-caste paced the distance between fence gate and car and found it to be little more than fourteen yards.

About five hundred yards beyond the fence was a house belonging, he was informed, to the Rabbit Department farm, and then occupied by the farm foreman. Also beyond the fence, and on the farther side of the railway, was a farmhouse occupied by a farmer named Judd.

Gray was disappointed when Bony failed to run about like a hunting dog, as all good detectives are supposed to do. For a detective he seemed too casual, and his blue eyes too dreamy. Yet Bony saw all that he wanted to see, which was that the backing of the car from gate to pipeline was done quite naturally, with no tree stumps to make the act a matter of chance.

"I hate the word, but I must use it," Bony said softly. "I am intrigued. Yes, that is the word I dislike. The railway crossed by the rabbit fence makes a perfect cross. On all four sides the land is cleared of timber and now is supporting ripe wheat. Here is difficult country in which to hide a human body indefinitely; for, supposing the remains of George Loftus were hidden somewhere among all those acres of waving wheat, it would be only a matter of time before a man driving a harvester machine came across them. Assuming that Loftus was killed, what object could his murderer have in hiding his body for only a few weeks, excepting, perhaps, to put as great a distance between himself and it before the body was discovered. And to carry the body weighing twelve stone to the nearest timber, which I judge to be not less than three-quarters of a mile distant, would be no mean feat."

"It's mighty strange what's become of him," the Fence Inspector gave it as his opinion.

"I shall find him alive, if not dead."

"You think so?"

"I am sure of it. My illustrious namesake was defeated but once — at Waterloo. I was defeated once … officially, at Windee Station, New South Wales. I shall not meet my Waterloo twice."

Inspector Gray hid his face with cupped hands, which sheltered a cigarette-lighting match, to conceal his silent laughter. Bony proceeded, unaware of the effect his vanity was having on his companion. Pointing to the fence, he said:

"I see several posts which want renewing. I suggest that you employ me cutting and carting posts and replacing those old ones. It will give me both opportunity to look about and time to study this affair. Now, please, take me on along the road Loftus would have taken from here to his house."

Proceeding southward west of the fence, the land to left and right appeared as a golden inland sea caressing the emerald shores of bush and timber. The drone of gigantic bees vibrated the shadowless world — the harvesting machines were at work stripping fifteen bushels of wheat from every acre.

Crossing the old York Road and then continuing straight south, the truck sped up a long, low grade of sandy land which bore thick bush of so different an aspect from that familiar to Bony in the eastern States that he was charmed by its freshness. Here this bush, by its possible concealment of the body of Loftus, presented a thousand difficulties: for in it an army corps could live unseen and unsuspected.

"What is your real opinion of this case?" Gray asked.

"Tell me your opinion first," Bony countered.

Silence for fully a minute. Then:

"This is the twelfth day since Loftus disappeared. It is my firm belief that he didn't just wander into the bush and perish. As you see, there is as much cleared land as uncleared bush. Loftus was not a newchum, and even a newchum hopelessly slewed would surely come to the edge of cleared land, where nine times in ten he would be able to see a farmhouse. I think he was killed for the money he might have had with him — anything from a shilling to a fiver — either where his car was found or at some point on his way home, possibly as he crossed the old York Road."

"Muir informed me that the vicinity of the York Road gate, as well as the edges of the wheat paddocks around the wrecked car, was thoroughly searched."

"Doubtless that is so," Gray assented. "Still, the possibility remains that Loftus may have been killed by a man or men possessing a car, who could have taken the body miles away to hide it in uncleared bush north of the one-mile peg beyond the railway."

"There is solidity in the composition of your theory," Bony said slowly, his eyes half closed, yet aware of the quick look brought by his ponderous language. "I am beginning to think that tracing Loftus will resemble the proverbial looking for a needle in a haystack. However, we must not rule out the possibility that Loftus disappeared intentionally. How did he stand financially?"

"He was as sound as the average farmer."

"And how sound is the average farmer—I mean in this district?"

"Distinctly rocky. Nearly all are in the hands of the Government Bank."

"Was Loftus an — er — amorous man, do you think?"

Inspector Gray took time to answer this pertinent question.

"Well, no," he replied deliberately. "I should not consider him amorous. To an extent he was popular with the ladies, but, nevertheless, he was a home bird. And, as I said before, Mrs Loftus is still young, good-looking, and a good wife. There you see the Loftus farm."

They had reached the summit of the long slope. Before them lay a great semicircle of low, flat country chequered by wheat and fallow paddocks: to the east and south-east reaching to the foot of a sand rise similar to that on which they stood; to the south far beyond the horizon; to the south-west extending to a sand rise which drew closer the farther north it came. The Loftus farm was situated immediately to their right as they slipped down the grade. The house lay not quite half a mile from the road at the foot of a long outcrop of granite with oak- trees growing in the crevices. A tractor driven by one man, which pulled a machine operated by a second man, moved with deceptive slowness round a near paddock.

"That will be Mick Landon driving the tractor," Gray said when he had taken in all the view. "The man on the harvester is Larry Eldon. He comes out every day from Burracoppin on a bike."

With narrowed eyes Bony examined the scene spread out before him, for the land dipped a little to the foot of the granite outcrop. Silently he regarded the small iron farmhouse, the stables beyond, and the stack of new hay beyond them. Over all that vast belt of brown fallow and golden wheat here and there moved the humming harvester machines like giant sloths, feeding on the grain voraciously and flinging behind them the dust of their passage. Gray said:

"That's Mr Jelly's place. You remember I mentioned him. He's a mystery, if you want a mystery. With him mystery is added to mystery. Most of us when we go away come back poorer than when we leave. He comes back richer than when he goes."

"Mysteries!" Bony sighed as though greatly content. His eyes were almost shut when he said: "Always has my soul been thrilled by mystery."

Seated at the table in his room at the Rabbit Department Depot, Bony slowly read once again the collection of statements gathered by John Muir. The most important of these statements was that signed by Leonard Wallace, the licensee of the Burracoppin Hotel. It appeared to be a straightforward account of his movements and actions from the time he left Perth to the moment he entered the room in the hotel occupied by his wife and himself. There were three statements which in part corroborated this, in addition to that rendered by Mrs Wallace.

One was signed by Mavis Loftus, giving the date of her husband's departure for Perth, the nature of his business there, the date of his expected return, which was 4th November— two days after his actual return. Michael Landon stated over his signature the orders that Loftus had given him before he went away and the fact that he had not seen or heard Loftus during the night of 2nd November or at any subsequent time.

The story, in full, of the finding of the wrecked car was given by Richard Thorn, employee of the Water Department.

From the mass there was nothing to point to murder, nor was there anything in them to make Loftus suspect of wilful disappearance. As far as Bony could then cull from his collection of facts the missing man was remarkable for no one habit, vice, or virtue.

Seated there in the quiet peace of late afternoon, idly examining each signature, noting the badly formed scrawl of Leonard Wallace at one extreme and at the other the neat calligraphy of Mick Landon, he experienced the sensation of elation he always felt when a baffling case, by great good fortune, came his way.

Questions poured through his mind as water through a pipe. He declined to halt the flow with a mental tap to find an answer to any one of them until he had cast his net in the still water about this small wheat town. When the fish had been landed for his inspection, then would he search for the deadly stingray which, if found, would prove that George Loftus had been slain.

Hearing the Depot gate being opened and a horse-drawn dray enter the yard, Bony rapidly collected the documents and placed them in his grip, which he locked. His bed was made, and from beneath clean clothes folded neatly for use as a pillow, he produced a book, then lay on the bed and pretended to read.

He heard the horse and dray cross the yard, saw horse, vehicle, and driver pass before the open doorway. Came then the sound of a dog racing over loose gravel. The door of the chaff room next his rattled when a speeding animal passed through the small cut opening at the bottom. A dog scratched and sniffed loudly. A man whistled and shouted:

"Ginger, come here!"

Into the room swept the whirlwind. His clothes were covered with a greyish dust; his face and neck and arms were whitened by the same dust. Hazel eyes, reddened by dust, gleamed good-humouredly.

"Ginger! Hi, Ginger! You callused-jawed pork sausage! You chase cats! You kill the boss's cat and get me sacked! You—you—you——!"

A dog, a red-haired cross between a whippet and an Irish terrier, came to heel, to stand with lowered head and uplooking soft black eyes which so plainly said:

"You're only kidding now."

"Lay down, you callused-jawed slaughterer."

Ginger lay down, head resting on forepaws, shortened tail thumping the floor.

"What kind of a day have you had?" Bony asked.

"Lovely ... lovely! I've been breathing chaff dust for eight and a half hours. It's got under my clothes, and tomorrow I'll be a red rash. See you later. I'm headed for a shower. Come on, Ginger!"

Whirlwind and dog departed, to return with equal speed ten minutes later. Bony continued to read while his room-mate dressed in clean clothes, and when Hurley finished lacing his boots he happened to look at the cover of Bony's book.

"What's that? What's the name of that book?" he asked.

Above the lowered book Bony's blue eyes twinkled.

"It is entitled," he said, *"A Contribution to the Natural History of the Australian Termite,* written by a little-known but really clever man named Kurt von Hagen."

"What's it all about?"

"About the Australian termite."

"Who's he, when his hat's on?"

"Do you refer to the author or the termite?"

"The termite. What's a termite?"

"A termite is a white ant."

"Oh! Then why the hell didn't you say so in the first place? You interested in white ants?"

"I am interested in everything," Bony replied grandly. "Art, philosophy, the sciences. At present my leisure is devoted to the study of the termite, which is the most wonderful of all living creatures. Its civilization is so simple, yet so complex, so strong as to defy every other creature save man, yet so vulnerable as to die in sunlight. We may be excused for thinking that what many regard as — —"

"Say, Bony, are you interested in murder?"

It was seldom Bony was trapped into visible astonishment. On this occasion it must be said in his defence that his mind was not then employed by the subject of homicide. Hurley's question actually brought him to a sitting position.

"Why do you ask such a question?"

"Because I am looking for a feller thoroughly in earnest on the subject of murder."

For a fraction of time Bony hesitated. His brain raced to supply answers to a dozen questions raised by Hurley's abrupt inquiry. Did the man know him for a policeman? Was it desired that he, Bony, should become a confidant? Did Hurley know that Loftus had been murdered and who murdered him?

"I believe," he said blandly —"I believe I can truthfully say that I am interested in the subject of murder."

Sighing deeply, Hurley leaned back over his bunk. Bony thought that the mystery of Loftus's disappearance was to be explained even before he had started his investigation. And the case had been so promising, too.

"Can you recite the names of Australian murderers since nineteen twenty?" Hurley persisted. "You know, like we did at school with the kings—William the Conqueror, ten sixty- six; William the Second, ten ... but can you?"

"Phelp, Trilby, Smith, and Low, nineteen twenty; Brown, Little, two Wills, Turner, and Love, nineteen twenty-one; Maynard, Ro— —"

"You'll do! You'll do!" Hurley was standing over the half- caste, thumping him on the back. "You'll do, Bony, old lad! You're meat for old Jelly! Hooroo! Saved—I'm saved!"

"Kindly explain the cause of your exuberance," Bony urged.

Eric Hurley snatched at the detective's tobacco and papers, swiftly rolled a cigarette and lit it. His face was beaming; his eyes were bright. Somehow Bony's liking for this impetuous man deepened.

"I'll tell you the tale," Hurley consented. "As a matter of fact, I'm in love with a girl. Her name's Lucy Jelly. She is the loveliest thing within a thousand miles of Burracoppin. Twenty years old, she is. Her father is a cocky four miles out. He doesn't seem to mind me courting his daughter, but he doesn't give me a chance to do any courting. That's Irish, but it's a fact."

Bony nodded sympathetically, his eyes veiled by the black lashes, the tablets of his mind wiped clean to receive new and startling impressions. Hurley went on:

"Every time I go to her place I get a moment or two with Lucy, and then the old man opens up on murder. He can't talk about nothing else. He knows the details of every murder case that has happened in Australia for the last ten years at least, how the blokes slipped and got caught, and how they behaved on the drop. Old Jelly sort of catches you by the ear and leads you off to his private little room. He pushes you into a chair, from which there's no getting out till it's time to come home. There's photographs of murderers all round the walls, and, as an extra treat, sometimes he'll show you the rope Merrier, the Bendigo killer, was hanged with. You simply got to stay put, and look at the pictures on the walls, and read bits with him out of his albums. You're his meat, Bony! You're his meat!"

"It sounds as though he were a cannibal," Bony interjected, his interest thoroughly roused, pleasure that this mystery was not so soon to be solved making him happy. "How am I his meat?"

"Why, it's simple enough. You come along with me this evening. I introduce you to Lucy and old Jelly. Then you recite your table of murderers. Old Pop Jelly will fall on your neck and take you into his chamber of horrors—he might even show you the rope—and I can go courting Lucy as she should be courted. Gee, I'm glad you got a job with the Rabbits!"

"Your description of Mr Jelly interests me," Bony said. To which Hurley replied:

"Jelly himself will interest you a thunderin' sight more."

Chapter Four

Mr Jelly

Eric Hurley owned a motor-cycle, to which was fitted a pillion seat, and, being a native of Australia, Bony should have known better than to take a ride thereon over country roads. He afterwards estimated that the two miles to the rabbit fence was covered in less than two minutes.

The rapidity of this locomotion certainly did not accord with the dignity of an inspector of police, yet he thoroughly enjoyed the rush through the air, warm yet from the sun which had seen set an hour. From the York Road gate they took the government track running east of the fence, roaring up the long sand slope, humming down the farther side. They passed the Loftus farm, tore onward another mile, swerved sickeningly to the left, and stopped with wickedly skidding tyres before a neat and comfortable farmhouse.

Two dogs welcomed them with much barking. Three turkeys fell off a tree branch, to which, with numerous other domestic fowl, they had climbed via a roughly made bush ladder. A cat came round the house with tail erect. Following it came a little girl whose age appeared to be about fourteen years. She was followed by a young lady alluringly cool in a white muslin dress. And behind her came Mr Jelly.

If you possess imagination sufficient to magnify a cigar to the size of a six-foot man you will obtain a pictorial impression of Mr Jelly. His head was small with a pointed crown, and his feet were small. From his head downwards and from his feet upwards Mr Jelly's circumference gradually increased till the middle was reached. He was between fifty and sixty years of age, bald save for a ring of grey hair which rested upon his ears like a halo much too small for him. His complexion was brick red, not alcoholic red, but the red of sunrays and strong winds.

"You will break your confounded neck one of these days," he told Hurley in the peculiarly soothing voice of a doctor addressing a rich patient. There was remarkable gentleness and kindly concern in that voice, a surprising vocal inflexion to be heard on an Australian farm.

"Not me, Mr Jelly. Hullo, Luce! Did you expect me?"

The girl's big brown eyes were clear and steady.

"Yes, of course. Have you forgotten that you said you would come tonight when you left last night?"

"Forgotten! Of course he's not forgotten."

"Hullo, Sunflower!"

"Hullo, Eric!"

"I've brought a new friend along because you ought to know him," Hurley announced easily. "Luce, this is Mr Bony. He has just started for the Rabbit Department."

Bony found himself being very thoroughly examined. Wearing no hat, he bowed as never man had bowed to Lucy Jelly. She looked upon his ruddy brown face illuminated by the keen, clean mind, watched the smile slowly break over it which swept aside her instinctive race prejudice, saw his teeth gleam whilst he said with polished grace:

"Mr Hurley insisted on bringing me, Miss Jelly. I am very happy to meet you."

Her eyes widened a fraction at his accent. Without pre-thought she said:

"I am glad you came."

"This is Miss Dulcie Jelly, known to her friends as Sunflower," came the next introduction.

Again Bony bowed, and this time he offered his hand.

"I hope you will accept me as your friend, for Sunflower is a very pretty name."

"I will think about it, Mr Bony," the young lady replied with unusual reserve.

"And now it is the old fellow's turn," put in Mr Jelly.

"Mr Bony—Mr Jelly."

Mr Jelly stared into the blue eyes of the Saxon, swiftly examined the features of the Nordic. He noted the rich, even colour of the face, in which he could see no vice. Returning the stare, Bony instantly knew that here was a man superior to his fellows, a man of great force, one who had plumbed the depths of knowledge if not the heights.

The introductions accomplished, Mr Jelly invited them into his house, saying:

"Well, come along in. We've just had dinner, but there's tea in the pot. I haven't seen you around Burracoppin before. From what part of Australia do you hail?"

"Queensland, Mr Jelly. I knocked up a good cheque there breaking in horses, and saw in it an excellent chance to visit Western Australia. Unfortunately, I stayed a little too long, and now must make a cheque with which to get back again."

"Horsebreaker, eh? Humph!"

While following his host through the kitchen door he glanced over his shoulder, to observe Hurley slowly following with one arm round the waist of Lucy Jelly and the other about the shoulders of little Sunflower.

The kitchen, evidently, was the dining-room. It was spotlessly clean, and austere in its furnishing. Bony was made to seat himself at the table and was given a cup of tea and offered a plate of small cakes. Mr Jelly lit the lamp. The world without was hushed to an unthrobbing silence.

"Bony is interested in ants, Mr Jelly," Hurley remarked in his pleasant way. "I found him reading a book about them which has more Latin words in it than English."

"Ah!" murmured Mr Jelly noncommittally, studying Bony in the lamplight.

"Ants always interest me," Bony confessed. "The termite especially is a wonderful insect."

The critical expression in Mr Jelly's eyes of light blue was replaced by one of pleasure.

"You are correct, friend. I am delighted to find in you a man of intelligence. The termite was living, as doubtless you are aware, millions of years before man appeared, even millions of years before the Australian bulldog ant, which is the oldest ant. You will agree that the termite's social laws are so far advanced beyond ours as to make ours merely the confusion of anarchy."

"I am glad I came tonight," Bony said, smiling.

"I am glad to meet a man who can discuss subjects other than horses, machinery, and wheat and the doings of our local society lights."

"You have followed Henry Smeathman?" Bony asked.

"No, but I have read what Dr David Livingstone said about the termites of Africa. A great naturalist as well as a great missionary. But, come! Let us go to my little den and leave these younger people to entertain each other. Coffee at nine-thirty, Lucy, please."

Again following Mr Jelly, Bony once more glanced back. Lucy Jelly was smiling happily. Sunflower Jelly was watching Bony with her big solemn eyes, the eyes of a Maid of Orleans or of a judge in ermine. Mr Eric Hurley closed one of his eyes as his generous mouth widened into a grin.

Carrying a lighted lamp, Mr Jelly led the way to a room at the farther side of the house. This room contained a plain oak bedstead with coverings, a desk, set against one wall angle, which was littered with papers and account books, a glass- fronted bookcase rarely seen in Australian farmhouses, and a large table set before the one window. The table was covered with a black cloth, and on it were several folio-size scrap or press-cutting albums, a pot of glue, writing materials, and an empty picture frame. Hanging on the walls was a gallery of framed portraits.

"This is Bluebeard's chamber," Mr Jelly was saying in his soft, soothing voice. "It is my private room. None of my household ever comes here. Well?"

"Here, I see, is the likeness of Maurice, the Longreach murderer, and there is Victor Lord, who killed a woman at Bathurst, New South Wales," came from Bony, who was examining the pictures. "Surely, Mr Jelly, you are not a criminologist as well as a naturalist?"

"Indeed I am," Mr Jelly admitted. "Of the two branches of science I am the more interested in criminology, but I do not neglect the science of agriculture. I do not permit my hobbies to interfere with the practice of my living. There are my children to be considered, and, my wife being dead, the responsibility is entirely on me. Yes, I have given much study to the lives of all those men whose pictures hang on those walls. All of them are murderers, and all of them have been executed. Study of the subject of homicide compels me to believe that it is the result of physical disorder. Sit down. If I can interest you, you will be an exception who will gladden my heart."

"I am sure you will interest me," Bony stated gently. He was actually more interested in Mr Jelly than he had been in a man for many years. To observe the farmer seated at the table with the soft light falling on his benign face, the ruddy complexion, the grey fringe of hair, and the light blue eyes, was to place him at a vast distance from such a hobby or life interest as homicide.

"Pardon my curiosity," Bony continued, "but how did you secure all those pictures, for they are studio portraits?"

"They are photographic copies of newspaper pictures," the farmer explained, adding with a sweep of his hand over the table: "Here I have their dossiers, accounts of their final trial and death. These albums are full of them, full of the greatest dramas in human life; accounts of men fighting for their vile lives, of women nobly swearing away their souls to save a man from the gallows, of innocent children facing a future where lies their father's sin ready to crush them at an unexpected moment. Here, let us look at them, these fools who kill."

Mr Jelly pushed aside the empty picture frame and drew towards him an album which he opened at random. Turning back a page, he revealed the original picture of a man named Fling. He said:

"Arthur Fling was the son of a parson and a highly respected mother. He had received a first-class education. He had great opportunities. Almost certainly he would have made his life successful. Why, therefore, should he coldly plan to and murder a man in order to gain two hundred pounds? Had his father known his need, he would have given his son the money. Result: the trap for the son, a broken heart for the mother, and an overdose of sleeping draught for the father." The pages flickered. "Now, Henry Wilde was born in a Sydney slum of vice-ridden parents. For nine years he committed minor crimes. He shot at and killed a man who surprised him when attacking an office safe. His parentage urged him to crime and finally to the scaffold. The minor crimes produced the major crime. You follow me?"

"Easily," assented the detective, who subconsciously was wondering at Mr Jelly's concise speech. It almost seemed that the man's speech was the result of training. He did not say, "cold-bloodedly plan and murder a man", and "shot and killed a man", but "coldly plan to and murder" and "shot at and killed a man". This subtle difference Bony was quick to notice. Mr Jelly continued:

"We have here two killers born in wholly different circumstances and living on quite different planes of life. On the surface the two are totally dissimilar, yet they are blood brothers to Cain. For a moment we will leave them. Here is William Marks who murdered three women at various times and places for their insurance money, and over here is Frederick Nonning of Charlton, Victoria, who killed five little children without motive. Nonning was a wealthy man; Marks was an artisan born of respectable parents.

"Now here we have four killers, no two of them in the same class of society. Two killed for money, one killed to avoid detention, and the fourth killed for the pleasure of killing. The question arises, why should all those men hang on my walls, why should they commit a deed which to you and me would be horrible even when contemplated? I'll tell you. I'll explain a theory which I think can be termed a fact.

"Murder is the visible expression of an hereditary trait. On these walls are the pictures of twenty-seven killers. Of those twenty-seven cases I have been able to construct the genealogical tables of nineteen back to the fifth generation. In all cases save two the tables reveal lunacy and self-destruction. The descendant of such ancestors today faces the probability of the legal death."

"I take it that you believe that murderers are mental defectives?"

"Undoubtedly."

"And, as insane people, should not be hanged?"

Mr Jelly was emphatic when next he spoke.

"Let us get down to brass tacks, as my old father used to say," he went on. "In the bad old days, when they hanged a man for looking crossways at the squire, it was considered that man was a free agent, able to distinguish right from wrong. In these days if a man brains his wife with a beer bottle, and more especially if the man belongs to the professional class, and he acts mad, the alienists will prove that he is, and their opinion is taken as accurate. You see, we have swung right round to the opposite outlook or viewpoint of crime and criminals."

Mr Jelly crossed his legs. Enthusiasm for his subject was warming him.

"The only man who ever really understood criminals was Lombroso, the Italian. He said, and could prove what he said, that a murderer, or any felon guilty of brutality, inevitably bore certain physical marks. These people can be picked out as easily as he picked 'em out in his day. I can pick them out: a very shrewd man, who wasn't a doctor, taught me how. Never mind who he was or where he taught me. The fact stands that Lombroso was right as regards killers. I give in to the oh-my- poor-brother fools when dealing with lesser criminals, because stealing and like offences are the result largely of environment; but, as I have said, if a man or a woman is a potential killer, either or both can be detected by physical abnormalities. So that, assuming you were branded, as God branded Cain before and not after he killed Abel, as many people think, you should be put away before you cut my throat, not after, because when my throat has been cut it can never again be uncut."

33

"But the difficulty would be in setting up the authority in the first place, and, in the second place, the examination of the people," Bony objected.

"I realize that," Mr Jelly agreed thoughtfully. "Still, the fact remains that many murderers should never have been allowed outside a lunatic asylum. Nonning and Fling, Wells and Mann were mentally unbalanced. I visited Wells and Nonning in jail and found the Lombrosian brand on them. Wilde, the burglar, was sane, but he was branded too. Like many criminals, his final crime was the culmination of a life of crime."

"You do not believe in the death penalty?" asked Bony quickly.

Mr Jelly's grey eyebrows became one straight bar. He said sternly:

"Every right-minded man must believe in the extinction of killers. The death sentence is a tremendous deterrent. It bulks large in the mind of a man who would like to kill, or who regards killing lightly, but himself fears death. No punishment would ever stop the subnormal or the abnormal, but abolish the death penalty and murders committed by sane men will increase mightily. No, what I think is that many murders need never have happened at all. I believe that penal control should be exercised over potential killers who have once come into a prison to serve a sentence for a lesser crime."

Mr Jelly was now fingering idly the empty picture frame. He talked on and on about his killers, interesting Bony with his wonderful memory of their trials, with, now and then, grim allusion to the manner in which it was reported that they died. Presently the detective's mind was jolted back to his business at Burracoppin.

"Yes, I am sure poor Loftus was murdered," Mr Jelly was saying. "He would not have disappeared voluntarily. I have got my own ideas, of course. It will all come out some day. Someone will find him under a stone or in a hole. I am a great believer in the saying 'Murder will out', and I am going to put the picture of Loftus's killer in this frame, after he is hanged. Poor old Loftus! He didn't ever do anyone a bad turn."

Yes, Bony was extremely interested in Mr Jelly. He thoroughly enjoyed his visit at the farm, and when he and Hurley reached the Rabbit Department Depot he said as much.

"I am glad you enjoyed yourself," Hurley said with a yawn. "I did— thank you!"

Chapter Five

Theories

The morning of the fourteenth day since the disappearance of George Loftus witnessed Bony dump a load of posts near the wrecked car. Somewhat to his annoyance Eric Hurley's dog accompanied him, the boundary rider having departed on his long northern trip of inspection.

It was a superb day—warm, cloudless, brilliant. What little wind there was came from the east. The air was filled with a low pulsating sound produced by the combined action of harvester machines and tractors in the wheat paddocks far and near. Already so early in the season the bags of wheat were being rushed by truck and wagon to the rail sidings. The land, having peacefully dozed for nine months, had quickened to feverish life.

To Bony, used to the solitudes of the eastern side of the great heart of Australia, this bustle and noise of Western Australia's wheat belt seemed to push him spiritually farther away from his aboriginal ancestry than at times had the roar and the bitter grimness of the cities. Here was the white man's life in all its naked virility, all its indomitable courage, its inventive genius. From the spot on which he was standing he could see mile beyond mile of land, which had been abandoned in its desolation by the hardy nomadic aborigines and now was one huge chequered garden. This morning Bony was proud that he was half white and wistfully longed to escape the environment of the mid-race for the upper plane of the white.

He had thoroughly examined every inch of the ground, giving only five minutes to the hunt for clues between spells of fencework in order not to raise unnecessary comment from the drivers of passing traffic. With hope in his heart he searched for the bones of recent history. He saw the masses of impressions made by motor tyres and the boots of those who had been attracted to the scene. He saw dog tracks, the tracks of a goanna, two snakes' tracks, and tracks left even by a centipede. He found a cigar end which at one time had been soddened by rain and now was tinder-dry and brittle. Matches, cigarette ends, an old boot, a half-inch spanner, and an old felt hat provided him with quite a collection.

Yet definitely nothing of importance. Bony hummed lightly whilst he cut out the old decayed posts, dug from the ground the rotted butts, and placed the new posts in position, rammed firm the earth, and bored the wire holes. The disappearance of Loftus presented possibilities of surprise and drama that made him happy. Now and then Ginger departed on a hunt for rabbits and was made happy, too, by the absence of restraint. He returned from these expeditions with heaving sides and lolling tongue and stretched himself in the shade to regain bodily coolness. A blowfly sometimes hummed near him at which he snapped, and always there was the higher, more persistent note of the machines stripping the wheat.

A goods train passed with roaring wheels towards Burracoppin, and the driver waved a friendly hand to Bony. The truck drivers who were forced to stop to open the gates in the longest fence in the world—1,350 miles—conscientiously closed them on seeing Bony working there. They were addicted to leaving open those gates, proving themselves good gamblers in betting against being caught and subsequently fined by a police magistrate.

At noon Bony filled his billycan from a tap at the government farmhouse and brought it near his work to boil for tea. The time he allowed the tea to "draw" he spent seated behind the steering wheel of Loftus's car. With the front wheels on level ground and the back wheels resting on the huge water pipe below ground level, the position in which he then was, although not comfortable, was not precarious. For a little while he imagined himself George Loftus, partly drunk, realizing slowly the stupid thing he had done.

As the farmer probably did, Bony groped over the back of the front seat and took from the car floor the two empty beer bottles he had obtained from John Muir. He pretended to drink from a bottle, tossed it to the ground as might a drunken man. He repeated the act with the second bottle before clambering out of the car to see then how easily Loftus could have swayed into the pipe trench, resulting in injury.

Retrieving the bottles, he passed over the road to his dinner camp, selected the shady side of a gimlet tree up which swarmed no ants, and sat down with the tree as a back rest. The lunch Mrs Poole had cut for him he opened on his lap and ate. Ginger had departed on another hunt.

Experiencing a real mental pleasure, the detective surveyed the disappearance of George Loftus. At the worst it certainly was no stereotyped murder case, with a dead body, a bloodstained knife, and fingerprints offering a dozen clues. It might not be—it probably was not—a case of homicide at all. Possibly Loftus had reasons for disappearing and had carefully planned his disappearance. Other men had disappeared from the impulsion of reasons to them of the utmost importance. Mr Jelly disappeared for varying periods, and no one knew where he went or why.

He was then sure that within a radius of one hundred yards of the wrecked car there was not to be found any object which could have become detached from the person of a human being through violence. He had found a once-sodden but now tinder-dry cigar end. It was not a very important clue, but it certainly formed a tiny brick of the structure Bony was building with his imagination. He had found the cigar end nine feet four inches from the car. It appeared to be about one-third the total length of the cigar. It added its quota to the imaginary history of Loftus's acts that night of rain.

With the extinguished cigar clenched between his teeth Loftus had driven his car. The rain on the windscreen obscuring his vision, his sight blurred by alcohol, and his mind heated by the recent argument, the farmer had not seen the fence gate in time to avoid a collision. The injury to the gate had been severe, but not sufficiently severe to prohibit repairs. The car's bumper bar was broken, and the front mudguards as well as the radiator damaged. Of course the car was stopped by the impact.

Loftus then had the choice of two courses of action. He could have driven on for three hundred yards where, reaching the entrance to the government farm, he could have turned the car, or he could have backed the car from the gateway along the road he had come far enough to give him sufficient room to take the right-hand turn south along the fence towards the old York Road and his home.

He had elected the second alternative, but in his then mental confusion had backed the car along a left-hand curve which brought it into the pipe trench. Once there it was impossible to get it out under its own power or with his own strength. Most probably Loftus cursed himself for a fool, yet made no immediate attempt to climb from his seat to the ground. Knowing the locality, being acquainted with the proportions of the pipe and its trench, and, therefore, having precisely the measure of his predicament, Loftus would experience a sense of anger. Then he would remember the extinguished cigar between his lips, and failing to light it, would fling it far from him. Possibly for a minute he then remained physically inactive and mentally struggling to regain equipoise. Memory of the beer decided him to drink. Still resenting the awkwardness of his plight, he had emptied both bottles and flung each from him with a vicious curse.

And so he arrived at the moment when he had clambered from his seat, possibly to sway on his feet holding the car for support, observing the danger of the yawning trench and summoning sufficient will power to lurch safely away from it.

Had Loftus been attacked whilst backing the car or when considering what he would do when he had backed it into the pipe trench, there must certainly have been a struggle, for he was a big and active man. And had there been a struggle, some object or some article of clothing would have been detached from the persons of the combatants to fall to the ground for the trained vision of the half-caste to discover. Whilst he rolled a cigarette the dog came back carrying a dead rabbit which it laid at Bony's feet. To Ginger, Bony summed up:

"Friend Loftus was not foully done to death at this lovely spot, my dear Ginger. We may decide that that is certain. He did one of two things. Either he walked on to his farm or he carried out the second part of a plan to disappear, the first part being the wrecking of the car, although why he should do that is not yet clear. I wish I possessed your keen nose. With your nose and my eyes I could perform wonders, despite the fact that fourteen days have gone by.

"With your permission we will now proceed to establish the man's preference in smoking. How often has tobacco hanged a man! We must remove the labels from those bottles and, if possible, establish the particular hotel from which they came. Our future activities will be directed to picking up tracks—if they exist—down along this fence which will prove one way or the other whether Loftus walked home as a dutiful husband should have done."

The dinner hour over, Bony went back to his work, the dog following with the dead rabbit in his mouth. Ginger really was over-conditioned to weather an Australian summer, yet, after laying the carcass at Bony's feet, he ran off on another hunting expedition. It was when Bony had dug out the old stump of the post he had last cut from the fence that Ginger returned with a second dead rabbit. He was reproved for his murderous appetite, and, before filling in the earth round the new post, Bony dropped the first of the dead rabbits into the hole and buried it.

Both Mr and Mrs Wallace were behind the bar of the Burracoppin Hotel when Bony entered at eight-thirty in the evening. They were waiting on a motley crowd of farmers, wheat lumpers, and government employees, who, after the first swift appraisal, took no further interest in the stranger. With a glass pot of beer before him, Bony lounged against the counter there to enjoy the study of humanity, always to him a subject of exhaustless interest.

Mr Leonard Wallace, of course, came first. The licensee was short of stature, grey of hair and moustache, weak of feature. He was an insignificant rabbit of a man, at first sight precisely the type cartoonists love to marry to an outsize woman. Yet even to the novice the first impression of Mr Wallace was superficial, for there were two points in his make-up oddly at variance with his general appearance. The hard black eyes belied the lack of intelligence indicated by the low and sloping forehead, and the deep tone of the voice was not congruent with the visible marks of timidity.

It was natural, because familiarity with the idiosyncrasies of our species make it so, that Mrs Wallace should be a woman weighing fourteen stone, yet handsome despite that and her forty-five years—despite, too, the stern forbidding expression in her dark eyes, which gleamed beneath straight dark brows. She watched her husband very much as a goanna watches a trapdoor spider.

Mr Wallace attended the main-bar customers, and his wife waited on the wants of several men standing at the slide counter in the parlour. To these customers her expression was one of demure coquettishness, but often she turned her head to look down on her husband, when into her eyes leapt contemptuous disapproval that was at once dispersed when she caught the eye of a visitor. Obviously little Mr Wallace's life was not a happy one.

"See you working on the rabbit fence today," a man said to Bony. "Have one with me?"

"With pleasure. Yes, I am now working for the Rabbit Department."

"Hi, Leonard! A cuppler pots."

Bony's new friend was prosperously stout, middle-aged, mellow-aged, pleasant-faced.

"Hi! Buck up, Leonard! A cuppler pots," he repeated in a voice that wheezed.

Mr Wallace then was drawing pots for a party of men at the far end of the bar. He was doing his job in the manner of an expert. Even so, Mrs Wallace thought otherwise.

"Oh, get out of the way, you slow-coach," she hissed, pushing him from the pumps. Winter then was vanquished by spring with amazing quickness: "Two pots, Mr Thorn," she exclaimed gaily, placing the drinks on the counter and accepting the shilling with a smirk.

Mr Thorn smirked also. When she turned her attention to the parlour customers he said to Bony, *sotto voce:*

"Poor ole Wallace! But don't you run away with the idea that Wallace is all mouse. He stands a lot over a long time and then suddenly bucks. When he does there's ructions; my bloomin' oath, there is. I was workin' late larst night, and when I got back to town about eleven the pub was shut. Any'ow, I sneaked over to see if I could rouse Wallace on the quiet and could 'ear her going off like a packet of crackers. She was telling 'im 'ow she knew he had murdered George Loftus, and he was tellin' 'er that if she didn't shut up he would murder 'er. No, by no manner of means is Leonard a nice little gentleman orl the time."

"Mrs Wallace must know something, surely?"

"She might, but I don't think so. That's just 'er nasty 'abit of mind. Now, if 'e murdered 'er it would be more like it. She's the sort of woman who gets surprised when 'er throat is cut slowly."

"It is very strange George Loftus disappearing like that, isn't it?" Bony remarked thoughtfully.

Mr Thorn became confidential. He breathed beer affectionately into Bony's face.

"There's nothing strange about it," he whispered. "He done just wot I'd 'ave done in 'is place. If you just thinks, it all comes plain. Orl these detectives and things makes a hash of jobs like this becos they 'aven't got no imagination. Now, I 'ave got imagination. I could write books about this township and the people in it. There's some bloomin' characters 'ere orl right. No, ole George Loftus disappeared becos 'e wanted to disappear. He was unfinancial. No, ole Loftus wanted the chance to get out, and 'e took it. 'E disappeared becos 'e was broke and saw the chance to get out with some cash. He went down to Perth to argue with 'is creditors, and then, likely enough, wangled a cuppler 'undred quid from them or the bank to carry on over the harvest.

"Two 'undred pounds sounds a lot to a man wot's broke, but it don't sound so much to a man wot's married and 'as a hungry farm waiting to swallow most of it. Says Loftus to 'isself: 'Well, 'ere's the boodle, and I'm orf. If I fades away, the bank' — or whoever lent him the money — 'will sool the Ds on to me, and me dinah will sool 'em when the bank gets tired. I gotta use me brains. I'll stage a nice mysterious disappearance, an' whiles they're all 'untin' for me corpse I'll do a get-over to the eastern States.' "

"In a case like this, all you gotta do is to put yourself into the other bloke's 'ead. It's simple, ain't it?" finalized Mr Thorn.

"It certainly is," agreed Bony delightedly. "Have a drink with me?"

"I don't mind if I do. I always — —"

"Hi, Dick!" boomed a bass voice. "Just seen your boss and he says there's a burst at the two-o-five."

"Then let 'er keep busted. I ain't movin' outter this pub till I gets chucked out," announced the Water Rat emphatically. To Bony, Mr Thorn whispered: "See 'im? Look at 'im. Just look at 'im."

Near the main-door end of the bar there stood with military straightness one who towered above the others. Seldom had Bony seen a finer human head. It was massive, crowned with a mop of snow-white hair, regally poised above massive shoulders. The keenest of steel-blue eyes were spoiled by the underlids, which drooped in half circles of vivid red, eyes which had suffered the agony of sandy blight, eyes that had glared at the dancing mirage in dreadful places. A snow-white beard fell down before the great chest clothed only with a flannel singlet, armless, revealing the arms of a giant.

"Look at 'im," implored Mr Thorn. " 'E can swing an axe orl day. 'E can put up a mile of fence whiles any ordinary main is putting up a cuppler strains. 'E can drink more'n me. Do you know 'ow old 'e is?"

"No," Bony admitted.

"No more do I. No more does anybody. But we know for positive sure 'e's over eighty. You wouldn't believe it, but 'e is. 'E ain't never gonna die. When we're stiff 'e'll be goin' strong. We calls 'im the 'Spirit of Orstralia'."

Chapter Six

"The Spirit of Orstralia"

The Spirit of Australia! What a name! How truly appropriate! Courage, strength, dependability; purpose, power, and unbreakable flexibility; dauntless and deathless. The Spirit of Australia! If any man was rightly nicknamed, this man was. Age rested on him as a crown of jewels, not as fetters of lead. More than eighty years old! It was incredible— till one peered deeply and saw that tremendous experiences had been the battlements which defied the onslaughts of Time.

"Who is he? What is he?" Bony at last inquired.

"'Im? 'E's a cocky ten miles out," Mr Thorn replied, wiping his lips with the back of his hairy hand. "'E drives sixteen 'orses in the old-fashioned way of two abreast, carting in ten tons of wheat every other day, when 'is sons get goin' proper with the harvester machines. 'Ullo! There's Mick Landon!"

"Where?"

"There," Mr Thorn said, pointing to a new arrival within the parlour. "See 'im?"

There was no need for Mr Thorn to point. Beyond the sliding counter the knot of men were welcoming a young and handsome man with fair hair and blue agate eyes. To Bony the classical features were marred by the eyes, for the pupils were of the one colour and had that strange deadness of expression to be associated with fish's eyes. Watching him, Bony was able to see them move rapidly from man to man, and from that group to Mrs Wallace, and beyond her to him and those who stood near him. A keen, alert, mentally vigorous man in the prime of life.

"'E works for Loftus," Mr Thorn carefully informed Bony, as a showman may describe his exhibits. "Terrible good farmer, too, is Mick Landon. Would 'ave 'ad 'is own farm by now, if it 'adn't bin for the wimen. They are orl mad on 'im. 'E can do wot 'e likes with 'em. Even the married ones get dopey when 'e looks at 'em. But for orl that, 'e's a good bloke and a good sport. No one can run a darnce like 'im. If ole Loftus 'as bin murdered, which I ain't sayin' 'e is, he might marry the ole woman. Mick could do worse. She ain't a bad looker, and she ain't a bad worker. Hey! Come on, Leonard. You're slippin'."

"Think I'm a scalded cat?" demanded Mr Wallace vehemently.

Mr Thorn chuckled like a devil.

"Watch me rile 'im and 'er up," he whispered.

"Hi, Mrs Wallace!" he shouted. "Wot erbout a drink? Two pots, please, Leonard—'e wants ter go to bed."

As a mantle might fall, so wrath fell upon Mrs Wallace. She swept aside her husband as though he were a fowl. She snatched up their tankards and with mighty arm worked the pump. The amber liquid fell into one pot and filled it to the brim. It half filled the second pot, when from the pump there came only white froth and a sound of hissing air. It was with an obvious effort that Mrs Wallace controlled herself sufficiently to say to her husband without stuttering:

"Go down and put on another barrel."

"Fill 'em up, missus," boomed the Spirit of Australia.

"Just a minute, Mr Garth."

"Slowest pub I ever bin in," muttered Mr Garth loudly.

"Get a wriggle on, Leonard, or you'll turn into a real creepy toad," urged Mrs Wallace with icicles behind her false teeth.

"The slowest pub I *ever* bin in," reiterated the Spirit of Australia.

The company laughed, and to Bony there was a hint of expectancy in the rolling sound.

Mr Wallace had now opened the trapdoor leading to the cellar. With an angry face but with a dignified air he descended the flight of six steps and, still maintaining the quickness of the expert, proceeded to tap a full barrel. Mrs Wallace was standing between the open trap and the parlour counter eagerly listening to one of "the upper class" retailing a questionable story. Someone near Bony asked for cigarettes, but the woman's attention was held fast.

Once again the Spirit of Australia vented his opinion of the Burracoppin Hotel in the matter of service. The cigarette smoker became insistent. Unable not to hear the end of the story, yet her full appreciation of it marred by the impatience of her customers and the apparent slowness of Mr Wallace, she at last swung round as a liner at anchor moved by the tide. Mr Wallace then was ascending, important work having been importantly done. His wife saw him emerge from the darkness of the cellar, and when he stood on the middle step, when his head was between floor and counter top, she cried in a loud voice:

"Lazarus, come forth!"

The hush of a moment fell upon the crowd. Slowly above the counter rose the pale, deathly face of Mr Wallace, his black eyes gleaming with an unholy light, his grey hairs entangling a ribbon of cobweb.

Roaring laughter bellowed out through the open doors and drifted far beyond the railway. It drowned the fall of the trapdoor. Laughing men beheld husband and wife standing face to face, the mighty woman with her hands on her bovine hips, the insignificant husband with his hands clenched behind his back.

"Murderer!" sneered Mrs Wallace.

"She-bull!" hissed her husband.

At this point either the little man's courage evaporated or experience had revealed to him the precise moment when to retreat successfully, because, with astonishing agility, he vaulted the counter, slipped between the customers, and disappeared through the main door.

Mrs Wallace threw the contents of a beer pot after her husband with exceeding poor aim considering the long practice she must have had. The beer descended in a shower over the Spirit of Australia, whose interest was captured by the darting Mr Wallace.

Now, an ordinary man would have wiped away the liquor from his whiskers, perhaps with an oath or two. But Mr Garth's experience of life would have been incomplete without a long course of bar-room education over all the Western Australian goldfields. To many present that evening it was unfortunate that Mr Garth did not know who was responsible for that deluge of beer. The Spirit of Australia, impatient as is the youth of the country, deemed the easiest way of finding the offender was to manhandle everyone within doors. Man after man was gripped with vicelike hands, lifted off his feet, and rushed to one of the doors, from which point he was propelled ten or twelve feet to the gritty roadway. Bony had his turn with the rest: but whereas the rest were content, being personally acquainted with Mr Garth, to arise in good humour, for really Mr Garth was not in one of his rough moods, Bony's black ancestry flashed to the surface of his dual nature, his white father's more civilized restraint submerged entirely.

Detective-Inspector Napoleon Bonaparte returned to the bar, his blue eyes like twin blue flames.

Standing on the step of the hotel door, Bony was confronted by a spectacle which so much surprised him that he went in no farther. In the very centre of the bar the Spirit of Australia faced Mrs Wallace, and the Spirit of Australia was most subdued. He was asking in pleading tones for "just one more".

"No!" thundered the lady, slowly advancing.

"Just one, marm."

"Get out!"

"Gimme a drink, and I'll go quiet."

"I don't care how you go, but get out."

Mrs Wallace was now like a liner steaming slowly out of harbour. Mr Garth was, indeed, a big man, but Mrs Wallace, if not quite so tall, was wider and deeper. Bony could see her face, and never before had he dreamed there could be such fury revealed in the human countenance. Mr Garth was unwise. He should have retreated gracefully. As he had rushed Bony out of the hotel, so was he rushed out by Mrs Wallace, his instincts inhibiting his exerting his strength against her.

The door was slammed. The other bar door was slammed with equal viciousness. Footsteps thundered along a passage, and yet other doors were slammed and bolted. Mrs Wallace was the triumphant victor holding the fort.

"She's a trimmer," announced the Spirit of Australia, chuckling dryly, in his voice no trace of his recent violence and anger. "Who heaved that pot at me?"

"She did," Mr Thorn said, as one who is bereaved.

"Then why didn't someone tell me?" Mr Garth asked with pained astonishment.

"We had a lot of spare time, didn't we?" a voice in the darkness pointed out succinctly.

Silence, broken presently by Mr Garth's dry chuckle.

"Well—well! We all enjoyed ourselves, so what's the odds? I'm off to feed me horses. Good night!"

With wonderful good humour, considering their rough handling, the small crowd dispersed to their homes, Bony walking towards the Rabbit

Department Depot. Arriving at the gate, however, he changed his mind about going to bed and sauntered south along the straight road hemmed in by the silent, brooding scrub.

He was feeling ashamed at his failure to control the flash of temper engendered by Mr Garth's assault, but when this wore away he began to enjoy retrospectively the human characters he had met that night. The circumstances of the evening he neither liked nor approved in general. He was not a drinker, not because he disliked alcoholic liquor, but because he hated to feel his senses dulled even for a short space of time.

It was not the want of human company or the craving for stimulants which had urged him to the hotel. His visit there was made for a quite different reason. He was aware—who is not?—that the masculine life of an Australian bush community centres about the hotel and the feminine life about the hall. Men accustomed to semi-solitary lives and performing open-air work are not naturally loquacious, but will become so when in the company of their fellows and mellowed by alcohol; while women from the lonely farms, when gathered inside a brightly lit hall at a dance or other social function, place no restraint upon their tongues.

Therefore, at the hotel and in the hall the real life of the community is to be seen in its nakedness for observant eyes to study with profit. As Bony knew, the essence of human aspirations, the virtues and the vices, are found in the humblest of the people. To Bony, thinker and student, the Spirit of Australia was of profounder interest than possibly could have been a member of royalty, for no king in history, who lived beyond eighty years, possessed Mr Garth's strength, freedom from diseases, and cleanness of mind which had guaranteed both. And surely the man clothed, nay, burdened with in the incrustations of pomposity, propriety, and power is of less interest than Mr Thorn with his vivid imagination, shrewdness, humour, and affability.

As for Mr Wallace and his wife, here was a study of the opposites revealing one of the greatest of human mysteries: the attraction for each other of people diametrically opposed physically and mentally. Bony asked the silent trees what it was in Mrs Wallace which once had been honey to the little bee, and what quality in him had aroused admiration, possibly passion, in the bosom of that majestic woman.

The still, warm air perceptibly cooled the fever produced by heat and artificial mental stimulation, and, while he walked oblivious of the time and place, the detective examined the fish brought to him by the first cast of his net. Separately he picked them up to find among them one which might resemble the stingray, putting each one down dissatisfied that the examination was inconclusive.

Leonard Wallace might have killed Loftus, for he was of that type whose nature is mild with the placidity of the supposedly extinct volcano. There was much in common in the characters of Dr Crippen and Mr Wallace.

Of his wife's melodramatic accusation Bony took little heed. Such an accusation as that her husband murdered Loftus seemed the visible expression of mere feminine unreasoning spite, feminine desire to hurt that which in other circumstances it would strive to protect.

On the other hand, there was reason behind Mr Thorn's bibulously inflamed imagination. While so far there was no apparent motive for anyone killing the farmer—other than a chance passing tramp—there could be many sound reasons or motives for Loftus to carry out his own disappearance. Having been a popular man, doubtless during the recent years of prosperity he had had money with which to support his popularity. Such a man would suffer distress from lack of money, and had he been able to secure a loan in Perth the temptation to disappear with it and start a new life in a different State might well have surmounted a love of home. Men have done worse things than deserting a wife, with less reason.

Yet, after all had been weighed in the balance of fact, the scales were even. The puzzle of Loftus's absence remained, and as hour succeeded hour the half-caste became more absorbed by it. He turned back when from far to the south came the low, murmuring roar of wind among the scrub, heralding the strong breeze which swept from the coast inland with the regularity of a clock at this time of night at this time of year. The "Albany Doctor" people called it, because the strong, cool wind from Albany way swept clear the bodily and mental languours brought on by the heat of the long day.

Bony was about a quarter of a mile from the Depot, the sound of the coming wind being then like the roar of surf, when the trunk of a white gum tree reflected the glare of approaching headlights behind him.

The machine was travelling at a high speed, the noise of the engine swamped by that of the wind which suddenly rushed through the scrub about him and raised a cloud of dust above the road.

Why Bony stepped behind a tree long before the driver of the car could have seen him was inexplicable even to himself, save that his maternal ancestry prompted the act, the impulse of the hunted, subjugated woman shy of the approaching stranger. Sheltered from observation, he now heard the racing engine and heard, too, the loud report which he quickly learned was caused by a tyre burst.

The car lurched dangerously and finally was stopped directly opposite the watcher. A man got down and examined the tyres with the aid of a flash lamp.

"A blowout," he said to someone still within the closed car.

The first man proceeded to obtain jack and tools. The second man alighted, a tall and big man dressed in dust coat and soft hat. Together they removed the deflated wheel and put on the spare, the first man grumbling all the time, the big man silent. There was no doubt in Bony's mind that the big man was Mr Jelly.

Within four minutes the change was effected and the car moved on. Bony watched the tail-light grow rapidly smaller. The car took the left-hand turn, the west turn towards Merredin and Perth.

Thoughtfully he walked on, wondering why Mr Jelly should be travelling away from his home at that time of night. He was still wondering when he reached the Depot gate, where he was halted by a voice outside the hotel.

"Let me in, Lizzie," pleaded a now subdued Mr Wallace.

No reply came.

"Hi! Let me in, Lizzie, old girl."

There was a light in one of the rooms on the first floor. It percolated through the drawn blind, revealing the substantial figure of Mrs Wallace standing on the veranda. Her arm was raised. Bony saw it swing forward and downward. Came then the crash of bedroom china on the roadway, and a startled exclamation from Mr Wallace.

When the licensee began to run towards the gate, Bony for the second time that night concealed himself, this time in the deep shadow of the corrugated-iron fence. Unaware of him, Wallace opened the gate and almost ran to the Rabbit Inspector's house. Inspector Gray appeared with a lamp held above his head in answer to the loud summons.

"Good evening, Mr Gray," Wallace said politely. "Will you please lend me your double-barrelled gun?"

"Sorry, Leonard, but the gun is at my son's place."

"All right." There was disappointment in Mr Wallace's voice. "All right! Sorry to knock you up. Good night!"

The door was shut. Wallace departed towards the rear of the hotel, probably to sleep in the stables, and Bony, now with further food for thought, walked slowly to his room thinking—thinking how strange it was that when asked for a gun at midnight Gray showed not the slightest surprise and had not sufficient curiosity to ask the reason prompting the request.

Chapter Seven

Within Another World

Before starting off for his post-cutting work, Bony wrote to the Commissioner asking him for details of debts owing on the Loftus farm, and if, when last in Perth, George Loftus had secured a further bank loan or any cash backing from other financial concerns. He also requested the Western Australian Police Chief to instruct the senior officer stationed at Merredin to report to him at Burracoppin as soon as was convenient.

A second letter he addressed to his wife, an educated half- caste like himself, who ruled their bush-girt home at Banyo, near Brisbane. Among other matters he wrote:

This case has many points in common with that which attracted me to the sands of Windee. Whilst remembering that in your goodness of heart and with your broadness of mind you could find nothing wrong with my final actions in that case, where I permitted sentimentality to cloud my sense of duty, resulting in an official confession of failure which has marred my unblemished record, I remember, too, your admonishment that the first and last duty of a crime investigator is to reveal the guilty criminal.

I shall not slip down that incline again. At Windee a lovely face and an understanding mind beat down my judgment and spoilt my greatest triumph. There is in this case, too, a pair of eyes lit by an understanding mind, but I shall watch and guard against my heart weaknesses. She is only fourteen years old and her name is Sunflower. I wish we had a fairy daughter.

Yes; there is in this affair much resemblance to that of Windee. There is no horribly violated body lying on the library floor, or anywhere else so far as I can ascertain. I am sure that murder has been committed; therefore, you will understand that, as in the Windee case, first I must prove the fact of murder and secondly reveal the murderer.

You know about that sixth sense which unerringly tells me that blood has been spilled. That undefined sense prompts me now. I believe that George Loftus was killed when I have no slightest evidence of it. There are in this case elements of peculiar interest. Quite possibly it may turn out to be one of those macabre murders such as those acclaimed by the lecturer in Thomas de Quincey's immortal essay, "On Murder Considered as One of the Fine Arts." The lecturer states:

"People begin to see that something more goes to the composition of a fine murder than two blockheads to kill and be killed—a knife—a purse—and a dark lane. Design, gentlemen, grouping, light and shade, poetry, sentiment, are now deemed indispensable to attempts of this nature."

How true, dear Marie, how very true! Modern killers often are real artists compared to the savage and crude practitioners of the early days. And as artistic beauty has evolved through the centuries from coarse crudity, so from the condition of low intelligence ruling the old English force known as the Bow Street Runners has become evolved the superlative genius of

Your ever affectionate husband,
BONY

These letters he posted when he had harnessed a horse to a dray and before calling on Mrs Poole for his lunch. He discovered his landlady flushed with anger.

"If you got up earlier," she snapped to the elder of her small sons, "that Mrs Black wouldn't have had the chance to milk her. You know what she is. If you don't get up tomorrow morning, I'll throw cold water over you."

"To beat that old cow I'd have to get up before daylight," was the stout defence of a lad about twelve years of age.

"Well, get up in the dark, then." To the detective Mrs Poole added:

"That's twice this week Tom has gone to milk the cow and found her stripped dry."

"Where is the cow ... during the night?"

"In bed. I suppose with that blackguard of a husband of hers."

Bony was puzzled. He said:

"I was not aware that cows had permanent husbands."

Obviously Mrs Poole tried hard to regain composure. "I was talking about Mrs Black," she said stiffly.

"Oh! I thought you were talking about the cow."

"So I was."

Bony's expression continued to indicate perplexity.

Young Tom laughed. "Mrs Black ain't a real cow," he explained, and was severely cuffed. It became Mrs Poole's turn to explain.

"We haven't any place to keep a cow at night. We keep her tied up with a bit of chaff till we go to bed and then let her loose to pick up grass and stuff about the town roads. Some mornings she's close by, and sometimes she's a mile away. Goldie is always going over the railway to Mrs Black's place. She feeds Goldie with sugar and things. And milks her before huntin' her away. I know it."

"Have you seen her actually milking the cow?"

"No. But isn't it obvious?"

"Where does the lady live?"

"Behind the hall."

"But there are other women living near the hall. Perhaps it is one of them who steals the milk."

"Oh! It's Mrs Black all right. She'd cut off her grandfather's whiskers to sell as horsehair."

Laughing silently, Bony went out to his horse and drove at a slow pace along the winding road flanking the railway and the pipe trench. At the rabbit fence gate he unharnessed the horse and put it in the farm stables for the day. Then, carrying a piece of paper and a pencil, he started off to examine every fence post between the railway and the gate across the old York Road.

Observant and curious eyes, had there been any, would have been satisfied that he was examining each post to ascertain if it wanted renewing, and that on the paper he was noting the number of the posts required over the stated distance.

Yet really Bony was less interested by the condition of the fence posts than he was by the surface of the little-used road adjacent to the fence on the western side. Assuming that George Loftus walked home during the early morning of O November, it was possible for evidence of his passing to lie on that track or beside it, despite the fact that it was raining and that the present date, 17th November, marked the passage of fifteen days.

The bush detective was aware of and appreciated one significant fact regarding the mentality of the Australian black tracker. Being an inherent fatalist, the aboriginal too soon gives up. Convince him that there are tracks to be found, and very pride in his wonderful sight will spur him to find and follow them more surely than a bloodhound. But the tracker who was brought from Merredin, twenty-odd miles westward, on 4th November, when it was definitely realized that Loftus was missing, knew that it had rained during the night of 2nd November right through to the dawn of 3rd November. And, observing by the condition of the ground search that even his eyes would not see tracks washed out by the rain. Once the idea that no tracks would be visible became firmly fixed in his mind, extraneous subjects of greater importance and interest would occupy his thoughts and blur his vision. Knowing there were no tracks, he would not think to look for objects which to the white man would become important clues.

Where the full blood would accept defeat without endeavour the white man would accept nothing for fact until it was proved. From his white father Bony had inherited the precious gift of reason, and from his mother the equally precious gift of patience. Reason and patience, developed by undying passion for knowledge, produced in this half-caste a force of good seldom found among the white races and almost never among the black.

While he walked slowly along the track he lived in another world vastly different from that known to the unscientific white man. He descended, or, perhaps, it should be stated, he ascended to the insect world. He saw innumerable ants belonging to a dozen species. The ferocious inch-and-a-half-long bulldog, whose sight was extraordinary, whose pugnaciousness at his approach was superbly courageous, and whose bite was venomous; the hurrying red ant half an inch long, which made beaten roads through the grass from nest to larder as represented by the carcass of some small animal; the tiny black ants but little larger than a grain of sugar, which swarmed along defined highways and up the trunks of many trees and into the branches, there feverishly to gather the honey from the blooms not much larger than themselves; the bigger black ants, long-legged, slow in action, which utilized sun-warmed stones with which to incubate their eggs; and the minute brown fellow of the size of a cheese mite living unconcernedly among this vast population of relative giants.

He saw the grey-and-black honey ants taking down into inconspicuous holes their loads of honey, which they crammed into the mouths of the store ants in their caves deep in the earth, crammed them so that their bodies were distended to the size of peas, the transparent skins making them appear like honey drops, living drops of honey unable to move, too huge to pass along the ant corridors had they been able, living only to regurgitate their stores during the winter.

Everywhere he saw evidence of the stupendous labour of the dweller in a world beyond even the insect world, the termite which lives in eternal darkness, without sight, without hope, the vast majority sexless, without individual purpose, dedicated solely to unending labour, governed by an inexplicable force originating from some inexplicable centre, creatures living the communistic ideal as never a race of super-Marxians could hope to do.

What has a detective to do with ants? What have ants to do with crime? They punish crime only in one way—death. The termite does not even violently kill. The order goes forth from the centre that the criminal must die, and not one unit of the vast population permits the sentenced to eat, and very quickly the doomed itself is eaten when death claims it. More than once had the ants presented valuable ideas to Bony; on more than one occasion they had given him a clue of great value.

Here and there, the rain not having soaked away, had formed overflowing pools, and, the ground slope falling eastward, the water flows had gathered twigs and dead grass into small beaverlike dams against the netting of the Fence. The accumulation of this rubbish was not overlooked by the termite, which works up from beneath the ground, and, working from within, plasters the object it attacks with a cement composed of sand and the juices of its body. Bony, also, did not overlook this rubbish, most of it now looking like thick ropes of rusted wire. He destroyed the careful work of the termites to maintain their loved darkness by kicking all this rubbish asunder, providing the voracious ants with a meal of delectable putty-coloured flesh.

It was in this way that he discovered a small notebook, the covers and the outer leaves of which the termites had eaten, a notebook which had been surrounded by debris, hidden from the eyes of the black tracker, when the rain had washed it against the fence. The few remaining leaves bore entries made without doubt by George Loftus when he was last in Perth.

It was irrefutable evidence that George Loftus had not been killed—at the spot where was found his wrecked and abandoned car.

Human dissatisfaction has been called divine, doubtless in those far-off days when the word was applicable to love and woman. Akin to worry, dissatisfaction has the same effect on the human being, in that men and women forever dissatisfied with their conditions of life are generally poor in physique.

Now Sergeant Westbury, the senior police officer stationed at Merredin, was wholly satisfied with his wife, his family of three boys, his official position, and the state of his bank account; and, in consequence, he was red of face, burly of frame, and generously endowed with flesh.

He came to Burracoppin on the 10 a.m. goods train, sought for and found inspector Gray, and induced the fence man to take him in his truck to interview Bony. The two men were more than acquaintances, for their wives were cousins.

"This half-caste bird. Is he a joke?" asked Inspector Gray.

"I thought so; I thought so," the sergeant replied in a harsh voice that absurdly contradicted the facial aspect of benevolence. The small twinkling eyes appeared as mere pinpoints of steel-blue light, so close drawn were the puckered lids. He talked as a man to whom talking is a necessary evil.

"Got a letter the other day. Commissioner himself wrote. Says give D. I. Bonaparte every assistance. Gives it him. Think Commissioner cracked. Two days ago along comes Mason. You know, D. S. Mason. I said: 'What's the idea?' He said: 'What idea?' I said: 'Who's this black on the job?' He said: 'Hush! I'll write it down.' … Fred—no, he ain't a joke."

"Seems educated," Gray asserted.

"Would be. Got to be. Mason says university. No social or colour bar in our unies, you know. We ain't that far behind the times."

"He told me he has failed only in one case."

Sergeant Westbury heaved himself round to face the other.

"Pulling your leg; pulling your leg," he snorted. "D. S. Mason—good man, Mason—says Bonaparte's never failed. Over east the heads think the sun shines out of his boots. Mason is thick with Muir, and Muir says the black is one hundred times cleverer than he is. And Muir's no mug, bee-lieve me."

"But if he is that smart, why haven't we heard of him in the papers?"

"It's a wonder we ain't heard of this damn road in the papers. He's a sight too clever to get his name in the papers. The underworld don't know him. Never heard of him. Never seen him as a detective. Don't dream that the real man who's bagged 'em is not the D. who invites 'em to take a little walk. A joke! No, he's not a joke."

They found Bony working on the fence midway between the railway and the old York Road, and after Sergeant Westbury had inelegantly backed down from the truck he faced Bony and with difficulty refrained from saluting.

"Headquarters' instructions to report, sir," he jerked out. "Ordered not to salute."

"Good! That saves me the trouble of asking you not to. The greatest tragedy of life is its shortness, and busy men have no time to waste." Bony was smiling. He shook hands with the sergeant. "Many people mistake me for a superior policeman, the most persistent being my own State chief. I regret troubling you to come all this way from Merredin, but there is work I wish to have done."

"All right; all right. No trouble. Pleasure, sir."

"Ah! I'm glad you remembered to call me Bony."

"Sorry, si — — Bony," the sergeant said with purple face.

"Quite all right sergeant. I once knew a millionaire who objected with much violence to being called sir or even mister. I liked him much. He was so refreshingly democratic. Have you any news of George Loftus?"

"No."

"Did your chief forward any particulars of the missing man's financial position?"

The sergeant struggled with a pocket. He was breathing heavily.

"The particulars are all set out on this document," he said.

For fully a minute Bony studied the memorandum. There was a note stating that the Agricultural Bank paid only on approved cheques as the credit was created by loan money. But a most important statement was that made by the manager of the Bank of New South Wales. Loftus's credit at this account, 30th October, was one hundred and seventy-three pounds, and on 1st November Loftus had drawn one hundred pounds in treasury notes of one-pound denomination.

"So it is probable that Loftus had on him a large sum of money when he arrived at Burracoppin," Bony said reflectively.

"Looks like it; looks like it," agreed the sergeant.

"Did you know Loftus?"

"No. Never remember seeing him."

"Were you with the black tracker when he was brought here?"

"Yes."

"How did he work?"

"Good! Good man. Intelligent."

"Did he track right along this road?"

"Yes, and all about the York Road yonder."

"He must have been half blind."

"Not him," objected the sergeant. "If you found anything you were lucky. I had a look along here too."

"Excellent," Bony said suavely, amusement in his eyes. "Observe that part of the roadway. You can, of course, see that within the last hour a centipede of medium size crossed it."

"Be hanged if I can; be hanged if I can."

Sergeant Westbury was stooping down, hands on knees. His face still was purple. His honesty delighted the detective.

"Look more closely," urged Bony. "See! There along this fallen twig."

"I can't see no tracks; no tracks."

"Nor I, because there are none."

Like a jack-in-the-box the sergeant stood up. "But you said——"

"I made no definite statement, but requested you to observe a set of tracks which do not exist. You admitted you could see no tracks when another man, knowing my training, would have said they could. I like you for that. I shall assist you in your career if possible. I feel now that I can rely absolutely on your silence regarding my identity and official position. Now, please tell me what you think of this case."

The Merredin man grinned his pleasure.

"On the face of it," he said, "Loftus disappeared on purpose. Why did he draw one hundred pounds in small notes just before he *left* Perth? I draw money from the bank *before* I go to Perth, and if another man had an account in Perth he'd draw money as soon as he got there and not just before he was leaving."

"Do you believe in intuition?" Bony inquired.

"Me? No, but my wife does. She gets an intuition fit every time I goes into a pub."

"Evidently your wife is a knowing woman. There are times when I permit myself to be influenced by a sixth sense commonly known as intuition. I feel sure, although I have no smallest tittle of evidence, that George Loftus was killed. Somewhere within a radius of five miles lies the body of the missing farmer, and in my mind there is no doubt that I shall find it. Never yet was the perfect crime, because never yet was evolved the perfect criminal, although each and every one of them think they are the brilliant exception.

"You can almost see Loftus's wrecked car down there by the railway. I know that he left his car in an angry mood, that he flung from him the remains of a nearly consumed cigar. I know that he walked from the car along this fence and that he remembered he had a fresh cigar when he reached the tall gimlet-tree just there. By that tree he lit it. I also lit a cigar there and smoked it quickly whilst I walked across the old York Road gate, and within thirty-seven yards of the spot where I threw away my cigar end I found the cigar end discarded by Loftus. I know, therefore, that Loftus reached the old York Road. Do you not now think it unlikely that George Loftus planned to wreck his car on the pipeline and walk then a full mile to pick up another on the York Road in which to decamp?"

"He might have planned to leave his car on the old York Road, and wrecking it on the pipeline was an accident."

"Certainly the wrecking of his car was an accident. He didn't plan to smash his car, or he would not have agreed to accept Wallace as a passenger. The argument between them started only after they had passed the garage."

"But Wallace might have been in the game," persisted the sergeant.

"Your reasoning is logical," admitted Bony. "Yet why was Loftus in such a towering rage? Governed by anger most certainly he was. The distance to which he flung two empty beer bottles, two cigar ends, and the fact that he used five matches to light the second cigar by that gimlet-tree goes to prove it, for angry men are far more energetic than calm men. In actual fact he was so angry that when he lit his second cigar he failed to note that his notebook fell to the ground.

"Yes, undoubtedly he was angry. The question presented to us is: Why was he angry when partly intoxicated? We answer: Because he had accidentally wrecked his car and was faced by a two-mile walk in the middle of the night when it was raining, and to that was added the certain knowledge that he had been a fool in not turning at the garage corner and so have avoided all his troubles. If he had planned his disappearance he would have drawn all the money from his bank account, and his plans would not have included wrecking his car and walking two miles in the direction of his home."

Sergeant Westbury was fascinated. Yet he further objected.

"But why did he draw that money when he did?" he asked.

"That remains to be discovered, Sergeant. We will proceed slowly. Never hurry Chief Detective Time. The first step, which we have accomplished, was to decide definitely whether Loftus deliberately disappeared or was either killed or abducted."

"You mentioned a notebook; a notebook."

"I did. I found it against the fence opposite that tree where Loftus stopped to light his second cigar and expended five matches in doing so. I found the used matches and the notebook buried in a mass of water-piled rubbish. See, here is the book almost eaten by the white ants, and here in these thin splinters of white wood we have all the ants left of five whole matches,"

"Anything important in the notebook?"

"Evidence that it belonged to Loftus and that he had possessed it when in Perth. As I just stated, the first step in this really interesting case is completed. Now, please, note a few instructions."

"Right. All set."

"I want all particulars regarding Mrs Loftus and the man Landon, who works on the Loftus farm. Their antecedents, their habits, and, if possible, their vices and their virtues. In fact, everything about them you can gather, and I am relying on you to be sure that your inquiries raise neither comment nor suspicion."

"I'll be careful. But you ain't going to accuse 'em of murder, are you?"

"Certainly not. And please find out from the Bank of New South Wales if the notes paid out to Loftus on November the first were old, or partly soiled, or new. That will be all."

Bony smiled at the burly sergeant, and Sergeant Westbury grinned back at him with eyes which were mere pinheads of steel in the centre of screwed-in lids. Before turning away to the truck he said:

"Very good. Yes, very good. Good day; good day!"

Chapter Eight

The Dance

At the invitation of Mrs Gray, Bony decided to attend the dance held at the Burracoppin Hall on the evening of 20th November.

Accordingly he dressed with care, in clothes sent up from Perth, and about nine o'clock left the Depot in company with Mr and Mrs Gray.

Into this hall from the town and outlying farms had come good-looking women and strong, well-set-up men, an A-1 standard of physique rarely seen in the older countries and the Australian cities. From the farm districts and from the vast bushlands beyond had emerged in NVNQ that Australian Army whose physical perfection had aroused the admiration of Europe.

Within the hall they discovered almost seventy people waiting for the M.C. to announce the first dance of the evening. The electric light was softened by strings of coloured paper festooned beneath the lamps. It fell on gaily attired women and well-scrubbed men in lounge suits. At the door people separated as though governed by established convention, women occupying the long forms set against one wall and the men taking their seats against the opposite wall. Near the door stood the contingent of unattached males.

Often Bony had observed this division of the sexes in the smaller towns of the Commonwealth, coming to regard it as a facet of the white man's psychology for which there was no adequate explanation. To him, an observer on the fringe, this sex segregation, far more marked than in the cities, was an unsolvable puzzle.

There was an undercurrent of excitement vibrant to his keen senses. Pleasurable anticipation glowed on every face. The members of the string band, minus coats and waistcoats, began to tune their instruments. From behind stage came the sound of crockery ware, and when Mick Landon jumped from floor to stage the flutter of anticipation was general.

"Ladies and gents," he said in a clear voice, "I have been asked by the committee to express their pleasure at the large number who have turned up so early. As you know, this dance is being run to benefit Mrs Loftus, who is financially embarrassed by the strange disappearance of Mr Loftus. The fact of the matter is that until it is known what has become of Mr Loftus his financial affairs cannot be settled. So let us hope his disappearance may be soon cleared up. When Mrs Loftus arrives, let us give her a rousing welcome, considering how popular she is."

" 'Ear, 'ear!" someone applauded, whilst the gathering expressed approval with much hand clapping.

Conscious of his position, Landon raised his hands to secure attention.

"We will start the night, then, with a foxtrot," he shouted.

The band struck up a rollicking tune. Men and women gravitated to each other on the floor, the women not waiting for an invitation or an escort. Evidently partnerships had been arranged before ever they entered the hall.

Without coat or waistcoat, with blue braces vivid against white shirt, Mick Landon looked like a clerk in a heated warehouse or a stockbroker digging up his garden. He was perfectly proportioned. The light gleaming on his fair curly hair showed his face to be really handsome. Once he had got the dance started he swept into his arms a young lady who made no effort to disguise her pleasure and conducted her round the floor, whilst his strangely fixed blue eyes looked down on her in a masterful way. Fifty pairs of feminine eyes watched his every movement; even those women dancing looked at him when he was in their line of vision, regarded him with narrowed eyes, their hearts moved by envy of his partner.

Bony decided that the women and girls could not be blamed. Sight of such a man could excusably arouse emotion in the heart of any woman. He was dominant, the master there. Mick Landon might rise high — directly the sex influence of women waned and gave place to worthy ambition.

Watching the crowd with absorbed interest, Bony caught sight of Lucy Jelly, calm-eyed, composed, and refreshingly cool in a becoming gown of white muslin. She was dancing with a young fellow about her own age whose eyes sparkled with pride and whose well-brushed hair gleamed with oil. Mr Thorn hopped around with a woman as fat as himself. She, Bony decided, must be his wife, because he studiously refrained from breathing beer into her red face. An active middle-aged man, whom Bony knew to be a Snake Charmer, was proving a worthy partner to spritely Sunflower Jelly, and the Spirit of Australia was dancing with youthful grace with a little woman about forty years old who actually appeared to be no older than nineteen.

"You working for the Rabbit Department?" asked a rugged six-foot Scotchman. It was more a statement of fact than a question. Bony admitted it. "Glad to see you here. Good crowd. Know many?"

"A few, yes. Mr Thorn, there. And that big man I have heard called the Spirit of Australia. Is it a fact that he is over eighty years of age?"

"Must be. I bin out here ten years, and he don't look a day older than when I come. Several of the old identities swear that he must be nearer ninety than eighty."

When next Bony spoke he said:

"I see Miss Jelly and Miss Sunflower, but not Mr Jelly. Does he not dance?"

"No, he ain't around," the Scotchman replied without accent. Had Bony been a fellow countryman no Englishman would have understood him. "He's a queer card, Jelly. Every time I think of him I am reminded of Dr Jekyll in the book. His going away without ever telling folk where he goes, or why, is very strange. 'Course, it might be a woman. He's a widower, you know. Some men are like that."

"Yet Mr Jelly did not strike me as being that sort of man."

"He don't really strike me that way either. But why does he go? Sometimes he's away for three of four weeks, and at other times he only goes for a few days, It wouldn't be so bad if he said he was going and when he would be back. But no one ever sees him go or knows that he is going, not even his daughter, who worries herself to death about it. It's a bit thick in a way."

"Who does the farm work during these periods of absence?"

"Old Middleton carries on, He works for Jelly. Well, I'm in on the next dance. See you after."

When the dance was in full swing Bony saw Mrs Gray trying to attract his attention, and after much adroit manoeuvring he gained her side. Mrs Gray was one of those women whose souls kept unblemished by the rouge of social ambition and the lipstick of snobbishness.

"Don't you dance?" she asked when Bony sat down between her and her husband.

"Yes, madam, but it is not often I have the chance," he told her gravely, refraining to add that the average white woman was shy of accepting him.

"May I have the pleasure of your partnership?"

"I would consent if I could dance," she said, regarding him frankly. "If you would like to meet them, I am sure there are one or two women here who would be pleased for you to ask them."

"Thank you! That is a suggestion I will gladly accept. Yet before you so kindly make the introductions, I am going to take my courage in both hands and ask Miss Lucy Jelly to favour me. I have already been presented to her. Permit me to go to her now before my courage trickles away between my fingers."

When he had risen, bowed, and departed towards Lucy Jelly, then sitting with Sunflower farther along the wall, Mrs Gray said to her husband:

"He's not working for you because he has to. What is behind your putting him on?"

Inspector Gray smiled at her and winked an eye. Slowly, distinctly, and emphatically he said to her:

"Find out."

"All right. I will find out. You never tell me anything."

Standing before Lucy Jelly, Bony was saying:

"I do hope you remember me. Might I have the next dance—a waltz, I believe?"

He saw doubt cloud her clear brown eyes, knew she would refuse before she uttered the excuse so difficult to evolve. He even detected her displeasure about the necessity to make the excuse.

"I'm sorry, but I'm engaged for the next dance."

Bony smiled his disappointment, saying:

"I, too, am sorry."

He was turning away when Sunflower's voice arrested him.

"You might at least ask me, Mr Bony. I won't tell a fib," she said softly.

"Dulcie, how dare you!" the elder sister exclaimed with scarlet face.

"I shall be charmed," Bony announced, offering his arm as the band started to play "The Blue Danube".

Sunflower's head came to Bony's shoulder. Permitting him to hold her in the approved style, they glided away among the crowded couples, and he, looking down on her golden hair, was thrilled by the pure glory of it. She was a born dancer. Music and poetry lived in her soul. Looking up at him with no sophistry in her dove-grey, limped eyes, she said to him, almost in a whisper:

"You dance wonderfully. Did you learn at the corroborees?"

"No. I learned to dance in Brisbane when I went to high school."

"And did they teach you elocution, and good manners, and all that?"

"No. I took much trouble to teach myself. Who taught you to dance so nicely?"

"Sis did," the maid said gravely before falling into a silence of very ecstasy that was in part a compliment to him. Minutes passed before she spoke again.

"You must forgive Lucy telling that fib, because she is so worried about Father," Sunflower said softly. "You see, the other morning we found that he had gone away, and he never tells us that he is going or when he expects to come home. It is not so bad his going, but when he comes back he brings strong drink with him and he shuts himself up in his room for days."

"You really do not know where he goes to or why?" Bony asked.

Sunflower shook her head with emphasis. The strange behaviour of her father was a heavy cloud masking the sun of her life. The music stopped. They stood almost in the centre of the floor waiting for a possible encore. People began to clap their hands. Little Sunflower said at last:

"No, we don't know about Father. If we did, it wouldn't be so bad, would it? Perhaps you could find out. You are a policeman, aren't you?"

Astonished that his identity was known to this unsophisticated young lady, Bony was hardly aware that the band had started playing and that the dancers were swinging off in rhythmic step. Sunflower, unabashed because unconscious of the shock she had given him, caught his hand before he responded to the music.

"So you know I am a detective?" he said softly, in his eyes an expression of quizzical interest.

"Yes, we have known about you ever since you came to our farm. You are not angry, are you?"

"I could not be angry with you, Miss Sunflower; but how did you find out?"

"Eric told us when you were with Father in his room that night. He said we must keep it a secret."

"Ah! And how did he find out?"

Sunflower laughed gaily, her mood lightened when at last she saw the gleam of laughter behind his blue eyes, from which she knew she could keep nothing back.

"Guess," she commanded teasingly.

"Did Eric hear me talking in my sleep?"

"No; guess again."

"I give up," Bony announced. "Tell me, quick, before I faint with curiosity."

"All right. Eric said he picked up a letter in the Depot yard which was written to Inspector Gray. He showed it to us the evening you came with him. Of course we were thrilled, but Lucy said it was wrong of us to read a letter that did not belong to us. She made Eric put it into the kitchen fire and made him and me promise to tell no one. We haven't, either."

"Not even your father?"

"No. Not even Father."

They circled the polished floor before she spoke again, saying:

"You know, you do not look like a detective. You look much too kind. Not like two of them I saw here before I met you. They were big, stern men with fierce eyes which make you shiver. Even when you are angry you don't look like they look at people."

"I am not stern. And I'm not angry. I am surprised at your knowing I am a detective, that is all. I thought that only Mr Gray knew. As you and Eric promised Miss Lucy not to tell, will you promise me not to tell?"

"Of course," Sunflower said, as though she were a past master in the art of keeping secrets. And then: "Do you think poor Mr Loftus ran away from Mrs Loftus?"

"Why should he? Why do you ask that question?"

"Well, you're here to find out, aren't you? And because if I was Mr Loftus I'd run away from her. I hate that woman."

"Dear, dear! Surely you cannot hate?"

"I hate her, anyway. I couldn't tell you why exactly. Do you think he ran away from her?"

There was no evading her question the second time. Bony was frank.

"I cannot find out," he said.

"Will you stay until you do?"

"Very likely."

Presently she said: "Will you come to our farm some day and tell me all about the blackfellows' corroborees? I would like to hear tales about them, and, perhaps, you could find out about Father. Would you try?"

"Yes, if your sister would like me to do so," Bony replied, studying the swiftly changing expression on her face. "We must defer to her, you know. She is the elder. Possibly she might not like my trying to find out."

"Oh I think she would. Father makes her so worried."

"Very well. I will put it to her later on."

The music came to an end. The dancers stopped. There was much laughter whilst people thanked each other, followed by a general movement to the seats.

"Will you ask me to dance again presently, Mr Bony?" Sunflower asked, not attempting to conceal her anxiety lest he should forget.

"It will give me great pleasure to ask, not once, but several times. Let me take you back to your sister, now talking to——" There was sudden commotion beyond the main entrance.

The knot of men who appeared as though glued to that part of the hall, seemingly content merely to watch—and criticize—raised a cheer which was taken up by the dancers. They parted into a lane, and into this lane flashed a sparkle of pink which resolved into a woman's dress. The wearer came along the lane, to pause at its innermost end while the crowd cheered and clapped.

Bony saw a strikingly pretty woman whom he guessed correctly to be Mrs Loftus. Her age, he knew, was twenty- nine. She was dressed in a frock of pink crepe de chine, which seemed oddly to contrast with her supposed financial difficulties, which this dance was being held partially to relieve. In height slightly above the average, her frock showed to perfection a well-moulded, supple figure. Her face was flushed, and her eyes—he thought they were dark hazel— reflected the lights. Her expression was one of strained anxiety, the whole giving a total effect of pleasure at being there and doubt of the proprietary of it when her husband was so strangely missing.

The band struck up "For she's a jolly good fellow", and the crowd roared the lines as Mick Landon gallantly escorted the guest of honour to the stage end of the hall, where he turned aside, leaving the woman alone to accept the welcome.

It was spontaneously given, and, Bony's admiration of the beautiful aroused, he added his mite to the general uproar. When almost any woman would have cried with a full heart, this woman smiled with the calmness of a queen. And then Bony's penetrating vision pierced deep behind the now smiling face, and he saw an iron-willed woman, sure of herself, selfish and sensual. His first impression was quickly revised. The loveliness of feature and form was marred in the eyes of the beauty worshipper by a will too strong, a composure too ably controlled, a mind too clever, too calculating.

The singing died down. The hand clapping ceased. Mrs Loftus said with charming simplicity:

"You are all very kind to me. I thank you from my heart."

Again the clapping and the cheering. It surprised Bony to observe how popular Mrs Loftus really was. Mick Landon came forward, holding a sugar bag. He shouted in order to gain complete silence.

"Ladies and gents! Ladies and gents! In this bag are the entry tickets. I hope all the holders of them wrote their names on them, because the ticket Mrs Loftus will now draw from the bag here will entitle the owner to the honour of the first dance with her. If the ticket owner cannot dance, he may nominate a gent who can, and if a lady draws the honour she may name any gent she chooses. Now, Mrs Loftus, please draw."

Watching with his never failing interest in human beings, Bony saw that when she placed her be-ringed hand into the bag she looked not at it but into the eyes of the man who held it open. When she had taken the ticket, the M.C. tossed the bag to the back of the stage and then politely took the ticket from her. There was a hushed suspense. Studiously Landon slowly looked up with the name on it in his mind, paused for precisely five seconds, and then shouted:

"Mr Garth!"

Again the cheering broke out, above which men shouted: "Good old John! The Spirit of Australia!"

The band began to play a foxtrot. Gath's booming voice rose above the din.

"I'm taking a ticket in Tatt's," he roared whilst stalking through the throng now surging on the floor towards the waiting woman who hid her disappointment behind a laughing face. The Spirit of Australia was dressed in a navy- blue suit. His bearing, his face, shrieked the lie regarding his age. Towering above Mrs Loftus, his courtly bow and the manner in which he offered her his arm shrieked, too, the lie of his wild rough life on the gold fields and the farms.

Bony was about to propose another dance to little Sunflower when Mrs Gray came up and expressed a wish to introduce him to a friend. Smilingly he accompanied her, yet not before he had au-revoired Sunflower and had seen the look of regret in her big soft eyes.

He was presented to a matron belonging to that type known as "gushing", yet was no whit abashed or discomfited. She danced moderately well, and, although his mind was occupied with Mrs Loftus, she did eventually confess to Mrs Gray that he was "a perfectly charming man, you know, in spite of his being unfortunately black, my dear".

It was not till after supper, at which the Jelly girls were attended by two young men, both of whom obviously strove to gain the elder's favour, that Bony found the opportunity to approach them.

"I have been hoping that you might now find an empty space on your dance card," he said suavely to Lucy. "Am I in time to ask for this waltz?"

Without smiling the girl regarded him steadily while he bent over her with deference. Her eyes searched his face, held his eyes with a steady look of one who would like to trust him but hesitates. Her decision to do so was reached abruptly. Still she did not smile when rising to her feet to say:

"Very well, if you wish."

There was no more opportunity to talk, because at the last minute Landon changed the waltz to a foxtrot. They do that sort of thing at country dances. And it seemed at the last moment, too, that Mrs Loftus stepped down from her place in his mind, giving way to Mr Jelly.

Chapter Nine

Mr Poole

The strange behaviour of Mr Jelly was not in itself of great interest to him. Knowing human nature as broadly and as deeply as he did, Bony realized that the occasional disappearance of the man from his farm might well be caused by the drink demon, woman, or some human vice the indulgence of which was irresistible. On the other hand, indulgence in vice is far more costly than the practice of virtue, and the fact could not be overlooked that Mr Jelly always returned from his absences with money and whisky.

That the disappearance of Mr Jelly had nothing to do whatever with the disappearance of George Loftus, Bony was convinced. For years before Loftus disappeared Mr Jelly had unobtrusively departed into the void and had returned unannounced. While other men had and do live double lives, the case of Mr Jelly was remarkable on one point: his return to normal existence with money.

It was a pretty little mystery wholly unconnected with the case then occupying his time—his holiday time, too—and his decision to unravel it was really based partly upon Sunflower's sweet beauty and partly on his passion for the mysterious which gave him such keen mental exercise. To Lucy Jelly he presently said:

"Sunflower tells me that you know what I am and that you are both worried by the occasional absence of your father," and later: "If I could be of any assistance I should be very pleased to try to help you."

"My sister talks too much, Mr Bony, but she is extraordinarily discerning in her judgment of people. Most of us require time to reach a proper understanding of a person's character, but she sums up a person in a minute. Her judgment always has been right, and I think I will rely on it regarding you."

When again she and Bony came together in the dance she said a little wistfully:

"I am worried about Father. I do hate mystery, and he seems mixed up in a mystery of some kind. I would like privately to know what Father does, so that if it's anything very awful I might be able to help him. I'd like to talk to you about it. Would you care to come to us for afternoon tea on Saturday?"

"You are exceedingly kind. I shall be delighted. Will four o'clock do?"

"Yes. We will expect you."

While escorting her back to her seat he observed that the cloud of anxiety was lifting. Even Sunflower noted and remarked upon it when next they danced.

That evening Bony thoroughly enjoyed himself. He danced with Mrs Poole, who with two vertical lines between her brows pointed out to him Mrs Black, suspected of milking her cow, and other notabilities of Burracoppin society. Mr Thorn invited him to run across to the hotel before Mr Wallace went to bed, and was most regretful when Bony declined. The small circle of people in which Mrs Gray had a place accepted him, thereby removing the impression that he was a stranger in a strange country. Yet other people, whilst interested in his personality and admiring his dancing, made no overtures, and he was shrewd enough to perceive that this was not so much on account of his colour as that he in Mrs Gray's circle rotated in a distinctly different circle from theirs. It was another phase of the white man's psychology which both interested and amused him.

Towards the end of the evening Mrs Loftus made a little speech.

"Friends, everyone," she said a little nervously, "I thank you all for your great kindness to me. It is comforting to have your sympathy during this trouble made by my husband's disappearance. I feel sure, though, he will be back one day, because I do not believe anything has happened to him. Thank you very, very much."

"You give old Loftus beans when he does come back," a man shouted above the hand clapping.

Mrs Loftus smiled wanly, but there was in her eyes a glint of purpose.

Bony escorted the Jelly girls to the car owned by a neighbour who was to take them home. After they had gone he walked along the footpath across the railway property and thence to the Rabbit Depot with his mind pleasantly occupied.

It was not three weeks since George Loftus disappeared from the face of the earth, or that part of it around Burracoppin. John Muir had communicated with the South Australian police, asking them to examine ship passengers from Western Australia, and had, too, telephoned the widespread station homesteads along the overland motor route the second day he had been put on the case. From the first the possibility that Loftus had planned to vanish, probably leave the State, was not overlooked.

Such a disappearance is the effect of one of several causes. He might have elected to disappear merely to desert his wife or escape his creditors with the balance of his credit, or he might have committed a concealed crime and fled to evade possible arrest.

Meanwhile Bony's investigations were not progressing as rapidly as the Western Australian police chief considered that his eastern States reputation demanded. Which, of course, gave Bony no concern. It was the lack of time sense when on a case, a mental trait bequeathed him by his maternal ancestors, a real gift of infinite patience, which was his greatest asset. The most painstaking white man would not have spent precious hours looking into trees, grubbing under half-rotted logs, or poking about beneath low and prickly bushes.

With extraordinary thoroughness he searched every yard of ground east and west of the old York Road gate in the rabbit fence. He discovered in an apparently impossible place a Bank of England five-pound note, and the only solution to account for its being wrapped about a twig at the extremity of a branch twenty-seven feet above ground was that a passenger on one of the Perth-Adelaide mail planes had dropped it in mistake for some useless document or paper. The bank note, although dilapidated, was still passable as currency.

Of any clues to the passage of Loftus, Bony found none, save the notebook and the cigar ends about which he had talked with Sergeant Westbury. From the wrecked car the bush detective had tracked the missing man to the old York Road, a distance of one mile, but he could discover no evidence that Loftus had proceeded farther south or, in fact, east or west. It appeared almost certain that the missing farmer had met a violent end or had departed in a car at the rabbit fence gate, crossing the old York Road.

Sergeant Westbury proved a rapid worker. The cashier at the Bank of New South Wales, who had cashed Loftus's cheque for one hundred pounds, remembered the transaction. He could describe the farmer in general outline and could state without doubt that the notes issued were brand-new one-pound notes. He had kept no record of their numbers and had paid out over four hundred that day, but he could give the series.

The tracing back to the places of purchase of the two beer bottles found near the car had been an equally simple matter. They had been imported into Western Australia from a Melbourne brewery and sold to Leonard Wallace at one of the hotels at Merredin. This particular beer was not sold at the Burracoppin Hotel. It was one of the many clues that occur in every criminal case which eventually prove to be unimportant. More time was required compiling the dossiers of Mick Landon and Mrs Loftus, and to these Bony gave little thought because he had sufficient on his hands to occupy his time and mind and not a little to amuse him.

*

In his own way, Mr Joseph Poole was as delightful a character as were Mr Thorn and the Spirit of Australia. He was tall and lank, a drooping willow, for his body drooped, his straggly grey moustache drooped, and his hair drooped down his high and narrow forehead. To observe him was to consider him a martyr to dyspepsia, but actually his life was one long delight at the oddities of everyone with whom he came in contact.

He was having his dinner when Bony arrived at Mrs Poole's famous boarding-house the second evening following the dance. Fifty yards from the weatherboard and iron building the detective first heard the raised voice of Mrs Poole commenting on the woodpile, the stove, Mrs Black and the cow, and all the remaining annoyances of life, including her husband.

"He doesn't care," she complained to Bony when he entered the kitchen by the back door. "The useless hulk! Just comes home and won't do a hand's turn. Go in and sit down, and I'll bring in your dinner."

"Do not allow your mind to dwell overmuch on the unpleasant things of life," was Bony's calm advice. "Remember only the nice things. Remember the dance the other night and how nice you looked in the blue frock. Remember the particular dance you danced with me."

"Go on with you! My husband's in there."

"Perhaps I'd better run away instead," he said, laughing.

"Have your dinner first," suggested Mr Poole from within the dining-room.

"I will," decided Bony, smiling again at Mrs Poole, whose temper could never be maintained at white heat.

Mr Poole's drooping brown eyes regarded Bony anxiously when the latter took his seat opposite.

"You'll do," he said, as though he were examining a beast.

"In what way?" Bony asked, observing the good-humoured gleam in his eyes.

"Yes. You'll do."

"Idiot!" Mrs Poole said. "Been away two weeks and think you've saved up a few jokes. What about the wood? It's getting dark. The kids have had to cut it up while you've been away enjoying yourself, but they aren't going to cut it now their lazy father's home."

Mr Poole continued to gaze at Bony with even more intensity.

"Yes. You'll do," he said again.

"You sniggering fool! What d'you mean?" demanded the now exasperated woman.

Joe had been angling for the question direct. Now he pointed a broken-nailed index finger at Bony and managed to say seriously:

"You'll do for a co-respondent. It'll save me the trouble of cutting 'er throat."

Then he leaned far back in his chair and guffawed, whereupon his poor wife rushed away to the kitchen and banged the dishes.

"You the new boarder?" asked Mr Poole at last.

Bony admitted that he was. Joe waved his hands as a dancer illuminated in the spotlight.

"Home," he said while he drooped into his chair. "I always enjoys meself at home. The cow and Mrs Black, the blank stove, and the blanker woodheap makes me happier every time I comes home." Clawing his way to his feet with the aid of the chair, he added: "See you after. If I don't chop the wood now the old 'un will start whispering love words to me just as I'm falling off to sleep."

Mysteriously he winked at Bony and went out. Later the detective helped poor Mrs Poole to wash the mountain of plates and dishes and afterwards joined the Pooles and the two garage-men in the dining-room, where the gramophone was constantly played, and they shouted to each other to command the noise of the machine and the two little boys who played on the floor.

"They tell me old Jelly's cleared off again," remarked Mr Poole conversationally.

"Yes, been gone some time," agreed one of the garage-men. "Queer old bird, to be sure. What the devil he gets up to beats me. Is it correct he's got a mania for pasting murder trials in scrap albums?"

"Too right," Joe assented without removing the drooping cigarette from beneath his drooping moustache. "He got me out there one night and fair give me the shivers."

"Funny kind of hobby to have," the second garage-man put in.

"No funnier than some of them perfessers have. They collects 'uman bones and things," Joe argued good-naturedly. "Knoo one once who collected 'uman skulls up Laverton way. He gimme fifty quid to go out and dig up fifty blackfellers' skulls off'n a tribal battlefield where the slaughter mustah been somethink awful. Why, the old perfesser handled them skulls like a tart handles jooles."

"Oh no! Jelly's harmless enough. He does keep off dead men's bones and things." Mr Poole lit another drooping cigarette and drooped farther into his chair, the better to expand. "I'll tell you what I think about old Jelly," he proceeded. "Old Jelly clears off on a temporary honeymoon and then gets terrible sorry for himself and swamps his remorse in grog."

"Go on with you!" Mrs Poole said sternly. And to the children: "Go to bed—go to bed, do you hear? It's ten o'clock, and that cow's got to be milked in the morning before Mrs Black gets her. Off you go!" When the children had sullenly departed she added—giving her husband a dark look—"You and your honeymoons before the kids! Old Jelly goes off just to get drunk like you'd do if you got the chance."

"I gets the chance all right, but you take jolly good care I don't get the money," countered her husband calmly.

"Yes, and I'm going on taking care."

Bony left before the discussion became one-sidedly acrimonious, for nothing that his wife said appeared to disturb Mr Poole. Out in the night the air was calm and warm. The frogs down in the pipe trench croaked and piped as though impatient for the arrival of the Albany Doctor. From far in the east a train puffed laboriously up the long incline, and its brilliant headlight lit the sky as the lights of a distant city.

Passing the hotel, Bony could hear the laughter of men within, but the doors were shut, although light streamed from window and fanlight. In the middle of the road he could distinguish the outline of a big woman, and at his approach she walked swiftly to the Rabbit Depot. He reached the gate when she was knocking on Inspector Gray's door. He was in time to see Gray open the door and to hear Mrs Wallace, whom the inside light revealed, say fiercely:

"Lend me your gun, Mr Gray, will you?"

"Sorry," the Inspector told her, "but the gun is up at my son's place."

"Oh!" Mrs Wallace hesitated. Then: "Oh! All right. But I'll get a gun off someone one of these nights, and I'll blow his head off. He's locked me out again. The little crawling runt! The snake!"

"Better get a bed at Mrs Poole's place," Gray advised calmly.

When she had gone, Bony went on to bed amazed at the Inspector's calm. He would not have been less calm had she asked him for a candle. From inside the closed and barred hotel came the burst of laughter which proclaimed Mr Wallace's temporary victory and the celebration he was making of it with his special cronies.

Chapter Ten

Bony Is Entertained

During the remainder of the week Bony worked hard without securing any result or making a single step towards the solution of the disappearance of George Loftus.

The men riding the harvester machines in the adjacent paddocks kept a sharp lookout for the body of Loftus lying among the wheat straws. Daily the squares of russet and gold grew smaller and the fringing borders of pale yellow straw ever deeper. Daily the iron sloths crept round and round with a low, humming whine and the ever-present cloud of dust forced from them by the thrasher fans.

The summer was now well begun. Each day the brilliant sun heated the ground and drove the ants from the shadeless patches. As early as nine o'clock the sun had sucked the night damp from the wheat-ears, allowing then the machines to start the long day's toil.

The wheat tide pouring into the rail siding was now in full flood. From eight to twelve hundred three-bushel bags were dumped into the Burracoppin wheat stack every day.

Twice Bony examined the road and the bordering land from the gate at the old York Road to the summit of the long south sand rise, and once from the summit down the farther side to the Loftus farm gate. He found nothing; not a single track or any object which possibly could have been left by Loftus the night he walked to the York Road.

More than once he had watched Mick Landon and the extra man, who cycled daily out from the township, at work in the wheat paddocks; noted how all the farmers bagged the wheat at opposite corners of the wheat squares, forming long dumps in echelon ready for the bag sewer and the carting trucks.

Saturday came. At noon precisely he parked the dray in the Depot yard and freed the horse in the smaller yard beyond. The working week being completed, he left town about half-past one dressed in white sports shirt, belted grey trousers, and polished shoes. Without jacket or hat, he set off for the Jelly farm with plenty of time at his disposal, taking the south road from the Depot.

When he had walked down the road for three-quarters of a mile he reached the old York Road. Here he turned to the left and presently passed the head of that road based at the vacant garage, the road Loftus should have taken. Proceeding a further quarter mile, he came north of a great granite rock rising two hundred feet at its highest point and itself situated on high land. The rock covered hundreds of acres and on its topmost ridge bore the inevitable surveyor's trig.

From this point Bony commanded a splendid view of the wide, shallow valley through which runs the Perth-Kalgoorlie railway, and from it obtained a wider impression of the vast wheat belt than he had done before. There were several gigantic outcrops of granite masses here and there beyond the valley, the higher of them bearing the rock-built surveyor's trigs which form the base lines from which the country had been accurately mapped.

Facing due east, he could see where the York Road faded into tall timber, wherein was the rabbit fence gate about which he had spent so many fruitless hours. Slowly he turned a little south of west, and, although he could not see it, he knew he then faced directly towards the rock mass lying behind the Loftus farm. A swift glance at the sun, a second glance to observe the angle at which his shadow fell to his right rear, and he set off for the hidden rock some two miles distant.

No one desiring a quiet stroll to contemplate the philosophy of Spinoza or the profound problems discussed by Haeckel would have undertaken that pathless journey. Bony undertook it in preference to the easier roads because the nature of the country and the timber was beyond his eastern States experience. The granite masses, sometimes hidden amid a tangle of wattle trees, the bushes in flower, the trees with trunks scored like a gimlet, the sight of a banded anteater and the glimpse of a brush kangaroo, the tracks of a pack of wild dogs, the scratch marks of a fox, were all part of a vastly entertaining scramble over uneven ground, round thickets of dense scrub, and across unsuspected open glades.

The long and gentle ground rise and the dense scrub gave him no warning of being near the Loftus farm rock until he suddenly stepped on it, walked up to a low ridge, and there looked down on the farm a hundred feet below, the rabbit fence beyond, and the vast sweep of flat country chequered by wheat and fallow paddocks, a scene so intensely brilliant as to make him shade his eyes with his hands.

For nearly an hour he sat on the ridge. Government employees might work only their forty-eight hours, but the wheat farmers work from dawn to dusk—during the three months' harvest.

Leaving the rock and presently reaching the lower and level ground, he sauntered along the edge of stripped and crushed wheat straw till he came to the rear of the Loftus homestead. Idly he examined the new haystack, wondering how many tons it weighed and how many acres the contents once had covered. He noted the poor-conditioned bush-built stables, the three chained dogs, the open water dam, and the small corrugated- iron house. Beneath a rough bush shed was erected a box- shaped tent, and this he guessed was Landon's quarters.

When he came in view of the front of the house he saw a woman carrying a basket in the crook of one arm, on her way to the men in the paddock with their afternoon lunch. He observed, too, that the house possessed but one door, and noted this peculiarity in a land where a house almost always had two doors to permit a draught of air to pass right through in summer. Standing at the one door was Mrs Loftus.

"Would you be so kind as to give me a glass of water?" he asked her.

In daylight he saw that her eyes were like diamantoids, blue and green lights flickering in their depths. Dressed in gingham overalls, her hair scrupulously tidy and her face faintly dusted with powder, George Loftus's wife was even in the light of day fresh and pretty. She took a tin pannikin from a nail and, giving it to him, bade him drink his fill from the rain-water tank.

Bony quenched his thirst whilst she silently watched him. A proud woman, he thought, a hard woman, because the afternoon-lunch tea had just been made and she might have offered him a cup of tea.

After thanking her he walked to the main south road, crossed it, and passed through the strip of low bush to reach the rabbit fence, and there, looking back, saw that she still watched him from the door. When he jumped the fence and turned south towards the Jelly farm he thought of Sunflower and smiled happily.

When Bony approached the Jelly homestead the two dogs came racing round the house, followed by the cat, with tail erect, which in turn was followed by Lucy Jelly. Neither Sunflower nor Mr Jelly appeared. In their stead came an elderly woman whom Bony had not seen before.

"I am glad you have come," Lucy told him. "If you hadn't, Sunflower would have been disappointed. This is Mrs Saunders, who is staying with us until Father comes home."

After the introduction had been acknowledged, Bony said with a trace of concern in his voice:

"Sunflower!"

"She has had an accident and is lying on the sofa on the veranda."

"An accident!" he cut in quickly.

"It's nothing very serious, although it was most painful, Mr Bony. She upset a pot of hot water over her foot. Mrs Saunders being here at the time, and being such a good nurse, the foot doesn't pain now and should be well in a week."

On the south veranda, where the shade was cool, Bony saw the slender form of the girl lying on the cushioned sofa and the bright face flushed with the excitement of his arrival. With eager haste he reached her side and, drawing a chair close to her, said:

"I am sorry to see you like this. I did not know."

"It was silly of me to be so careless," she told him with a radiant smile. "It happened at teatime on Thursday." She now saw plainly that which her feminine intuition had told her at the beginning of their acquaintance. She saw the gentleness and compassion of his basic nature; saw, too, the bigness of his heart and his lovableness without being conscious of his colour.

"If you had known, what would you have done?" she asked provokingly.

"Come straight here to see you," was his instant reply.

"I believe you would. Really, I knew you would. But I will be all right soon. There is no pain now."

Bony related how, when once on walkabout with his family, his youngest son's foot was scalded and what was done to effect a cure.

Sunflower was now lying on her side, her head resting on the palm of her hand, her soft eyes holding his gaze with their purity.

"Is little Ed brown like you?" she asked innocently.

"Oh no! His skin is white. It will become faintly dark, but never brown, like mine."

"You are not sorry you are brown, are you?"

"Sometimes I am. Sometimes I am glad."

"But why are you sorry sometimes?"

"You really must not ask such personal questions, dear," Lucy said, looking up from her needlework.

"You are not vexed, are you?" the maid asked of him.

"Decidedly not. You may ask me as many questions as you like."

Slowly Sunflower put out a hand and timidly touched his arm.

"I won't ask any more now," she decided. "Oh, I am glad you came! Tell me some stories of the blackfellows; about their fights and corroborees. Please do."

So Bony told her much of the folklore and many of the legends of the aborigines, speaking softly in vivid sentences and charming vocal inflexion. The quietly observant elder sister listened with equal interest, sometimes looking up from her work with growing wonder at the picture presented by Bony and the child. Any distrust of him on account of his colour, any doubt there may have been in her heart of the wisdom of confiding certain matters to a police detective, vanished during those never-to-be-forgotten moments. Alike with Sunflower, she became unconscious of his colour.

Mrs Saunders brought out the afternoon tea and set it on a small table at the foot of the sofa. She was a pleasant and placid woman of fifty, and with the solicitude of a lover Bony waited on the invalid.

He described to them his wife and his three sons; how little Ed was going to school at Banyo, near Brisbane, how the restless Bob had answered the call of the bush and was working on a far western cattle station, and of the pride of his life, Charles, the eldest, who attended the Brisbane University and so was closely following in his father's steps. He went on to describe the working ants, and the wonderful termite, and from the insects passed to the stars when the evening star shone faintly from the darkening eastern sky.

Mrs Saunders and Lucy were as firmly held by the magic of his personality as was Sunflower. To them his well-stored and cultured mind was a revelation. He spoke to them as never a novel or a play could have done; escorted them into worlds unknown.

When the silence of nature fell upon the land during those few minutes between twilight and night, Lucy suggested that he might like to accompany her when she shut up the fowls from the prowling foxes. Together they left the veranda, watched wistfully by the invalid while they drew farther away into the reflected glow of the pink and emerald western sky.

"Do you still wish to help us with Father?" she asked presently, glancing into his face.

"Certainly, if you still would like me to."

"I—I hope——" she said hesitatingly. "Supposing Father is doing something terrible. You would not act against him, would you?"

"Everyone will think I am a policeman," he protested.

"But aren't you? Aren't you a detective?"

"I am not a policeman. I am an investigator of crime. I am looking into the disappearance of George Loftus. I cannot think that your father has anything to do with that, and, consequently, I can say that whatever lies behind your father's absences will be dealt with discreetly and with every regard to your feelings. Whatever the mystery behind Mr Jelly, I will lay it bare before you only."

Realizing how stupidly rash he was in saying all this, knowing he was slipping down the incline which at Windee ruined his greatest triumph, still he persisted. As the dipsomaniac who hugs his bottle although aware of the inevitable result of his indulgence, Bony allowed his heart to govern his mind. The girl at his side and the lovely Sunflower had asked his help, and he could not but give it, even if by so doing he blasted his reputation and humbled his astounding pride.

"Tell me," he urged, "how long now has your father been going away like this?"

"About seven years."

"Does he always go away without warning you of his intention?"

"Yes, always."

"And does he always return without warning?"

"Always."

"Does anything happen before his goings that is made significant by repetition?"

"Yes. He always receives a telegram."

"Ah! That is something of value. Have you ever chanced to read one?"

"Two. One early this year; the other several years ago. The last one I read said, 'Come Sydney', and the other said, 'Come Adelaide.' Neither was signed, and both were dispatched from Merredin."

Can you be sure that your father received a telegram before he went away this time?"

"I did not see one delivered," she said in a manner which left no doubt in his mind that she was sure her father had received the usual telegram.

"Now, please, describe how he returns."

Lucy Jelly did not immediately reply. She shut the fowl- house door and closed another door on some sleepy ducks.

"He always comes home at night," she said slowly. "Sometimes early, sometimes in the middle of the night. He comes in a car, but I have never seen the car as it always drops him at our farm gate near the rabbit fence. Those times he comes in early we have seen him bring in a parcel of whisky. It is all wrapped up, but I know it is whisky, for I have watched him bury the bottles. Sometimes he says good night before going to his room; sometimes he says nothing to us, not a word. Once in his room he locks the door, shuts himself in for several days, and won't open to see me and take in anything. When he comes out he looks awful."

"He has money?"

"Yes. Always he has money. After he becomes normal he pays all our small debts."

"I suppose he gives you some money too?"

"No. Strangely enough, he will never give Sunflower or me a penny after one of his absences, although at ordinary times he is most generous to us. Somehow I cannot help thinking that he is mean with the money he brings home because it is dirty money. You understand?"

"Yes, fully."

"You will help us?"

"Surely. I shall find out where Mr Jelly goes and for what purpose, and in what way he obtains the money to bring home."

"You will tell me when you have found out, won't you?"

Bony became silent. She repeated her words. Then he said slowly:

"I will tell you if I can tell a lady, Miss Jelly. Men are such strange, illogical creatures. They can do terrible things, things I could not even tell my wife. Yet be not greatly disturbed. Having met Mr Jelly, I cannot believe that he is doing anything dishonourable. He may be a secret drinker or addicted to some terrible vice which holds him with an unrelenting grip. If this proves to be so, and you are told precisely what it is, you will, most likely, be able to help him. Whatever it is, you may rely on both my discretion and my assistance. Do not worry. Every shadow is caused by brightness."

"Thank you," she said gently, and having by then come near to the house, they spoke no more of Mr Jelly.

Mrs Saunders had moved Sunflower into the living-room, and the girl was waiting to ask Bony to write something in her autograph album. When he had written a verse of Shelley's and had added his signature beneath it, he said, looking up at Lucy:

"By the way, this afternoon I saw a woman leaving Mrs Loftus's house with afternoon lunch for Mick Landon and the other man on the harvester. Who is she?"

"If she was a tall, thin woman, that would be Miss Waldron, Mrs Loftus's sister. She has been staying with Mrs Loftus ever since her husband disappeared."

"She wasn't staying there before Loftus disappeared— when he was in Perth?"

"No. Oh no!"

He remarked the stare she gave him when she answered that question. It was as though the question had created the link completing a chain of incidents. In the presence of Sunflower he refrained from pressing the subject and began to talk of the wild things of the bush, beginning with the great battle he had once seen between two eagles and a fox; how the eagles in turn swooped and knocked the fox over with their wing pinions until they had beaten it to death.

The golden yellow lamplight fell on his animated face. Mrs Saunders was knitting, but Lucy had forgotten her needlework, being as fascinated as her sister. Through open fly-netted doors and windows came drifting and soft distinct night sounds: the constant clickings of the cicadas, the honk- honk of the bullfrogs at the edge of the dam, the whorl-whorl of a fox daintily padding the far sand ridges. And then the dogs barked suddenly.

Bony continued to talk, but he wondered why the dogs barked. Twenty seconds later he heard the low hum of a motor engine. Five seconds after that he saw the flash of fear spring to Sunflower's eyes and knew that she, too, now heard the car. Still he went on talking, not seeing, but aware that Lucy had quietly gone out of the house.

Happiness and tranquillity went away with her, and in their place came fear. A quick glance at Mrs Saunders showed him the fixity of her eyes whilst her mind was projected beyond the house to the rabbit fence and the roads. Waiting— she was waiting to hear the car stop. Outside, Lucy was waiting to see the car stop. She watched the headlights winking whilst the machine passed beyond the roadside trees, watching and wondering if the car was travelling south on the main road beyond the fence or along the government track their side of the fence, which Mr Jelly would have to take to reach his home. The car did stop—at the farm gate.

Those within the house heard the engine hum die into silence. They could see with mental eyes, as clearly as though they stood against the fence, the tall figure of Mr Jelly getting out of the car. They gave him time to say a word or two to the driver. And they heard the engine hum into song when the driver let out the clutch and began to change gear upward.

The car was returning to Burracoppin, and then, likely enough, on to Merredin.

"Father!" whispered Sunflower.

"Everything will be all right," Bony assured her. Lucy Jelly came inside and, without speaking, sat down and took up her needlework. Mrs Saunders continued to knit with the stoicism of a Madame Defarge. Bony proceeded to describe a native kangaroo hunt, knowing that not a word he said was heard by the other three, who, with straining ears, were listening for footsteps above the barking of the dogs.

Sense of time became distorted. The dogs raced away from the house. Their barking quickly gave place to whimpers of welcome. A man commanded them to keep down. Then footsteps on the veranda.

Quietly Bony stood up, taking position at the foot of the sofa facing the door. The cigar-shaped figure of Mr Jelly was revealed by the light before he entered. He halted just within the door, a raincoat flung carelessly over one shoulder, a suitcase held by one hand, the other hand and arm cradling a large stoutly corded parcel.

The farmer's ruddy complexion had been replaced by a sallow greyness. It was but half a shade darker than the halo of hair that appeared to rest on his ears. His pale blue eyes, that reminded Bony of Landon, were black-ringed and strangely glassy.

Without giving any greeting, he stalked across the room to the passage leading to his den.

"Father! Sunflower has badly scalded her foot. Won't you speak to her?"

Lucy said with brave calm.

Retaining hold on all his impedimenta, Mr Jelly halted with obvious reluctance. He then crossed to Sunflower's side, to stand mutely looking down at her. The child valiantly smiled up at him, into his ashen face, her hands tight clasped upon the autograph album.

"My foot is getting better now, Daddy. But it did hurt," she said as calmly as her sister had spoken.

Mr Jelly's lips moved. Just for a second his hard, glassy eyes softened.

"It is a time for courage, Sunflower," he said, and without kissing her or touching her, he turned and left them. They heard him lock his room door. Sunflower began to cry softly. With a little fluttering rush Lucy fell upon her knees beside the sofa and cried with her.

Chapter Eleven

Dual Mysteries

The dual mysteries at Burracoppin were getting more interesting. Detective-Inspector Bonaparte was realizing that the disappearance of George Loftus was a little more profound than a pavement murder. The case presented features that made it stand out from other cases of human disappearance or even of murder. He had traced the farmer for one mile along a little-used track to a gate crossing a busy highway, a lonely tree-girt place from which the nearest habitation was more than a mile distant.

At this time the Loftus case comprised three main questions. Was the man killed near the York Road gate and his body cleverly hidden? Did he plan his disappearance and board a car for the purpose of leaving the district? Did he walk on and finally reach his farm?

The problem of Mr Jelly was even more extraordinary. What lay behind his absences? In what business was he engaged which during a time of financial stringency supplied him with money? What could that business be which so remarkably affected him? From what Mr Jelly had said, he and Loftus were friends. Certainly they were near neighbours. Was there any connection between them, their absences from their homes, the strange business of Mr Jelly?

These questions engaged Bony's attention during the Monday afternoon following the return of Mr Jelly. He sought answers to them while slowly he drove his horse and dray along the east side of the rabbit fence south of the York Road.

At this time he believed that the Jelly case could be cleared up with ease, and he decided that before dealing with it he would test the third significant question relating to the Loftus case. Did Loftus reach his home?

Could he prove that George Loftus never had reached his farm, and lack of evidence went a long way to prove it, he would be obliged to follow other avenues of investigation, avenues he would follow if he spent a year of time, sent his chief, Colonel Spender, to his grave with worry, or received permanent dismissal from the Queensland Police Force. Death only would draw him away from this absorbing case.

On the Loftus farm the two men were still stripping the wheat. The land east of the farm and the fence was uncleared, the bush comprising tall white gums standing in thick- growing scrub. Arrived at the camp site half a mile south of the Loftus gate from which Hurley had heard the dogs howling the night Loftus disappeared, Bony unharnessed the horse when the dray was pulled into the best shade and kept level by propping its shafts with the drop sticks. Giving the horse the four buckets of water it needed, he secured it with a neck rope to a tree from which he suspended a bag feeder. Quite accustomed to being tied to a tree all night, the horse was content to feed, and Bony made sure that the length of rope permitted it to lie down when it wished.

The sun was still high and hot. He made a fire and boiled the billy for tea. He moved the water tank to the front of the dray, pushed his swag against it for a back rest, and then sipped his tea whilst seated on the floor of the dray away from the ants.

A rabbit which came from a bush and nibbled chaff dropped by the horse recalled to Bony the absence of Ginger, who had departed with Inspector Gray three days before to join his master. And it was memory of Ginger which recalled Hurley's statement that he had heard the Loftus dogs howling when last he camped here. It was to test this statement made to Mrs Poole, and to grasp opportunity, if presented, to learn more about the Loftus household that he was here.

All dogs will howl, but not all dogs will bark. A dingo will howl, but never bark as a domesticated dog does. The wild dog, the cross between the domestic dog and the dingo, very seldom barks, delighting to howl in concert with the pack or when alone in answer to another dog. Domestic dogs will howl at the moon for no special reason of which man knows, and it is not yet established that they howl only when saddened or grieved.

Yet, despite all this, there remains the fact that domestic dogs will howl when unable to accompany a loved master. Very often they howl when the master dies, irrespective of the master's colour. Where the subject provokes discussion is in the question:

Does a dog howl because it knows its master has died?

When the sun went down, Bony ate his supper of cold mutton chops, bread, and butter from the enamelled billy, which was wrapped in hessian, saturated with water, so that the evaporation might keep the contents hard.

Whilst he ate he watched Mick Landon coming over the stripped stubble, wondered if he was coming to speak to him, and wondered where he was really going when Landon jumped the fence, wondered till he saw him cross the fence track and made for the Jelly farmhouse, half a mile east.

Landon returned in the dusk, carrying a machine part which he had borrowed from Mr Jelly or from Lucy. He came to Bony's camp, to say pleasantly enough:

"Good night! Didn't I see you at the dance?"

"Yes, I was there," Bony replied, looking up from his cigarette making. "A good dance, too," he added.

"Too right. We are having another next Saturday night at the Jilbadgie Hall. Sure to be a crowd from Burra. You could get a lift in a car."

"Where is Jilbadgie Hall?"

"The hall is close to the Ten-mile Gate. Try and get down. It'll be a good dance."

"I'll try," Bony compromised, casually examining this open-air worker, whose magnificent body was boldly outlined beneath the armless cotton vest. The man's face, chest, and arms were whitened by the harvester's dust, yet he appeared clean, most certainly he had shaved that day.

"Was that you walking over our rock Saturday afternoon?"

"Yes. I was asked to tea by Miss Jelly, and I walked a straight line from Burracoppin."

"Rough country."

"Very. Yet I preferred it to the dusty roads."

"You could have got a truck ride."

"I could, but I like using my legs. It is what they were given me for. If I come to the dance I might walk the ten miles."

In the fast-falling light Bony was carefully scrutinized. "You must like walking," Landon said. "You're lucky to get a job with the Rabbits these bad times."

"Influence, my dear man, influence, not luck," Bony told him lightly. "The Black Hand Society, you know."

Landon laughed at this, and the laughter enhanced his good looks. Yet somehow the laughter did not remain long. It subsided abruptly, as though Landon was unused to laughter and felt its strangeness.

Again he searched Bony's face with those light, evenly coloured blue eyes of his, gazing at the detective as though tantalized by a memory of having met him somewhere before. Bony offered him a pannikin of tea, and his cigarette material when the tea was declined. Whilst Landon's supple fingers worked at tobacco and paper, the half-caste said:

"By the way, when I passed Loftus's house the other day and called for a drink, I could not but admire the expert manner in which that new haystack was built. I wondered how many tons of hay it contained. Can you give an estimate? I guess fifty tons."

"The haystack!" Landon ejaculated sharply. "Oh! The weight? About sixty-four tons as near as nothing. Interested in stacks?"

"I am interested in everything about here. You see, this wheat country is all strange to me, for my home is on the Queensland cattle stations," Bony blandly explained.

"Never been up there. Ah well, I'll get along. See you at the dance most likely. Good night!"

"Good night," returned Bony pleasantly.

At eleven o'clock the moon rose. At eleven-thirty the Loftus dogs howled long and mournfully. It was so quiet that Bony could hear Mick Landon shouting at them to stop.

Late the next afternoon, when Bony reached Burracoppin, he called at the post office, and there received three envelopes, two of which bore the Brisbane postmark; the third came from Perth.

Having parked the dray and fed the horse, he read his mail in the privacy of his room. The first envelope opened contained a copy of a telegram sent by John Muir care of the C.I.B. It read:

GOT HIM. LEAVING BRISBANE TODAY. SAW MISSUS. SAYS YOU COME BACK AT ONCE. TOLD HER YOU AMUSING YOURSELF.

JOHN

The message was stamped with John's impulsiveness, a quality that annoyed Bony, who had his career at heart. He was at the time so impulsive that he was unable to write a clear message. The content of the second envelope was a letter signed by Colonel Spender, Chief of the Queensland Police Force. Without preamble, the typed part ran:

Please curtail your leave and return at once. Important case out at Cunnamulla requires your services. Suit your abilities. Must be undertaken.

Below the signature, in the Colonel's handwriting, was this:

For God's sake come back quick. Every fool here falling down on his job. Can't succeed in convicting common drunks. I'm the only policeman among the damned lot of them.

[Initialled amid scattered blots] *G.H.S.*

The image of Colonel Spender's choleric face and his violent manner that so adequately disguised a generous heart flashed on Bony's brain, causing him to laugh softly. The letter was dated. 11th November, two days after Bony had met John Muir in Perth. By now the Western Australian detective would have explained the Burracoppin case to the Colonel and have been energetically cursed for introducing it to the half-caste.

The third letter was from his wife, the last paragraph reading:

I hope that you are enjoying your holiday. The long train journey would have been too much for me, and you have always wanted to see Western Australia. Have you met John Muir by now?—John is very nice, isn't he? He will never grow old; always will he be a rampageous boy. Is that the right word?

Bony's smile was softer now and his eyes were faintly misty. His wife, a mission-reared half-caste like himself, possessed those splendid maternal qualities of gentleness, sympathy, and deep understanding. Twenty-two years married and sweethearts still, there never had been a moment's anger or distrust. Where no white man, and no black man either, would have understood Bony or Marie, their understanding of each other was perfect.

The next morning the detective decided to take a day off and pay a visit to Merredin to investigate the source of Mr Jelly's telegrams. Accordingly he boarded the guard's van of the nine-forty-five goods train.

At the Chicago of Western Australia (a flourishing centre and the railway terminus for several branch lines) Bony inquired his way of a small boy and eventually entered the police station, where he found Sergeant Westbury seated at a plain deal table.

"Good day! Good day!" jerked out the senior officer at Merredin, heaving his bulk upwards and outwards to seize a chair and place it invitingly near him. "Pleased to see you— pleased to see you."

The screwed-up eyes regarded Bony like the naked points of blue steel rapiers.

"I am taking a day's holiday from manual labour," Bony explained gravely. "I dislike manual labour intensely. It may be suitable for the white men, but I am not wholly white. Have you made any progress with the dossiers I asked for?"

"Slowly—slowly. Had to take care; take care. Have 'em here, but not complete".

Taking the sheets, Bony quickly sorted them and learned what had been painstakingly gathered. Landon had been born at Northam, Western Australia, in 1901. He joined the A.I.F., 7th August 1918, and was discharged 19th July 1919. In May 1923 he joined the Police Force and was dismissed the following year for trouble with a woman. After that he worked in the mines about Kalgoorlie until he went to work for George Loftus in 1927.

"So Landon was in the Force?"

"Yes. Mason—D. S. Mason—was here yesterday. Says he remembers Landon. Smart man—promising—mad on women—women his downfall. I heard the other day in Burracoppin that he's a sheik around there!"

"Undoubtedly he is a sheikh with the ladies," assented Bony. "Yet there appears nothing against him. What was the trouble with the woman when he was in the Force?"

"Maintenance."

Mrs Mavis Loftus—so the dossier stated—was born at Cobar, New South Wales, in March 1902, of pastoral people. Her career, as far as the sergeant had ascertained, had been uneventful. She married Loftus at Cobar, Ond May 1924.

Leaning back in his chair, Bony pinched his lower lip reflectively. The dossiers were barren of important information. It seemed as though he had figuratively reached a high and blank wall over or round which there was no possible way.

"Know anything?" asked the sergeant wistfully.

"Nothing," Bony confessed.

"No reports from South Australia, either, but that don't mean that Loftus didn't keep hid on a boat when at Adelaide and went on to Melbourne—Melbourne."

Bony smiled frankly at the perspiring sergeant.

"He did not go to Victoria. He did not leave this State."

"How do you know, how do you know?"

"I know by the same reason or agency that permits your good wife to know you have been in a hotel."

91

Westbury broke into a roar of laughter, saying when he could:

"Then you must be right. Loftus must be in Western Australia. My missus is always right; always right."

"We are both of us always right, sergeant. Now, does it chance that you are friendly with the postmaster?"

"It does."

For four seconds Bony studied the other's red and jovial face. He wanted to know how much Sergeant Westbury was really governed by that brain-stunning material, red tape. When he spoke it was with deliberation, for much might hang on it.

"I am going to ask you to grant me a favour. I want you to give me a letter of introduction to the postmaster telling him who and what I am requesting him, firstly, to keep my identity a secret, and, secondly, to oblige me in a little matter I will make clear to him. If he will oblige I shall be saved much trouble and time which would have to be expended to gain what I want through official channels. There are occasions, sergeant, when the official manner of doing things makes me intensely annoyed. Will you write the introduction—and remain dumb?"

"Certainly—certainly. And no questions asked."

"You are a man of perspicacity."

"Eh?"

"Of intelligence, sergeant."

Sergeant Westbury beamed—and wrote the desired introduction.

Having read what Westbury had written, the postmaster gazed searchingly into Bony's smiling countenance. Within his private office he said:

"What is it I can do for you?"

"Show me the telegram lodged at this office for transmission to Mr Jelly of South Burracoppin before 17th November. That is all."

The official was absent in the main office for ten minutes. When he returned he carried the desired telegraph form. Bony read:

"Come Perth."

On the reverse side, in accordance with post-office regulations, was written in a bold hand the name and address of the sender:

"Miss Sunflower Jelly. South Burracoppin."

"Thank you," Bony said courteously, and walked out to the street.

Chapter Twelve

Note Series K/11

During the return journey to Burracoppin in the guard's van of the goods train which leaves Merredin at five o'clock, Bony mentally reviewed the two cases now absorbing his interest. The guard was busy checking his sheets and bills, and there were no other passengers to disturb the peace with their caustic observation about the wheat market and the Government.

The dark mystery of Mr Jelly was in no way lightened by Bony's trip to Merredin. The telegram produced by the postmaster was both baffling and astonishing, astonishing because the sender of it certainly was not Dulcie Jelly. Bony had walked the streets of Merredin for an hour, had then returned to the post office to secure if possible a description of the person who had sent the telegram in Sunflower's name.

The clerk who had accepted the message could not recall the person who had passed it in for dispatch. He was not positively sure, but had a faint recollection of seeing the name "Sunflower" before. Much questioning, however, could not dig from the depths of his mind the purpose for which the name had been used, and Bony felt sure it was used in sending similar telegrams calling Mr Jelly to the various cities of Australia.

He was sure, too, that Dulcie Jelly had not dispatched the telegram, neither had her sister nor Mr Jelly himself. The farmer must have known, though, what the summons to Perth implied, and he must have known who sent the summons in his daughter's name.

Of course it would have been a woman, for had a man signed a girl's name the fact would have been remembered by the clerk. Undoubtedly a woman had sent the command to Mr Jelly. She had handed it to the clerk at 2.20 p.m., 16th November.

Bony's progress in the affair of George Loftus appeared to have been stopped by a wall as unscaleable as that which so effectually hid the strange absences of Robert Jelly. He began to doubt the efficacy of that sense of intuition upon which, as he told Sergeant Westbury, he so much relied.

The scales had been slightly tilted towards the fact of Loftus's murder and now seemed tilted the other way to the man's planned disappearance. Sergeant Westbury obstinately clung to this latter theory, and, despite the sergeant's placid and contented outlook on life in general, he was, nevertheless, a shrewd and clever policeman. Against Westbury were opposed both Inspector Gray and Mr Jelly, who had expressed belief that George Loftus had been killed, but they were not in the position occupied by the trained Westbury, who had been first on the case. Even beyond this circle were people like Mr Thorn and Mrs Poole, equally divergent in their opinions.

So far Bony had no more than they on which to base a definite opinion. Yet despite this he was far from hopeless. This philosophy taught him, and experience had shown him, that of all classes of crime murder investigation is assisted the most by time. It would be a matter of time only when the thoughts of two people would clash and produce a result commonly known as coincidence, to become another link of an incomplete chain. Bury a stone how deep you will, and Time will bring it to the surface. So it is with secret crime. Time will reveal it, no matter how deeply it is pushed into the black pit of mystery.

While the train was slowly losing speed in its climb to the summit of the highest ridge of the railway system, Bony produced his notebook and turned up those entries under the date 16th November.

That day he had thoroughly examined the wrecked car and the surrounding ground. It was the day Ginger, the dog, caught two rabbits, one of which Bony had buried. During the evening of this day he had met Mr Thorn and the Spirit of Australia and, later, had watched Mr Jelly and another man change a tyre and proceed towards Merredin. It was now reasonable to assume:

That at 2.20 p.m. on 16th November a woman had handed in at the Merredin post office a telegram directed to Jelly, South Burracoppin, after having complied with the regulations by writing a name and address on the back of the form. One minute later the telegram was dispatched to Burracoppin by telephone, since at Burracoppin there was no telegraph instrument. The person to whom the message was directed lived four miles south of the town, yet he must have received it shortly after its transmission, for he had obeyed the summons that night. Either Mr Jelly, expecting the message, had waited for it at Burracoppin or had arranged with a truck driver to bring it out, an act which proved that he expected it the day it was sent. The point made clear was that the farmer knew the summons would probably arrive that day and had made his arrangements to obey it. Had he been positively sure it would arrive when it did, there would have been no necessity for its having been sent at all.

The car in which the farmer had departed doubtless was the car in which he had returned. Bony had noted that it was a four-door sedan, probably of English make, because its outlines were not American. The fact that no number plates were attached was not singular. A good many car owners in the bush and country are like the wheat-truck drivers, who leave open the gates in the rabbit fence in a gamble against being caught.

Actually cheerful, for the greater the mystery the more he enjoyed it, Bony left the train at Burracoppin when the sun was setting. The wheat traffic had stopped, and the lumpers were gathered in a group near the weighbridge smoking a hard-earned cigarette before dispersing for a shower bath and dinner. The hotel bar was crowded with drivers and farmers when he passed. Inside the Depot yard Mrs Gray waited with a letter.

"This came for you this afternoon," she explained. "A truck driver brought it in from Lucy Jelly. Are you cutting Eric Hurley out?"

"Madam, I am a married man," Bony told her with smiling reproof. "I am expecting an invitation to play bridge, and this must be it."

"If you are going out this evening you might be able to secure a lift with Mrs Loftus as far as her gate. She's come to town to take Mr Loftus's damaged car home from the garage."

"It has been moved from the pipeline and repaired?"

"Yes. The police gave permission last week."

Knowing this, Bony continued to feign ignorance.

"The damage could not have been so great as it looked," he ventured.

"Oh no! The garage-men have had it only two days. Go along and find Mrs Loftus now, if you are going."

"Please excuse me. I will accept your advice," Bony said, raising his hat and smiling. Again on the road, he opened the envelope and read the note. It was signed with Lucy Jelly's initials.

Please come out this evening. Father is very strange, and we are all frightened.

With pursed lips he rounded the hotel, declined Mr Thorn's invitation to enter the bar with him, and, walking on, came to the once wrecked car, now staunch, but still dilapidated, standing outside one of the stores. Here he waited five minutes till Mrs Loftus came out of the store, followed by the storeman, carrying a heavy parcel of goods. Bony said:

"I have been invited to spend the evening at Mr Jelly's house. I wonder if you could find it convenient to give me a lift as far as your gate."

The greenish-blue eyes of this pretty woman stared into his beaming blue ones. She saw a mild, guileless personality behind the sharp-featured brown face.

"Very well," she said, consenting with a smile. "I shall be leaving about six o'clock. I cannot wait a minute later than that. I have seen you before, haven't I?"

The question was asked in the superior manner of one who looks down from a social height. There was that inflexion of voice which proved that the woman often had spoken to aborigines from the plane of a squatter's homestead veranda. Still beaming, Bony replied:

"Yes. You kindly gave me a pannikin of water when I called one afternoon."

"Ah yes! You were on your way to the Jellys' that afternoon, were you not?"

"Yes, I spent the evening there."

"A very nice girl, Lucy Jelly, isn't she?"

"Very," he agreed seriously, adding: "Miss Dulcie is equally charming."

Mrs Loftus turned away, but not in time to prevent Bony seeing the sneer disfiguring her mouth. The expression was so different from the impish smile Mrs Gray had given when she surmised Bony was cutting out Hurley.

Passing through the railway enclosure, he reached the garage when the two owner mechanics were washing the grease from their hands preparatory to closing the building for the night.

"Hullo, Bony! You've got a good job. A Sunday today?" asked the elder.

"No. I took the day off because the weather fatigues me," Bony answered with a chuckle. "I've been to Merredin, and there I meant to send my wife five pounds. I quite forgot about it. Can you change a ten-pound note? I must retain a few shillings for myself, you know."

"A ten-pound note! Hi, Fred, he's flashing ten-pound notes!"

"It's about time we saw Gray and got a government job. Private enterprise is dead," complained Fred, a shock-haired pale-faced man of forty.

"Well, you're always lucky," announced the other. "Some of these cockies do pay up sometimes. We had a bill paid this afternoon, so we can fix your little difficulty. Wait a tick."

"I saw Mrs Loftus standing by a car just now," Bony said to Fred. "That's not the car Loftus smashed, is it?"

"The same, Bony. It cost her fifteen quid, and, knowing how she's placed financially, we wasn't going to let her have it till she paid up. But up she comes with the wad, fifteen of the best, and six pounds off the old bill."

Fred's partner returned with a sheaf of pound notes. He counted into Bony's untrembling hand ten of them and accepted the ten-pound note in exchange.

"Thank you very much," Bony said calmly. "See you at dinner, I suppose. I must go now, as I have an appointment with a lady at six o'clock."

Fred grinned. Bony actually chuckled and winked. All three laughed.

On his way to Mrs Poole's boarding-house he examined the notes with which Mrs Loftus had paid her garage account. They were quite new notes, and all were of one series—K/11. It was from this serial number that the cashier of the Bank of New South Wales had paid George Loftus one hundred pounds.

Chapter Thirteen

Bony's Invitations

It was half-past six when Mrs Loftus came along to the car beside which Bony waited, and he was thankful to see her accompanied by the woman he had learned was Miss Waldron. The back seat of the car was given him, and after some arrangement of the numerous parcels he made himself fairly comfortable, whilst Miss Waldron sat beside her sister who drove.

He was thankful for the presence of Miss Waldron because it obviated the necessity of talking with Mrs Loftus at a time when his mind was busy with two developments of this dual mystery. What lay behind Lucy Jelly's call for assistance he resolutely deferred to the time she herself should explain, leaving his mind clear to decide the matter of those new notes received by the garage-men and of the serial K/11.

The possibility of the notes paid out by Mrs Loftus from the same serial as those paid by the bank to her husband being a coincidence was more than probable. Notes of the same issue very likely were being handled by a dozen banks in Western Australia and a hundred business arms. The total number of one serial may be tens of thousands. Yet there was a significance in the fact that Mrs Loftus, for whom a benefit dance recently had been held which produced for her the sum of seven pounds and two shillings, was able to pay a debt of some twenty-one pounds and had bought heavily from one storekeeper whom, too, she might have paid money off a long-standing account.

What was the source of Mrs Loftus's affluence? Her father, a pastoralist near Cobar, might have sent her a cheque. Or she might have sold a valuable piece of jewellery in order to meet the expenses of the farm, for it was a fact that she had been financially much better off before her marriage to Loftus.

Still, supposing the notes she had paid away at the garage were identical with some of those paid out to George Loftus by the bank cashier. In this case how did she come in possession of them? Not being a woman stupid enough to act without thinking, it seemed unlikely that she had come by them through any crime, because she was intelligent enough to know that the police would take great pains to ascertain how much money her husband had on him when he disappeared and to trace the source of that money. The most obvious explanation—the obvious very often is correct—was that George Loftus had sent the money to his wife.

Bony's faith in intuition further waned. Sergeant Westbury must be right. There was no other logical explanation than that Loftus was alive to send the money to Mrs Loftus. It was possible, nay, probable, that she knew his precise whereabouts; knew, too, the reason behind his disappearance.

It was not long after this disturbing conclusion was reached that they arrived at the open gate giving entry to the Loftus farm. The crimson reflection from the western sky was quickly turning to purple.

"Thank you very much," Bony said when he stood on the road beside Mrs Loftus.

"That's quite all right. I hope you enjoy the evening. Convey my regards to Miss Jelly, won't you?" she said sweetly, yet unable to keep the mockery from her voice and laughter.

"I shall not forget, madam. Again thank you."

The car sped away down the stubble-bordered track leading to the house, Bony looking after it with a quizzical smile touching his lips and pain in his heart. Whenever he came in contact with this type of Australian woman the ever- present wound of his mid-race broke open to red rawness, recalling his inferior parentage which was the real foundation of his vanity. Knowing that snobbery is but the mask of ignorance, the sign of mental shallowness, the sole crude weapon of the stupidly spiteful, nonetheless an exhibition of it hurt him as nothing else could.

In this lay the explanation for his one failing as an investigator of crime. It explains his admiration of Mrs Thornton of Barrakee, of Miss Marian Stanton of Windee, and of the two Jelly girls. Women as these were the salve to the wound of his impurity of race which so fiercely at all times attacked his pride, and it was his pride which kept him aloof from the savagery of his aboriginal ancestors.

The tint of wine in the still air was being slowly replaced by the grey-blue tint of early night whilst he walked rapidly southward along the rabbit fence. His mood lightened as the distance between Mrs Loftus and himself lengthened and shortened between himself and little Sunflower Jelly.

A narrow ribbon of the palest yellow lay along the western horizon, and the sky was aglitter with stars when he reached the Jelly's farmhouse. Although he did not see them till they were jumping up against him, he knew that the two dogs had come racing round the house corner. He knew that Lucy followed after them, although he did not see her white dress until she was close to him.

"Thank you for coming, Mr Bony," was her simple, heartfelt greeting. "Please come in, and if you should see Father let him know that you called quite casually, will you?"

"Yes, I will manage that," he told her with assurance. "How is your father?"

"We haven't seen him since he went to his room last Saturday."

"Dear me! And today is Wednesday. Have you heard him moving about in his room?"

"Yes. Moving about and talking to himself. He has taken in the food and drink I have been leaving outside his door, and we have heard him leave and re-enter the house long after we have gone to bed." When she placed a trembling hand on his arm he could see her white and troubled face upturned to his. She began to speak more hurriedly.

"This time has been no worse than some of the other times, but this time I have thought much of you and of your promise to help. Before, I have had to bear it alone; wonder what he has been doing to worry him like this. I have kept on smiling and trying to be brave for Sunflower's sake; but it is hard to smile now she is growing up, and harder now to answer her questions. Oh, I have wanted someone to help, someone I could lean upon! Eric I cannot wholly trust, even though I love him. We have known each other such a little while. I know you even less, but I felt that I could not go through another night without calling on you, and I am so glad you've come. You don't think me silly, do you?"

Bony detected the hint of hysteria in her voice. He forgot entirely the sneering Mrs Loftus. He wanted to place an arm about this girl's shoulders and comfort her as he could have comforted Sunflower and would have comforted little Ed. From the low-born half-caste in the presence of Mrs Loftus, in this girl's presence he was again Detective-Inspector Napoleon Bonaparte, his chief's most trusted officer, the friend of a State governor.

"Leave your father to me," he said quietly. "There is no further need to fear or to worry. Let us go in and see Sunflower and Mrs Saunders, who, I suppose, is still with you."

"Thank you. Thank you very, very much."

He felt the pressure of her fingers on his arm before her hand was taken from it. The little friendly gesture so plainly told him of the load of responsibility she had had to bear since her mother had died. On the top of the veranda steps they found Sunflower waiting, her burned foot still swathed in bandages.

"Why, it's Mr Bony!" she exclaimed, her dove-grey eyes alight with pleasure. "Oh, I am glad you have called!"

"Really, I have called especially to see you," Bony valiantly lied. He was triumphantly escorted to the dining-room and urged to be seated on the sofa at the child's side. When Mrs Saunders offered a cup of tea he said: "Thank you—thank you!" and was reminded of Sergeant Westbury's jerky repetition of speech.

"How is the poor foot?" he asked.

"Better. Much better. Lucy says I may leave off the bandage on Friday."

"Can you? That's splendid, because I wanted to ask you and Miss Lucy and Mrs Saunders to accompany me to the dance at the Jilbadgie Hall on Saturday evening. Will you?"

Sunflower gazed at her sister with shining eyes. Lucy's eyes were misty.

"You can take me for one, Mr Bony," announced Mrs Saunders with emphasis.

"I shall be delighted," agreed the detective. To the maid he said with raised brows: "Well, what shall you do?"

Again Sunflower regarded her sister appealingly.

"Oh, Lucy! Say yes, please," she almost whispered. And Lucy said:

"We shall be very glad to accept your invitation, Mr Bony."

"Good! Then that is settled," he said lightly, with assumed relief in his voice. "The dance is timed to start at nine o'clock. I will call for you at half-past eight, so be ready."

"How are we going?" Sunflower asked.

"Why, we will go in a car. Fred, the garage owner, has a beautiful car."

"That will be lovely. Will he wait to bring us home?"

"Certainly. And we will not come home until you are tired or the dance stops for the night. If you will excuse me for a little while I will go along and invite your father."

"Father!"

"Of course. We must persuade Mr Jelly to come along too."

"If only he would!"

"He'll come after I have invited him." Bony rose to his feet. "I'll not be long," he told them smilingly. "When I return to you we'll arrange the dances you will give me, for if we leave it until we reach the hall other men will quickly snap them up."

Yet the lightness of his voice failed to bring back the happiness his mention of Mr Jelly had banished. In their eyes was expressed horror when he slowly backed towards the passage leading to the farmer's den. Whilst he walked the short passage to the door at its farther end cold rage entered his heart against the man whose extraordinary behaviour was blighting the lives of his two daughters. On the closed door Bony knocked peremptorily, as though the law itself knocked.

No sound came from within the room.

Again he knocked, as the law impatient of denial.

"Lucy—go away!" ordered Mr Jelly in his low, tuneful voice.

"It is I, Mr Napoleon Bonaparte," Bony said loudly. "Let me in, Mr Jelly. I wish to speak to you."

"Go away!"

"Open the door, please, Mr Jelly."

"Go away! D'you hear?"

"I will not go until I have talked with you on a most important matter. I am a persistent man, Mr Jelly."

To this last statement Mr Jelly made no answer. Bony waited for ten seconds.

"You must have heard me, Mr Jelly," he said, and there was just that hint of a threat in his voice to tell any man that he was not to be turned away.

With startling abruptness the door was flung back. The soft lamplight silhouetted the cigar-shaped proportions of Mr Jelly's tall figure. Vicelike hands gripped the detective's arms. He was swung round like a weathercock. Cunning hands pinioned his wrists with steel handcuffs. He was dragged into the room. The door was shut with a crash.

The red-shaded lamp on the table appeared as a lighthouse amid the raging sea of albums, newspapers and clipped cuttings, a pot of paste and scissors, two empty bottles and one partly full, several glasses and a water jug, enlargements of photographs and picture frames, and slices of bread and butter on a plate. The tinted light above the shade appeared to magnify Mr Jelly's proportions to an alarming degree.

The farmer was dressed only in his shirt and trousers. The halo of grey hair was a tangled mass. His complexion was as white paint patchily laid over dead features, and whilst he regarded the manacled Bony his light blue, red-rimmed eyes were the only indication that he lived. In his voice, when he spoke, there was no anger, and because there was none, Bony sensed the man's dangerousness.

"Now that you are here, say your little piece," Mr Jelly commanded.

"Sit down and let us talk," Bony urged him quietly.

"It would be for your ultimate good to lower your dignity a little," the farmer said, as though explaining a difficult point. "Like all your kind you are too presumptuous. When white people are foolishly decent to your sort you think them weak enough to put up with unlicensed impertinence. You will say why you have forced yourself on me, or——"

"Sit down and let us talk," Bony said for the second time. "I came here as a friend, so let us remain friends."

The corners of Mr Jelly's mouth were sucked slightly inward. During a period of ten seconds he examined Body as one might a horse at a show. Then he turned back to the tallboy chest of drawers, rummaged among the contents, and brought out a tapered whip of rhinoceros hide. Returning to Bony, he said:

"Will it be necessary for me to persuade you?"

Bony stood up. Mr Jelly took another step towards him. Slowly Bony's hands came round his sides, and casually he tossed on the table the pair of handcuffs.

Mr Jelly's steady gaze at the detective's face wavered and fell down to the glittering steel bands. They were, he saw, still locked—he had locked them on Bony's wrists. Without haste the half-caste backed round the table, but Mr Jelly did not follow. He stood looking at his own handcuffs as though the gleaming points of reflected light hypnotized him. Silence and absolute cessation of movement for several seconds, and then Bony walked round the table back to Mr Jelly's side, when he reached away for a chair and drew it opposite that on which he had been forced to sit.

For the third time he said: "Sit down and let us talk."

The farmer's gaze lifted from the handcuffs to the detective's face. They stood staring into each other's eyes as might two boxers before a bout. Mr Jelly was on the brink of a mental breakdown brought on by some strange excitement and hard drinking. The man's nerves were all quivering, jerking little patches of skin on face and neck. He was as one coming out of a terrible fit of masked epilepsy; presently his muscles began to tremble in all his limbs. For the fourth time Bony said:

"Sit down and let us talk."

Now he deliberately turned his back on the farmer to clear a space on the table and reach for whisky and glasses, expecting to feel leaping agony beneath the stroke of the whip. The weight of a hair would decide the scales in favour of Mr Jelly becoming a madman or a cowed, prostrate man. Bony began to pour whisky into the two glasses. The drinks he set, one at each end of the cleared space, and the water jug exactly between them. Slight movement behind him was almost too great a temptation to turn and fight for his life before the dreadful whip fell, and he could have sighed audibly when the following movement told him that Mr Jelly had collapsed into the chair Bony had placed for him.

Without looking at the farmer, he produced tobacco and papers, sat down, fell to making a cigarette. Not till the lighted match was held against the tobacco did he look at Mr Jelly, encountering then the pale blue eyes regarding him with an admixture of astonishment and curiosity. Bony leaned back in his chair with the freedom of one who had known Mr Jelly for a very long time.

"I used to do a lot of tracking for the Queensland police a few years ago," he said easily, thankful that he was mastering this extraordinary man. "Sometimes they played jokes with me, catching me unaware and securing me with their handcuffs. The regulation bracelets used here are better than the American type. Yet I agree with you that yours of the new French pattern are superior to both. Here's luck."

Mr Jelly continued to stare.

"Drink up," Bony said persuasively, examining an unmounted enlargement of a portrait study.

When Mr Jelly did speak his voice betrayed the struggle to regain composure.

"Why have you come here?" he asked.

"Because I am the father of three boys."

"What have your boys got to do with your being here uninvited?"

"I don't know how old you are, but I am forty-three," Bony told him, puffing at his cigarette. "I married young, and my wife and I and our three sons form an exceptionally happy family."

Abruptly he leaned forward and pointed beyond the other. Their eyes clashed. He went on. "The other side of that closed door your two children are living in fear for you because of you. They were kind enough to ask me in to tea last Saturday. I was here when you came home. This evening, in order to repay their kindness, I called to invite them to a dance at the Jilbadgie Hall next Saturday evening, and Mrs Saunders tells me that since you arrived home you have not left this room or permitted the members of your family to come into it. As a man and as a father, it was my duty to force myself on you for the purpose of telling you to your face that you are behaving shamefully."

"You have plenty of nerve, haven't you?" Mr Jelly said grimly.

"Little Sunflower gave me nerve enough tonight."

"And plenty of curiosity, eh?"

"I have always been of a curious disposition," was Bony's admission.

The farmer's hand, which had been idly fingering the glass of his untasted whisky, suddenly fell on Bony's right wrist. The half-caste made no effort to free his wrist from a grip which was as firm and as unbreakable as a clamp of bar iron. Instead he inquired:

"What prison were you in?"

Had he released a powerful spring beneath Mr Jelly the effect could not have been more startling. In the space of a fraction of a second the farmer was on his feet, glaring down at the detective, whose wrist he continued to hold in his enormously powerful hand. Bony noted with prideful pleasure that the result of his bombshell was to produce honest anger in the place of cold, simmering fury. Jelly's voice was harsh when he demanded:

"What do you mean, you coloured rat?"

"My question was but the logical outcome of the dexterity with which you handcuffed me, hustled me into the room from the passage, and the precise manner in which you are now gripping my wrist. If you so flagrantly betray your old profession, how can you blame me for correctly guessing it?"

"You seem to know a deal about my old profession," the other said.

"As I told you, I have mixed a lot with policemen and warders. However, we are drifting from the subject of ourselves as family men. Cannot you understand that your remarkable behaviour is really causing your girls much distress?"

If the former question had jerked the farmer to his feet like the spring beneath the jack-in-the-box, this last question acted like the box lid which compresses the spring and imprisons the jack. Mr Jelly dropped into his chair, fell forward over the littered table, buried his face in his arms, and began to weep. The following minutes were the most terrible Bony ever had experienced.

The pointed, hairless head of the crying man touched the enlarged photographic print of a young man about twenty-five years of age, clean-shaven and by no means ill-looking. The hair was ruffled as through by a sea wind, and the widely opened eyes looked out with charming frankness. Bony took it up the better to examine it, and presently, in idle curiosity, he reversed it and read in Mr Jelly's handwriting:

"Charles Laffer. Hanged, Fremantle— —"

It appeared probably that Mr Jelly was about to add the date of Laffer's hanging when Bony disturbed him by his insistent knocking. The morbidity of the farmer's hobby caused Bony to shudder, and after a little while he began to speak in a low voice, urging Mr Jelly to give it up. He described the effect this passion for collecting details of murderers and of their executions was having on the other's mind and what the probable end would be if it were continued. He spoke of the unhappiness it was causing Lucy Jelly and Sunflower but said nothing about the mysterious journeys undertaken at the call of mysteriously sent messages. Presently Mr Jelly became calmer, and when he raised his head his expression was bitter.

"I am an old woman, Bony," he said. "Sometimes I think I am a little mad. I am sorry for what I said about your colour. I have been mad for several days lately, and because you have come here pluckily to beard me in my own room, I will tell you a little of my life's tragedy."

Again he crossed to the tallboy, and when he returned to the table he carried a small silver-framed picture. Laying it down before Bony, he said:

"That is of my wife, taken about a year after we were married."

Whilst Bony was looking at an older edition of Sunflower the farmer took from the wall one of the framed photographic reproductions. When he laid this beside the picture of his wife he said in explanation:

"And this is the picture of Thomas Kingston, who murdered her when Dulcie was ten months old."

Bony turned in his chair to stare up at Mr Jelly. "Then your name isn't Jelly," he said.

"No. Afterwards I took my mother's maiden name. I had to, you see. I gave up my position in the prison service and finally settled here when the country was new. Like you and your wife, Hetty and I were sweethearts. I was lying on her grave, unable to shed any more tears, the minute they hanged Kingston, who walked to the trap singing hymns. They are dead, but old Bob Jelly lives on and interests himself in every swine who kills: sad when the alienists cheat the law, glad when the law cheats them."

"Nevertheless, you should give thought to your girls," Bony said sympathetically. "It is your duty to live for them and their happiness. Don't you see that by giving most of your thought to this strange hobby of yours you are enabling Kingston to strike at them through you? Let the past fade and the future shine brightly for all three of you." Mr Jelly's face became buried again on his arms. "When I asked your girls and Mrs Saunders to come with me to the dance their eyes sparkled at the prospect, and when I said I would see you and invite you, too, I saw uneasy fear replace their joy. Give all this up. Let us now collect all this material, all those pictures, and take the collection into the garden and burn it."

"No." Mr Jelly was emphatic. "But I am in the mood to compromise. I will cease to collect when I have filled the frame with the picture of George Loftus's murderer, and that will be directly he is hanged."

"You mean that the killer of Loftus will provide the final item?"

"I mean that; just that."

"Very well," Bony said, sighing. "You are, I think, a man to keep your word. And now shall we both go along to the kitchen and tell them that you have accepted my invitation to the dance?"

Mr Jelly raised his head.

"Not now," he begged. "I am unwashed, unshaven."

"I will bring hot water and towels," Bony declared, rising. "You and I will hear Sunflower laugh before another hour has gone."

Leaving the farmer still protesting, Bony passed out of the room, walked the short passage. When he entered the kitchen three pairs of eyes regarded him steadily, entreating him to speak quickly.

"A jug of hot water, a wash-basin, and a towel, please," he said.

"Father! Is Father hurt?" Lucy asked sharply.

"No, no!" replied Bony, laughing softly. "He is quite all right, and he will be with us in a few minutes as fresh as Peter Pan."

Mrs Saunders could not refrain from smiling at Bony's linking of that gay figure of childhood with the cigar-shaped Mr Jelly. The three assisted each other to supply Bony's wants, and in less than two minutes he re-entered Mr Jelly's den to see the farmer standing at the window and pouring whisky from the remaining bottle on a quite innocent flower plant. When Bony set down the basin and the water on the plain washstand Mr Jelly said, with wonder in his voice:

"You are a very strange man. Somehow I think I shall get to like you."

"Everyone gets to like me in time."

"Here, strop my razor. My hand shakes."

Yet, despite his shaky hand, Mr Jelly shaved with great care and thoroughness. After he washed the grey fringe of hair and combed it, when he had put on a clean shirt and over it a well-brushed coat, the transformation from the dream- haunted, drink-sodden man was amazing. But he said:

"I feel ashamed. I'd rather meet them in the morning."

"We will meet them together," Bony said firmly, adding in lighter vein: "Tell you what! Let's climb out through the window and go in by the kitchen door, as though we had been out to lock up the fowls."

For three seconds Mr Jelly gazed at Bony as though he was seeing him for the first time. He nodded his big head solemnly and crawled through the open window, as a little boy robbing the pantry. Together they reached the veranda steps; together they entered the kitchen dining-room. Beyond the threshold Bony halted. Mr. Jelly took one further step forward. His eyes were bright, and he blinked rapidly.

Sunflower, who was standing by the sofa, held by amazement, suddenly ran to him, oblivious of her bandaged foot. A little more sedately Lucy followed her, so that there stood Mr Jelly holding a daughter in each of his massive arms, kissing them in turn, whilst the tears ran unchecked down his weather-beaten face.

Bony wrote on a leaf torn from his notebook: "Will call for all at half-past eight Saturday."

Slipping the note on the dresser when sure that Mrs Saunders observed him, he nodded to her, pointed to the note, placed two fingers against his lips to enjoin silence, and silently walked out of the house.

Chapter Fourteen

Mr Thorn's Ideas

All day Thursday Bony cut and carted fence posts from the dense timber covering the eastern half of the government farm. For years posts had been cut from that area of timber when required, and he found that the posts suitable for the rabbit fence were not so plentiful as the uninitiated might think; for many trees, when dry, would easily become destroyed by the omnipresent termite.

Because he would need the horse for the afternoon trip to the timber, Bony stacked the posts among the trees near the gate beside the railway. He then parked the dray in deep shade, and, taking the horse out, tied it to a tree to eat its midday feed. Finally he made a fire, filled the billy with water from his canvas water bag, and set it against the flame to boil for tea; for no Australian could possibly eat a meal without the accompaniment of several cups of tea.

Trucks passed towards Burracoppin loaded with wheat and re-turned empty. The sun flooded the road with heat and seemed to hold the white dust level with the treetops. A long train came roaring down the grade to the fence, Bony observing with interest the long rake of wheat-loaded trucks on its way to the seaport.

Whilst waiting for the water to boil he leaned against the fence, near one of the new posts he had erected. The wheat train having passed, his gaze dropped to the flame-wrapped billycan and from it to a number of blowflies settled on the ground at the base of the post. When he moved his foot near them they took wing, but immediately his foot was withdrawn they settled again.

The question arising in Bony's inquisitive mind while he waited for his billy to boil was: Why were those flies so much attracted to the earth around that one post? There was not at that place more moisture than anywhere else. So absorbed was he by his problem that he automatically flung a handful of tea into the boiling water and omitted to remove the billy until the question had been answered several minutes later, when the liquid had become blue-black.

That was the post at the bottom of which he had buried one of Ginger's rabbits many days before. Fifteen inches below rammed earth lay the body of a rabbit, and it was the process of its decomposition, throwing off a strong smell, penetrating through the packed earth right to the surface, which was attracting the blowflies.

Unheeding the inky-black liquid his tea had become, he lifted the billy from the fire with a stick and thoughtfully carried it to the dray, on the floor of which he was to eat his lunch safe from the ants. He had not long been reclining with his back against one of the sides of the dray when he saw Mr Thorn reach the fence on his patrol bicycle and dismount. The Water Rat looked at his watch, then at the sun, and then round him, whereupon he saw Bony, and, after waving his hand in greeting, fell to unstrapping his billycan and lunch from the machine.

"Bit of luck, sightin' you," he said on reaching the dray. "I'll shove me billy on your fire, if you don't mind."

"Not a bit," Bony cheerfully assured him.

"Wish it was beer," Mr Thorn said, filling his billy from Bony's water bag.

"Tea is better at this time of the day," the smiling half-caste pointed out to the Water Rat arranging his billy on the fire.

Mr Thorn was emphatic when next he spoke, proclaiming the fact that he knew precisely of what he was talking.

"Beer is best at any time of the day and night, and all through the year. It is especially best on a hot day like this. But I never was lucky. Even the blarsted pipes won't bust now, but they'll keep on busting in the middle of winter when the water freezes stiff. Going to the darnce Sat'day night?"

"At Jilbadgie Hall? Yes, I expect so. Are you going?"

"Well, I haven't been aiming to, seeing as 'ow there's no pub handy. I can't darnce much on coffee. But the old woman says I've got to take 'er, and I love peace enough never to argue." Mr Thorn's face brightened with hope. He said: "Perhaps we could manage to take along a few bottles with us?"

"We might."

"How are you going?"

"In a car. I am taking the Jellys."

"Oh!" Mr Thorn uttered the exclamation very slowly and most distinctly.

Then he whistled. Then he said: "Old man got money, eh? Just come outer smoke, eh?"

"I really don't know when he returned," Bony lied expertly, and yawned.

"She's right," announced Mr Thorn, referring to the billycan. "Give us your pannikin," he requested when due time had been allowed for the tea to "draw".

"How did you enjoy the benefit dance?" Bony asked him.

"Good-oh!" Mr Thorn's round red face lost its creases of anxiety regarding the beer supply at the coming dance. Into his small grey eyes flashed an expression of sweet memory. He added with faint expostulation, "You oughta 'ave come with me acrost to the pub when I gave you the oil. We 'ad a good time for nearly an hour. But I nearly made meself sick eating peppermints to take orf the fumes; and then, when I got back, the old woman swore I was drunk, and a disgrace, and a low, swilling beast. You married?"

"For more than twenty years."

"Poor blighter," murmured Mr Thorn sympathetically. For a little while he did not speak, and then presently he burst out: "The driver of Number Ten goods this morning told the lumpers in Burra that George Loftus 'as been located at Leonora. He heard about it in Merredin, and the bloke 'oo told 'im was the yardman at one of the pubs 'oose sister is married to one of the policemen. I knoo old Loftus 'ad done a bunk!"

"But why did he do a bunk?" Bony asked calmly, yet feeling deeply disappointed.

"Dunno, I'm sure. Any'ow, they can't do nothink to 'im for clearing orf. Doing a bunk ain't no crime. Between me and you, I think he did a get because he was fed to the teeth with his flash wife. 'Course, she's very popular in Burra, but there's them 'oo thinks she ain't so popular with them. My missus don't think much of 'er for one. Mrs Loftus is too stuck up for gov'ment workers, but she's backed by a clique 'ere 'oo'd crawl under a snake at the bottom of a hundred-foot mine shaft.

"Expect now Mrs Loftus will sue for divorse. My missus always did reckon that if Landon got the chance he'd marry 'er to get 'er—and the farm. Got 'is 'ead screwed on right, has Landon, but he'll do better when he loses interest in the skirts."

Having finished his meal, Mr Thorn proceeded to replace pannikin and cloth in his lunch tin and then slowly and with concentrated interest to fill and light his pipe. Having got the tobacco to burn to his satisfaction after the expenditure of four matches, he continued his monologue, for Bony was lying back with half-closed eyes.

"Talking about that benefit darnce reminds me," said he. "The Wednesday before, my missus drawed five one-pound notes from the bank. Come Sat'day night she reckons that the last three of them would be safer in 'er 'andbag than under the mattress at 'ome. And as she says it she's looking 'ard at me. So the notes goes with 'er to the darnce, and sometime about the middle of it she must needs open 'er bag to powder 'er dial and drops the folded notes without knowing it. There went a 'undred and twenty nice cold pots down some other bloke's neck, 'cos we never found 'em.

"She quite calm when she tells me. If I 'ad lorst a deaner I'd have got hell for a week. I see Mick Landon without a girl, and he reckoned the bank might 'ave kept the numbers. Most obliging chap, Mick. He was in the next day squaring up the darnce, and he sees the bank manager and arst 'im, and the manager told 'im that they never keeps the numbers of pound notes.

"Good bloke, Landon! Good spender, too! If 'e does marry Mrs Loftus they'll make a good pair as far as looks go. But she'll find that Mick Landon won't be as easygoing as old Loftus was."

And so on and on about people in Burracoppin, whilst Bony silently listened and wondered about Landon being so interested in the numbers of lost notes and about the news that Loftus had been discovered at Leonora, away up in the north-east of the State.

At last Mr Thorn announced the end of his lunch hour and rolled off the dray.

"I must go," he said regretfully. "See you at Jilbadgie, Sat'day. Don't forget to bring 'arf a dozen bottles with you. I'll bring my share, an' we'll make a plant nice and 'andy so's we can nip out now and then on the quiet and 'ave a deep-noser!"

"A deep-noser!"

"Yes. A snifter."

"Do you mean a drink?"

"Of course I means a drink. A snifter's a pot, an' a pot's a deep-noser. Didn't you understand that?"

"No. I fear I did not. I shall know in future."

"You'll know all right when I whispers into your ear: 'Come an' 'ave a snifter.' We'll be all right if we makes the plant. Hooroo!"

"*Au revoir*," replied Bony pleasantly. While Mr Thorn's rotund, well-nourished figure waddled away Bony smiled quizzically. When the Water Rat had clambered across the pipeline, mounted his machine, and had pedalled away along the patrolman's stone-cleared path, he said softly: "Thank you, Mr Thorn. You deserve your plant Sat'day night."

Chapter Fifteen

Secrets

On the Friday before the Jilbadgie dance Bony received a long letter from Sergeant Westbury which revealed his prose to be less staccato than his speech. He wrote in a triumphant vein to state that George Loftus had been discovered in company with two other men sinking a shaft in the hope of striking a gold-bearing reef near Leonora. As no charge had been laid by Mrs Loftus on the ground of desertion, and as no serious damage had been done to government property through wrecking the car, no action could be taken against the farmer. He had been photographed, however, and copies would be forwarded for purposes of identification.

The man himself stoutly denied that he was George Loftus, giving his name as Frank Lovelace and stating that he was but recently arrived on the goldfields from South Australia. Yet his particulars were identical with those of George Loftus supplied by the Merredin police. In conclusion, Sergeant Westbury expressed pleasure that the case was almost finalized and hoped that Bony would call on him for a chat before returning to his native State.

Even his communication did not wholly convince the Queenslander that the missing man still lived. That sixth sense warned him against accepting a probability not backed by proof, and until proof was produced he would carry on.

With a disturbing sense of disappointment Bony admitted the probability of the man at Leonora being George Loftus, but there was yet to be explained the all-compelling reason for a man leaving a comfortable home, with all its attendant amenities and the society of a pretty wife, for the rigours of a gold-miner's camp in the heat of summer. There was no reason for a man deliberately to wreck a car to make that change in his life.

The passage of time had tangled the threads, broken them, made them more numerous. Day had succeeded day, and Bony could discover no clue of importance that would lead him to the heart of the mystery. There was growing in his mind a conviction, based on no tangible evidence, that the cause of George Loftus's disappearance was that which controlled the absences of Mr Jelly. He came to believe that could he solve the puzzle of Mr Jelly and placate the mind of Lucy Jelly, he would satisfy his own mind regarding Loftus.

By now Bony should have left for Queensland if he was to report for duty at the expiration of his live. Yet he found he could not desert this dual case. He had promised Lucy Jelly to make clear the mystery hanging over her father and which shrouded Sunflower's life and her own. He had promised to clear up the Loftus case for John Muir. In his heart he knew he would not give up, even had he not made those two promises, and indications pointed to his being once more dismissed from the Queensland Police Force for engaging in a case outside his State without official permission. Memory of a much-tried Colonel Spender caused Bony to sigh.

In reply to Sergeant Westbury's letter he wrote out a long message to be telegraphed to his chief, maintaining the secrecy of his identity, which such a message telephoned from Burracoppin would have destroyed. In view of the location of George Loftus at Leonora, Bony's request to Colonel Spender for a month's extension of leave to proceed with the Burracoppin case produced great astonishment in the mind of Sergeant Westbury.

Bony realized that he must depart a little from the straight line of his philosophy of crime detection and give Father Time a sharp nudge. It was almost certain that Mrs Loftus and Mick Landon would attend the dance at Jilbadgie. It was less certain, but likely, that Miss Waldron would also go, and if she did not an excuse could be invented to assure her attendance. The Loftus farm, therefore, would be guarded only by three dogs, two of whom appeared to Bony, when he called for a drink of water, to be capable of energetic action at night. In the house they would guard might be found the explanation of the farmer's departure for Leonora — if he had departed for the goldfields, which Bony's intuition compelled him to doubt.

When he had finished work for the Rabbit Department at noon on Saturday he paid a visit to the garage to hire Fred and his car for that evening. He then drew Fred's partner aside and opened negotiations for services of an entirely different nature.

These two men belonged to that small class who are habitually cautious in their dealings and in their speech. Bony had noted this reserve when they spoke with Mr and Mrs Poole and others, and he felt no unease when divulging his secret business to William. In the precise centre of the yard behind the big iron shed he said:

"I want you to do something for me, if you will. Fred is to take me to the Jilbadgie dance tonight, as you know, but the matter about which I wish to speak to you has nothing to do with his commission. I must entrust to you a little secret."

There was enquiry in his voice, and William nodded assent.

"It is a fact," Bony went on, "that I am a police officer engaged in looking into the matter of George Loftus's disappearance. I think it possible— —"

He permitted William to read the sergeant's letter.

"But they have found him, haven't they?" William cut in.

"They say they have, but I do not think they have," Bony said emphatically. "Even if the man at Leonora is Loftus there remains much behind this affair, and I believe I could learn at lot if I could but get an hour's freedom in Loftus's house. It is almost certain that Mrs Loftus and Landon will go to the dance tonight. If Miss Waldron does not go I must invent some excuse to persuade her.

"What I require of you is to leave here about ten o'clock on your motor-cycle and wait beside the main road, out of sight, about four to five hundred yards this side of the hall. At a favourable opportunity I will slip away and join you, because I want you to take me on your machine to the Loftus farm, leave me there, decoy away the dogs, and after about an hour take me back to the dance. Did you wish to attend the dance?"

"No."

"Excellent. Please tell everyone that you are not going. Fred will stay and dance all the evening. Consequently, curious minds will not associate my short absence with any person actually there, unless it is with Mr Thorn, and the reason of his absences is well known, I think. Will five pounds be sufficient remuneration?"

"You bet. That job's mine."

"You will keep the secret of my identity?"

"Even from Fred. And he's close-mouthed enough."

"Good! I will fetch a little parcel later, which you must be sure to bring with you. *Au revoir!*"

Punctually at the time appointed Fred waited on Bony with a roomy and comfortable car. To placate the friendly Water Rat, six bottles of beer and a glass were packed securely among the tools under a seat. Bony was smartly dressed in dark navy blue.

Reaching the Jelly homestead a little after half-past eight, Bony and Fred, who was dressed even more smartly than the detective, found little Sunflower and Mr Jelly waiting for the others to finish their toilet. Scones and small cakes were surrounded by teacups, and on the fire simmered a fragrant coffee-pot.

"Everyone ready?" Bony asked when he entered the kitchen.

"Sunflower is ready and so am I," announced Mr Jelly. "Lucy has a new frock and must not be hurried. Nothing in this world will hurry Mrs Saunders, and I doubt if anything in the next world will, either."

Mr Jelly was his usual complacent self. Benevolence and good humour radiated from his large face. Again he was the jovial farmer whom nothing could daunt.

Mrs Saunders appeared, placidly cheerful as always. She busied herself with the coffee. Gowned in white satin, Lucy Jelly came into the kitchen, cool, controlled, and calm.

They were all laughing at something Mr Jelly had said when the car sped away to the fence, where they turned southward along the government track. It was a happy party which reached the Jilbadgie Hall.

Bony danced twice with Sunflower and once with Lucy Jelly and told them he had business to do which would occupy him an hour, begging them to excuse him and not remark his absence.

"Father!" exclaimed Sunflower.

"No. Mr Loftus is the cause."

"Father?" inquired Lucy.

"No. Mr Loftus. Your father will give up his strange hobby and mysterious journeys in the near future. He promised me that he would."

"You make me glad," she said, sighing, and was smiling happily when Mr Jelly claimed the next dance.

The building was packed. Mrs Loftus was receiving congratulations from many about the report of her husband. Mick Landon, of course, acted M.C. and worked with enthusiasm, minus coat and waistcoat, the red braces over white shirt adding colour to the women's dresses. And there was Miss Waldron dancing with the Spirit of Australia, whose passion for dancing evidently had not cooled with age.

The only difficulty in the way of Bony's quietly unnoticed departure about ten o'clock was presented in the Falstaffian figure of Mr Thorn. The Water Rat's difficulties were appalling. His objective was the six bottles of beer which with Machiavellian cunning he had concealed in a clump of dense bush one hundred yards from the hall. The obstacles presented to him were represented by the equally Machiavellian Mrs Thorn and by Bony, who cussedly enough appeared to be the actual needle in the haystack. There were moments when Mr Thorn almost pricked himself with the illusive needle, but not until late that night did he even so much as touch it.

"Blast!" he ejaculated when at last he had surmounted the obstacle, in the person of his watchful wife, and had successfully managed to sneak away from the hall. "I wonder where that coon's got to.

"Don't seem like 'im to 'ave a plant all on his own, and until I'm sure he's brought no beer I don't like having a Jimmy Woodser."

Yet in the end he was forced to copy the example of that detestable fellow, Mr James Woods, and drink without company precisely at the instant Bony, dressed in mechanic's overalls to save his clothes from dust, reached the Loftus farm gate on the back of William's motor-cycle.

There he unwrapped the small parcel the garage-man had brought, producing an electric torch, a black silk handkerchief, a pair of roughly made sheepskin boots, large enough to slip over his dancing pumps and made with the wool on the outside of the soles, and a bottle of aniseed to the contents of which had been added five drops of essence of roses, a ball of worsted yarn, and a long length of stout string.

The sheepskin boots would enable him to move about without leaving tracks. To the end of the string he attached the ball of yarn, and on the ball of yarn he poured a quarter of the aniseed oil and the oil of roses. The lamp and the handkerchief he pushed into the single pocket of his overalls.

"Now, I think, we are ready," he said to the deeply interested William. "Listen carefully, please. The strong smell of this mixture of aniseed and essence of roses should be a sufficiently powerful decoy to entice away those barking dogs. This end of the string I will tie to the pillion frame. You will now take me to the Loftus house, keeping carefully in one of those wheel ruts on the farm road. Where the farm track reaches the hard ground near the house, turn sharply about and drive slowly back again, still being careful to keep in a wheel rut. When we turn near the house I will drop the doped ball of yam when it will be trailed behind the machine. The dogs will pick up the scent and follow, and when we get about halfway back to this gate I'll slip from the machine. The dogs will not bother about me.

"Now, remember, give them a good run right back to Burracoppin. Run the trail to that empty garage, of which, you say, you have the key, unlock the main door, go in, machine and all, and pass out through the back door, which, of course, you will instantly reclose. Then slip round the building to the front, and when the dogs arrive and go in, lock them in. It is now twenty minutes past ten. Time yourself to get back to this gate at half-past eleven. Is all that clear?"

"As rainwater."

"Very well. Let us go."

Riding on the pillion whilst William steered the machine with difficulty along one of the deep wheel ruts was not easy. The truck which was moving the Loftus wheat, as well as the Loftus car, kept to one set of wheat tracks, which now were six or seven inches deep. The tracks ran over ground proved to be clear of tyre-destroying roots; and, therefore, what marks the motor-cycle would make could certainly be wiped away by the wheels of Mrs Loftus's car when she returned from the dance.

At the house end of the farm track the three dogs met them with yelps and savage snarls. As William turned the machine on the hard ground near the house Bony dropped the treated ball of worsted yarn which at once became trailed. In the darkness he could see the dogs, and when they had covered fifty yards of the return journey to the gate the animals suddenly ceased their noise, telling the detective that they had crossed the powerful decoy and were following it. The odour of roses added to that of aniseed would draw them till they dropped with exhaustion.

Bony slipped from the machine and darted several yards into the wheat stubble, there to stand motionless while the dogs passed, noses on the trail William was laying.

With a handful of straw he obliterated his tracks on the roadside made when he had left the machine. Hiding his white collar with the black handkerchief, after making sure that his sheepskin boots were securely on his feet, that the torch was in the overall pocket, he moved towards the house, carrying in his hand a short length of tempered wire.

When Bony approached the homestead for the second time the buildings looming out of the darkness were strangely silent now that the dogs were decoyed away. The dwelling house was like a large square box, so few and slight were the attempts at decoration.

Silently Bony circled it, eyes and ears at straining point to note the possible presence of a human being. He observed how the narrow veranda partially protected the front of the house, which faced east, a veranda so narrow as to be almost useless for the purpose for which it was built. The wider south veranda, enclosed by wooden trellis-work up which climbed sturdy grapevines, was the only softening effect, the whole building appearing to reveal George Loftus as one who spent all his money and thought on the land at the expense of a comfortable home. During his stay in the wheat belt Bony had seen many superior farmhouses and many much worse.

Again reaching the front, satisfied that the house was empty of human beings, he stepped carefully across the rough- floored veranda and inserted the hooked piece of wire in the door lock of common make. Ten seconds later he was inside the house, the door just ajar behind him, listening to make positively sure he was alone. Then the white shaft of his torch flashed out across the room.

To Bony was revealed a large kitchen, which also was made to serve as a living-room. Beside the long dining-table in the centre and the stiff-backed chairs against the wall there were two leather lounge chairs, a cane-grass sofa, and, in one corner, a glass-fronted bookcase filled with volumes. White crockery gleamed from the shelves of a big dresser. The glint of polished fire irons came from both sides of the cooking range. A room most comfortable, although the walls were covered with hessian stretched and tacked to the wooden frame. A clean and neat room, obviously ruled by a woman.

There was but one door leading from the living-room. Crossing to it, Bony's light showed him a bedroom which, like the kitchen, seemed oddly to contrast with the poor appearance of the outside of the house, There was no further room leading off this one. Living-room and bedroom were all that the house contained. The windows of both rooms faced eastwards, either side of the solitary door, and at the west side of each room long narrow fanlights which could be opened were built in high up near the ceiling.

The bedroom more accurately described the character of Mrs Loftus than did the living-room. The living-room she was obliged to share with others, but her bedroom was her own, the more completely since her husband had vanished. Here was her secret world wherein she spent most of her time; here was the world in which she dreamed her dreams and thought her secret thoughts. The furnishings, the pictures, the little books tossed carelessly on the writing table proclaimed the aspirations of this woman for things higher than are found on an Australian farm.

The cream-painted double bed with the lace-edged quilt above the coverings, the cream-painted long dress mirror and the dressing table, and, in sharp contrast, the black oak pedestal table and the antique escritoire of time-dulled walnut, all bespoke a woman of artistic taste in furnishings.

Two seascapes in watercolour hung in ebony frames on the walls, attracting him by their portrayal of light and wind. Low in the right-hand corner of each were the initials M.L. Mrs Loftus was without doubt something more than an amateur artist. Upon an easel was another picture, this in the making.

The writing table was next to claim Bony's attention. It was a plain-topped affair, having no pigeonholes or drawers, heavy, and firmly held by the carved pedestal supported by three claw-shaped legs. Now seated at the writing table, the detective proceeded to examine every article on it. There was a photograph of a young woman in tennis kit who might be Mrs Loftus's sister, for there were lines about the girl's mouth claiming relationship. There was a framed photograph of Mrs Loftus herself, seated before an easel beyond which was the wide-shaped veranda of a large house. Was that house her childhood home?

A volume of poems in leather covers held the detective's attention for several minutes. Written by an Australian poet, they breathed of love and passion, and, according to the wording on the title page, the book had been given to Mavis Waldron by the poet. Idly turning the well-thumbed pages, he came across a piece with some of the lines heavily underscored, read it through, read it again, and for the third time. Unrequited love was the theme of the poem, describing in mounting intensity the things the poor poet would do if his love was not reciprocated, things ranging from self-mutilation to homicide. Extraordinary verses, indeed, to capture a woman's fancy.

A black, gilt-edged, cloth-covered notebook was the next article to be examined. Almost all the pages were filled with neatly penned verses about love and hate, sorrow and joy, passion and dead flowers, and small pencil sketches of dreamlike magnificent houses, of nude male figures, and of several heads among which were copies from life of Mick Landon and the Spirit of Australia. This notebook and the volume of poems spoke plainly of a woman's passionate heart amid harsh, uncongenial surroundings.

Every inch of the table was examined. Far from being an expert, Bony yet recognized its age although unable to tell the period to which it belonged. The piece suggested secret hiding places in the thickness of its surface, the carved pedestal, the curious claw legs. And in one of the three claws he did discover a long shallow recess which contained a small, intricately fashioned key.

Obviously the key was regarded as valuable, since it operated a lock behind which presumably were articles of greater value. Bony spent ten precious minutes searching for a drawer or chest or box with a lock which this key opened. He found no such object either there or in the kitchen, but, coming across a box of candles that were softened by the heat of the house, he made a set of impressions on one of them, placed it in a dish of water to harden, and replaced the key in the secret cavity in the table leg.

An exhaustive search of the escritoire produced no result. There was nothing other than papers and books and accounts relating to the management of the farm; no smallest clue to the whereabouts of George Loftus, not a letter from him, no address, no written word of his intention of going to Leonora.

Bony raised the carpet in sections and examined each of the floor-boards, finding none loose or capable of being moved. The walls were equally barren of result. The bed he left until the last.

Here he paused with indecision, because the make-up of this bed was outside the ambit of his experience. He felt that should he disarrange the coverings he might be unable to replace them precisely as he found them. The dainty lace- edged pillows, the artistically silk-worked counterpane, made him feel that to touch them would be an act of sacrilege, something that never could be fashioned again once he destroyed the symmetry of its virginal lines. And yet he could not leave the bed unexamined.

With great care he folded downward still farther the bedclothes. With his light he patiently searched the pillows and the sheets, for in his mind was born a suspicion begotten by the poems and the sketches. The close-held torch threw a circle of light no larger than a cheese-plate. Inexorably it covered every inch of pillows and sheeting, and at the end of one pillow, entangled in the lace, he found a hair, yellow in colour, about two inches long. It might well have come from the head of Mick Landon.

At the dressing table he was fortunate enough to secure from the woman's brush one of her hairs measuring more than a foot in length, but when he compared it with the short hair he could discern no difference in colour in the light of the torch. The two hairs he placed in folded paper, and the paper within his pocket book.

Back again at the bed, he began to examine the flock mattress, slipping his arms beneath it and above it, feeling every inch of its surface with his fingertips, taking remarkable care not to disorder the clothes. And there at the foot of the mattress he found with his fingers a sewed-up incision of about seven inches, and, at the end of a minute, located a foreign substance among the flock about fifteen inches in from the edge.

Several minutes were expended trying to work that hidden thing nearer to the edge of the mattress. With great care he exposed the incision to the light of the torch, when one swift appraisal told him that were he to cut the herringbone stitches he would never be able to put them back, because despite his intellectual gifts, despite his bushcraft and his acute vision, it would take him years of practice to acquire Mrs Loftus's sewing ability.

Balked, he stood thoughtfully biting his nether lip. He came to realize that here inside this house he was outside his element. In the open bush he might be supreme, but his knowledge became limited, and his craft useless, within a lady's boudoir. It was impossible for him to reopen the incision as he could not reclose it again without betraying the fact to Mrs Loftus, whilst if he cut a fresh incision she would notice it when she made the bed.

He was limited, too, to one other thing, and that was time. Eighty minutes he had given himself for the entire examination, and already thirty-five had passed.

Sighing with regret, he rearranged the bed coverings before passing out to the kitchen. Five of his precious minutes he gave to searching the kitchen, which offered no clue. Other than the living-room and the bedroom, there were no further rooms in the house to be searched, and when he closed the house door behind him and locked it with his piece of wire he would have been wholly satisfied could he have known the secret of the flock mattress.

Round the corner of the house to the south veranda he moved as soundlessly as a shadow. At the doorway in the centre of the trellis he paused a moment, listening, before opening the door and passing within and henceforth being most careful of his torchlight.

He saw a black wrought-iron bed, a plain deal dressing table with silver-mounted appointments, a cretonne-covered, roughly made washstand of casing boards. Beneath the bed was a large tin trunk on which were painted in large letters the initials E.W. The trunk was unlocked, and he had no time to bother with its contents. Evidently this was Miss Waldron's bedroom, and, there being here no object having a lock that the hidden key might fit, he went out into the night and silently made his way to the tent room occupied by Mick Landon.

Here he found a stretcher bed neatly made in readiness for the night. For a farm worker's bed it was luxurious. Landon slept between sheets. His head would rest on a linen-covered feather pillow. Silk pyjamas lay folded on the pillow. A pair of red leather slippers were left on the strip of carpet beside the bed.

At the head of the bed was a chintz-covered, case-made table on which were several books, a looking glass and shaving kit, a silver-framed photograph of a man Bony had never seen, an alarm clock, and knick-knacks inseparable to a bachelor's existence.

Opposite the bed was a leather suitcase, unlocked and containing clothes, a packet of letters all bearing an English postmark. That was all. There was nothing of importance. Idly Bony, looked at his watch and saw that he had six minutes left.

Without purpose he picked up the photograph the better to see the face of the man wearing plus-fours and carrying a bag of golf clubs. The frame was exceptionally heavy, exceptionally thick. It created curiosity, and he put down the light on the table the better to use both hands to feel it, turn it about. Then he saw the little sliding clip which, when pushed up, permitted the frame to open outwards like the covers of a book. It was a double frame, and the picture revealed inside was that of Mrs Loftus taken, according to the note written in pencil at the bottom, at Bondi Beach, 1923.

The detective became a thief. He stole two hairs from Landon's comb.

Decidedly, when he reached the gate and then was obliged to wait several minutes for William, he had much food for thought.

Chapter Sixteen

Mr Thorn's Plant

I had a game with the dogs," William told Bony on his return. "After I left you I kept the bike down to five miles an hour. Turning west at the old York Road, I saw a car pulling up at the gate the other side of the fence, so I went on for a quarter of a mile fairly quick and then stopped and got off. By that time the car was through the gate and coming up behind me, and in its headlights I saw Loftus's three dogs nosing my trail like bloodhounds.

"As per instructions, I set sail for the pub end of Burra, trailing all round the town and ending up at the empty garage. In I went, trail and all, and once inside I picked up the trail and put it into the tool bag, opened the back door, pushed the bike outside, and left it leaning against the building. Then I slipped round to the front and was just in time to see two dogs, noses to the ground, going inside. Three more dogs followed them before the three from here, and nine more followed them eight.

"As I was leaving I seen Mrs Poole's cow, leading Mrs Henry's pack of goats, coming along the road right dead on the trail, and, between there and here, I counted two horses, another cow, four dogs, and about five million rabbits. By the morning there'll be a menagerie outside that garage. When Burra wakes up tomorrow the people will wonder how that garage got turned into a Noah's Ark."

"It wull be a graand sicht," murmured Bony, affecting a Scotch accent. "You did excellent work. Well, we must move off to the hall."

"How did you get on?"

"The time period was too short to secure satisfactory results, supposing there were results to be secured."

"Do you still reckon Loftus isn't at Leonora?"

"Between ourselves, I do, but ask no questions, because really I do hate to tell lies, even though I am an expert."

After travelling a quarter of a mile William pulled up. "Sorry, but I have got to tell you," he said, much hindered by his chuckling, "what a fool I was not to let into that garage Mrs Poole's cow and Mrs Henry's goats."

"There will be enough recriminations without adding to them," said the delighted Bony.

Fifteen minutes later William stopped the machine about four hundred yards from the hall. Bony got out of the mechanic's overalls, rolled up in them the bottle of decoy, and tied the parcel to the pillion seat.

"I shall not want you any more tonight," he said, to add with a low laugh, "I will try to get out early in the morning to see the animals gathered round the garage. Thank you for your assistance tonight. I am going to rely on your discretion."

"You be easy. The less in a joke the better the joke. Pleased to do any other jobs you want done. Hooroo!"

Bony waited till the cycle's tail-light had vanished up the wide straight road before walking the remaining distance to the hall. Long before he reached it the music of the string band reached him, and a little later the rhythmic sound of the dancers' feet slipping over the polished floor. The very first person he met was Mr Thorn.

"Where-in-'ell 'ave you been?" demanded the worried Water Rat. "I've been looking for you all the evenin'. I couldn't wait. I've drunk up 'alf me beer. Did you bring any?"

The reflected light from the hall windows revealed Bony plainly to Mr Thorn. The detective's shoes were speckless. No handkerchief, black or white, now protected his collar. He was an illustration of the lie he spoke.

"The heat of the hall affected me," he said blandly. "Sun heat never affects me as sometimes does the heat produced by massed human bodies. I have been for a quiet stroll."

"Well, thank 'eaven, I found you. Did you bring any beer?"

"I did bring a few bottles. They are in Fred's car."

Mr Thorn sighed his delight. His fat neck stretched up and down through his tight collar, reminding Bony of the needle's eye in which at long last the proverbial camel had become jammed. There was a note of entreaty in his voice when he said:

"Let's get 'em and take 'em over to my plant."

When Bony returned with four of his six bottles of beer it was with difficulty that he discovered the Water Rat sitting on the running board of one of the many parked cars.

"Hush! Go quiet," Mr Thorn implored. "Me old woman's taking a bird's-eye view out of the door. Don't speak, or she'll spoil the game." And then, after a minute, with relief: "Come on! She's gone. Foller me."

Mr Thorn marched off to the rabbit fence with extraordinary caution, walked north along the government track beside the fence until they reached a dense wall of bush, into which he vanished with Bony close on his heels. The detective was conducted, with all the secrecy of an initiate to a lodge, to a small clearing in which was Mr Thorn's plant. It was evident to the amazed Bony that that clearing was the site of many plants dating from the opening of the hall several years before. Empty bottles, dozens and dozens of them, littered the clearing, and if none had shared this plant with Mr Thorn, then that man's capacity for beer must be inexhaustible. With wonderful sagacity he found his two remaining full bottles and glass among the welter of empties.

"I couldn't wait," he said complainingly. "I been wanderin' round like a lorst dog all the evenin' 'cos I ain't got no real friends here. Open one of yours whiles I opens this one."

He drank, and sighed with ecstasy. He sighed again with equal appreciation after his second glass. Each bottle contained three glasses, and when Bony had taken one glass from his bottle he filled his friend's glass twice.

"I feel better," Mr Thorn stated when he had carefully concealed Bony's beer with his own. "I got to watch me chance now, and see that I don't darnce the next cuppler darnces with the old woman. A terrible nose for beer, 'as the old woman. She's my cross, she is."

"We had better go before Mrs Thorn begins to suspect," Bony advised, observing that Mr Thorn was loath to leave his plant.

At the hall entrance the Water Rat hung back among the usual crowd of young men always to be found stationed at the door at a dance hall, but the detective wormed his way through the bashful youths to discover that a dance had just started and that Mr Jelly was sitting it out alone. There being room, Bony sat down beside the farmer.

"Where have you been?" demanded Mr Jelly with mock sternness.

"I went for a walk because I was feeling unwell, and when I came back I was met by Mr Thorn, who persuaded me to accompany him to his plant."

"Plant! What plant?" Bony smiled.

"Near here he has a secret reservoir of alcoholic refreshment which he terms his plant. One cannot help but like the man, for he is a truly companionable spirit. In the course of a year he must drink much beer."

"In the course of one year he drinks one complete brew made by the biggest brewery in Western Australia. I should say about ten thousand gallons," Mr Jelly estimated with twinkling eyes. "Look at him now, dancing with Mrs Poole. His eyes are oozing beer, and Mrs Poole is trying hard to escape his breath."

"All of which is being noticed by Mrs Thorn," Bony pointed out, slyly directing his companion's attention to the grim lady watching her husband with gimlet eyes and a lipless mouth.

"She will jaw his poor head off going home, but likely enough he'll fall asleep," Mr Jelly murmured. "Do you think old Loftus cleared out for Leonora?"

Bony met the quick change of topic with trained facial control. "What do you think about it?" he parried.

"Why, that the feller at Leonora isn't Loftus at all." Mr Jelly was silent for a full minute. He spoke again only when he found his companion hesitant to give an opinion. "Why should Loftus clear out like that? There is no reason why he should, unless the reason was provided and waiting for him when he reached home from Perth at two o'clock in the morning a day or so before he was due."

"Ah! Just what do you mean by that?"

"I'll trust you not to pass it on," replied Mr Jelly slowly. "You just keep your eyes open like you did when you worked for the Queensland police. Watch how Mrs Loftus looks at Landon when he dances with another woman, and if she isn't jealous I'll hop on one foot from here to my veranda."

"You really think that she is in love with the hired man?"

"Sure of it—and he with her. He is better able to control it than she is." When Bony glanced round at Mr Jelly he saw that the farmer's lips were compressed into a straight line. Mr Jelly went on: "Supposing—I say, supposing—that when old Loftus reached his house he found that Mick Landon wasn't in his bed. Old Loftus might have turned back and got the first car driver he met to take him anywhere, from which place he could have took train to Leonora. Or——"

"Well? What would be the alternative?" Bony asked quietly, thinking how strange it was that Mr Jelly always referred to the missing farmer as "old Loftus", when Loftus was at least ten years his junior. Mr Jelly spoke with conviction.

"It's possible, if not probable, that old George Loftus, finding that Mick Landon was in the wrong bed, started to kick up a row about it, a row in which he got hurt. If so, the question is: What did they do with body?"

"Really, Mr Jelly, your imagination is boundless," Bony said, laughing outright but thinking rapidly. Mr Jelly was serious when he said:

"Not a bit—not a bit. It's more than likely that Landon was not in his right bed. It's more than likely that old George Loftus did reach home that night. As I said, Loftus could have done one of two things, and, knowing old George as I do, I am sure he would have used his bare hands in preference to sneaking away to Leonora."

"Yet you cannot be in earnest," Bony still objected, but, remembering the short yellow hair he had found in the lace of Mrs Loftus's pillow. "Surely you are not seriously suggesting that Landon and Mrs Loftus killed George Loftus because he came home earlier than was expected and found them *en déshabillé*?"

Mr Jelly remained obstinate.

"I am stating possibilities," he said. "Look at Laffer, and Smythe, and Thorpe. You wouldn't think them vicious enough to kill a fly. I tell you it only wants a particular set of circumstances to raise Satan in active blood fury in five men in every hundred. I've studied criminals. I've lived among 'em for years as a warder, as you know. I learned to pick out the killers long before they killed anybody, and most of them had those slate-blue-coloured eyes Landon's got."

Mr Jelly paused to nod and smile at Sunflower when she passed with her partner, who happened to be the drooping Mr Poole. Then he said:

"I have less experience with women, but I am glad that I'm not a fallen fighter in a Roman arena looking to Mrs Loftus, sitting in the Emperor's box, and hoping she will turn her thumbs up."

"You do not like her?"

"I don't. I never did. She always reminds me of a poorly baked cake covered with beautiful sugar decorations." After another short silence he went on: "I may not be as good a judge as the chief warder of one prison I was in. He used to run his hands over the head of every new bird who came inside, taking particular interest in first offenders. Used to feel their bumps and enter notes into a large book. More than once, when a feller was taken for murder, he would refer to his book and there find the murderer's name. If at the time the chief warder felt the killer's bumps it had been decided to keep the bird inside for good, the poor victim might have lived his or her allotted span. A couple of years back at a picnic I felt Landon's bumps for a joke. I didn't tell him just what they told me."

"What did they tell you?" asked Bony, whose interest was now aroused.

"That he was likely to commit murder at any time. And I won't be surprised to learn that he's done it."

Chapter Seventeen

After The Dance

There was no defined reason actuating Bony's decision to pay a second visit to the Loftus farm the night William decoyed the dogs away from Burracoppin.

Mr Jelly's suspicions—he had refused to impart to Bony the grounds on which they were based, if grounds there were—had strengthened his own created by the short hair found in the lace of Mrs Loftus's pillow and her own extraordinary poems written in a notebook.

Knowing that Landon was the secretary as well as the M.C. of the dance, Bony thought it likely that the Loftus party would be the last to leave. He, with the Jellys, had left immediately the dance broke up, and as he had politely declined to stop at their homestead to eat a light supper, he was aware that the Loftus party had not passed north on the public road. When a quarter of a mile past the Loftus farm gate, he requested Fred to stop and drop him, as he desired to walk the remaining distance to Burracoppin, and having speeded the astonished garage-man, he turned back, jumped the rabbit fence, and eventually arrived at the cart shed north of the Loftus house, wearing his sheepskin boots, his white collar camouflaged by the black handkerchief.

And here in the concealment offered by farm machinery he waited the arrival of the Loftus party, smoking cigarette after cigarette, his mind occupied by Mr Jelly's suspicions and his own discoveries. It was twenty-three minutes after two o'clock when the Loftus car turned in on the farm track.

The car stopped immediately in front of the house door, so that the lights, shining directly into the open-fronted cart shed, compelled Bony to keep hidden behind a small cart. When the lights were switched off he could see that the lamp had been lit in the living-room and the living-room window swung open. The figure of Mick Landon was revealed when he entered through the doorway.

Bony could hear one of the women laughing, and it presently became apparent that the party had no intention of retiring at once. He was as a black smudge of shadow gliding from the cart shed to the north wall of the house, where he disappeared into deeper shadow. Now he could hear the low murmur of conversation, which grew in volume as he edged his way round the corner. It became distinct when finally he reached the window and was enabled to look into the room through the gently swaying lace curtains.

"Make that wretched kettle boil quickly, Mick. I'm dying for a cup of tea," Mrs Loftus was saying. She was seated in one of the leather chairs, her back against the dresser, whilst she faced the window. Miss Waldron occupied the second leather chair facing the crackling stove, permitting Bony to see her rather fine profile. Landon was bending over the stove, coaxing the flames beneath the iron kettle. The farmer's wife, flushed by the cool night air after the heat of the hall, was looking her best while speaking to her sister.

"I saw you dancing with young Smedley more than once," she said in her clear, cold voice. " 'Ware! 'Ware! He hasn't a penny to fly with. This harvest will see the end of him."

"He's a nice boy, but I'm not mushy," Miss Waldron stated with emphasis. Not as good-looking as her sister, Miss Waldron was less brilliantly hard, less sophisticated, consequently more likeable to ordinary people.

"And whatever made you dance with that blackfellow?" asked Mrs Loftus, with just the suspicion of a frown she was careful always never to permit to mar her forehead.

"He asked me to very nicely," replied Miss Waldron coldly.

"But he is black, sis," objected Mrs Loftus.

"I prefer a black gentleman to a white boor."

"Oh! Please yourself, of course. What did he talk about?"

"Mostly about you."

"Me!"

"Yes. He said he thought you to be the most beautiful woman in the hall. He said he never had seen anyone quite to equal you, but — —"

"Well? Go on," commanded Mrs Loftus impatiently.

"He said—he said— —" Miss Waldron hesitated. It seemed that she was less desirous of offending her sister than Mrs Loftus was of offending her. "He said that although you danced well, he thought I danced better."

"How does he know? I never allowed him to dance with me."

"It would not be necessary for a judge to dance with a woman to see how she danced," Miss Waldron said with dangerous sweetness, knowing quite well that Bony had never asked to dance with her sister. "Anyway, he's not properly black. He's rather good-looking, and certainly is good company. I like a man who talks well and doesn't splutter and gasp all over you like some of the men did tonight. Oh! Make the tea strong, Mick, there's a good fellow. I had only one rotten dance, and that was with that man Thorn. Do you know, I think that man drinks."

The delighted Bony almost joined in the laughter of the others at this grave pronouncement on Mr Thorn.

"Oh, sis," Mrs Loftus gurgled, "how can you say such a dreadful thing?" To which Mick Landon added:

"Surely you are mistaken, Miss Waldron?" And then, seeing the indignant look in her eyes: "Drink! Why, he couldn't be drowned in beer."

"But there was no drink at the dance, was there?"

"No, but you may depend that old Thorn brought a few bottles with him in spite of his wife's watchfulness."

"I don't like her, and she doesn't like me," Mrs Loftus remarked with suddenly hardened eyes. "There are a lot in Burracoppin who'd like to cut me since George went down on this rotten farm. When we had money they crawled to us."

"They might crawl again if George strikes gold at Leonora," suggested her sister, now pouring out the tea Landon had made.

"No doubt about that," Mrs Loftus agreed. "People are funny when folk come down in cash values. But I don't care. They amuse me rather."

"The black seems well in with the Jelly crowd, eh?" Landon said.

"Yes. I thought Lucy Jelly was sweet on the fence-rider."

"So she is, or was, anyway," Landon replied. "He's a bit of a mystery, that black. Poole was telling me that he tracked a lost child for seventeen miles over rough country in Queensland once, and found the kid in time. How he got a job with the Rabbits when there's so many white men out of a job beats me. Pity they can't give a Burra man a chance."

"Somehow I don't like him," Mrs Loftus said, reaching for the carton of cigarettes. Landon struck a match and politely held it for her use. Between puffs she added: "And I don't like the Jellys either. The girls are stuck up, and the old fellow is too superior."

It appeared that Mrs Loftus did not like many people.

"Yet George thought well of him. When I was here last year they were great friends," objected Miss Waldron.

"Blow George!" Mrs Loftus murmured inelegantly. "Let's forget him. He ran away, so let him stop away for keeps. I don't want to see him again."

"But——"

"Don't argue, sis. I'm too tired."

"So am I. I'll go to bed. Give me a candle. My last one burned out."

Miss Waldron stood up. Mrs Loftus turned round in her chair and pulled open one of the dresser drawers, from which she removed a candle-box, opened it, and took out two candles.

"That's funny," she said, looking up at her sister. "Are you sure you didn't take one?"

"Of course I am. Mine was dying out in a splutter just as I finished dressing."

"But there were three candles in this box when we left," Mrs Loftus insisted. "I'm positive about it. I went to the drawer after I was dressed to get Mick some adhesive tape for a petrol leak, and three candles were halfway out of the box. Don't you remember, Mick? You were standing near me."

"Yes. You took candles and box out of the drawer. There were three candles there then."

"Well, what does a candle matter more or less? We're not that broke, surely," Miss Waldron exclaimed impatiently. "Give me one, instead of looking at them as though they were hundred-pound notes, before I yawn my head off."

"That's very funny," Mrs Loftus again said, giving one of the two candles to her sister.

"Don't let it keep you awake all night," urged Miss Waldron, laughing and yawning. "Good night, Mavie! Good night, Mick!"

"Good night!" Bony heard them reply while he slipped back to the north wall angle, round which he saw Miss Waldron emerge from the house, stand for a second looking up at the glittering stars, and then disappear round the south vine-protected veranda on which was her bedroom. Two minutes he gave her before he took the grave risk of her returning to find him at the window.

When again he peered into the living-room it was to see Landon standing with his back to the stove, smoking a cigarette and looking intently about the room. After a little time Mrs Loftus came out of her bedroom, when they regarded each other steadily for several seconds. It was he who spoke first.

"Anything disturbed?" he asked.

"Not a thing. Yet I am sure about those three candles."

"So am I. I'll look round in the morning and see if there are any strange tracks around the house."

Bony saw Mrs Loftus's eyes widen, whilst on her forehead gathered the forbidden frown.

"Mick!" she whispered.

"What?"

"The dogs?"

"What about them?"

"Oh, Mick! Where are they? They never met us tonight, and they have always barked and gone mad when we've come home late."

"By Jupiter! It is strange. I'll call them."

When he strode to the door Bony slipped back round the house corner. Landon came out and with index finger and thumb whistled shrilly. Then he shouted. He came to the corner, and Bony darted back to the west side of the house. Again he whistled, then stood listening for answering yelps, or, perhaps, for a distant bark. He whistled and called again before returning to the lighted room, Bony at the window two seconds after he had entered.

"I advised you to chain them up before we left," Mrs Loftus was saying. To which he replied:

"They were better loose. Gip would tear a prowler to pieces. Their being away is peculiar. I don't like it. They've never cleared out like that before."

"And I don't like it about that candle."

Now for fully thirty seconds the two stared at each other across the table. Then Landon laughed and said:

"We are imagining things, dear heart. There must have been two candles, after all. Who would steal a candle? As for the dogs, they have gone hunting; very likely a fox wandered too near, and they nosed his scent. They'll come back any time."

"I could have sworn — —"

"We are becoming afraid of shadows. There is nothing to be afraid about. Come, let us turn in. It's half-past three."

"Yes, I suppose we are foolish, dear." Mrs Loftus passed swiftly round the table to the man, who took her in his arms.

"I'll go to bed, but you will sleep lightly, won't you? I am very tired. You'll excuse me?"

"Certainly, Mavis. Kiss me properly, and I'll go."

Bony watched them embrace, thought of the absent Loftus and of Mr Jelly, whose suspicions were being proved fact before his eyes. The nudging he had given Father Time was certainly producing results. When they parted he slipped noiselessly back again to the north wall. He heard Landon utter a parting endearment within the room, and then, when outside the house and about to close the door, Landon said:

"Good night, Mavis! Pleasant dreams."

Waiting no more, Bony darted to the fence-enclosed haystack, in the impenetrable shadow of which he watched Landon leave the house and cross direct to the stack almost on his trail. At first he thought the man saw him and was about to demand reason of his presence there, but he veered to the north end of the stack, climbed a ladder, and from the roof slope pulled away half a dozen sheaves of wheaten hay. On reaching the ground again, Landon picked up the sheaves, one in each hand and two under each arm, and carried them to a small yard adjoining the stables, when the low "moo-o" of a cow explained Landon's movements. Until all the wheat had been stripped the cows could not be freed from the fenced narrow paddock running back to the rock and in which the grass had been burned off by the sun. From the cow yard the hired man walked straight to his tent.

During three minutes Bony watched his shadow dancing on the tent walls and low roof. The light was extinguished, and Bony settled himself to wait and see what happened next, if anything.

What he had seen in the living-room that evening had given him a fine opportunity to sum up the characters of these three people. He was now sure of Miss Waldron on several points. He was sure that she did not know the whereabouts of George Loftus unless he was at Leonora, and he was sure that she did not know about the hidden key and the object in the flock of Mrs Loftus's mattress, and he was sure that she did not know the intimate relationship between Landon and her sister.

What he had seen confirmed his opinion of Mrs Loftus. She knew where her husband was and was indifferent to him. She was a hard, selfish woman, sensual and snobbish, but she shared certain secrets with the hired man, who was strikingly handsome.

Regarding Landon, Mr Jelly was quite right. He was better able to control his emotions than could his lover. His personality was but little weaker than that of Mrs Loftus. He was cool, and, therefore, able to calculate and plan, and, consequently, could become a dangerous man. Despite his easing Mrs Loftus's fears with laughter which rang true, Bony knew that he was disturbed by the missing candle and worried at the absence of the dogs. He had gone to bed without delay when many men would have searched for traces of the dogs, and it was this point which indicated the probability that the man even then was watching from his tent door, his suspicions still strong.

Why were both he and Mrs Loftus made so uneasy by the absence of the dogs and by that missing candle Bony had taken on which to make impressions of the secret key? What did they fear? Was it guilty knowledge which made them fearful? Were they afraid of George Loftus, of his vengeance? Was it — —

Bony's keen eyes saw the shadow distinctly almost at the instant it left the cart shed. What was Landon up to now? Bony had not observed him leave his tent. He was creeping without sound towards the house.

Glad that he had waited on the chance of this development, his nerves leaping under the thrill of it, he saw a second shadow but a short distance from the hired man's tent. Who was that man? If it was Landon, then who was the first man? He watched the two shadows draw near, converge. He heard one of them utter a little grunt of surprise; saw a second later a red spurt of flame leave the side of the second shadow and heard the whiplike crack of the revolver and the cry of pain.

The second shadow shrank downwards, then shot up to its former height. The man began to run towards the road and the rabbit fence, speeding over the stripped stubble between the road and the homestead. Twice in rapid succession the red flame spurted from the man whom Bony guessed to be Mick Landon. Then Landon fell, stumbling over some concealed object, and when he got to his feet, swearing vividly, the other man had vanished.

Cries came from the house. Miss Waldron rushed into Bony's vision carrying a candle, which became a dim yellow speck when Mrs Loftus joined her carrying a lamp above her head. There was tense alarm in her voice.

"Mick! What has happened? Are you hurt? What did you shoot at?"

"I'm all right," Landon replied reassuringly. "I waited in the dark, and I saw him sneaking across from the cart shed. I winged him, but he got away, running towards the road."

"Was it a man? Are you sure?"

"Positive, Miss Waldron," Landon said coolly. "But he won't come back. He got a good issue. Come now. Don't stay out here in your night things. Both of you to bed before you catch a chill. If you wish it I will make down a bed in the kitchen. Shall I?"

"Oh I'll not sleep a wink—I wouldn't dare!" wailed Miss Waldron.

"It'll be all right, sis," Mrs Loftus said with wonderful command of herself. "Come and sleep in my bed. Mick won't mind sleeping on the kitchen floor."

"Of course not. I'll run over for my bedding right away."

Bony watched him run to his tent and return with mattress and bedclothes in his arms. The last he saw was Landon shepherding the women round the house corner to the only door. He gave them five minutes before he stole away—and his shadow could not have been seen by the keenest of eyes.

Skirting the stubble paddock, he gained the main road, removing the sheepskin boots when halfway up the long sand rise. The one question that occupied his mind was, where did Landon obtain the revolver? It certainly was not in the tent when Bony searched it. Did the man go armed to an entirely innocent country dance?

Chapter Eighteen

Bony Is Called In

Since it was twenty minutes to five on Sunday morning when Bony slipped into his bed at the Rabbit Department Depot, he made no attempt to rise in time for breakfast at the boarding- house, even though the meal was not served until nine o'clock. When he was awakened it was five minutes to eleven, and the man who awoke him was one of the last he expected to see.

"A log of wood is playful compared to you," Mick Landon said cheerfully. "Did you intend to sleep all day?"

"I certainly feel like it," Bony replied, at once mentally alert. "I don't know what time you went to bed, but I do know that it was a quarter to three when I got back."

"You were lucky. It was after four o'clock when I turned in. We were late fixing up about the dance. And there's been some queer goings on out at Mrs Loftus's farm. I took a shot at a feller."

"You took a shot at a fellow?" Bony echoed, reaching for tobacco and papers. "Did you kill him?"

"No. But I winged him. Look here, Bony—somebody told me that you did tracking for the Queensland police once. Would you do Mrs Loftus a favour? She's almost scared to death. Will you come out with me now and have a look round for the fellow's tracks? It's not serious enough to report to the police."

"Well yes, I could do that," Bony assented slowly. "I could go out after dinner."

"We want you to come out now. Mrs Loftus got me to drive the car in."

The detective feigned hesitation, although he felt electrified by this turn of the case. Then:

"All right. While I shave and dress describe these queer goings on you mentioned."

"In the first place," began Landon easily, "some time last night someone played what at first seemed a practical joke. When Sawyers, who took a crowd of Burra dancers to Jilbadgie, took the crowd home this morning he was stopped at the empty garage by all the town cows, six or seven horses, and umpteen dogs all walking around and sniffing at the place. Being dark and everyone tired out, they didn't take much notice, but this morning a Snake Charmer was passing, and beside the stock walking round outside he could hear a lot of dogs barking and snarling inside. When I came in I didn't turn down the garage road, and I thought it strange that several dogs, a couple of horses, and a lot of rabbits were messing about at intervals along the road right from Mrs Loftus's farm."

"It appears that the joker laid a trail, probably of aniseed," Bony said reflectively, "I remember it being done once in Queensland."

"I think there is more in it than a joke," Landon went on. "They ran the trail from Mrs Loftus's farm right to the garage and inside it. A lot of dogs that followed it, including the three out at our place, were allowed inside the garage and locked up there."

"The trail laid as far as Mrs Loftus's farm?" asked Bony.

"Yes, it was. After what happened later I think the trail was not laid for a practical joke. If it was aniseed they used it must have been terribly strong. Why, there were rabbits nosing along the farm track when I came out."

"What makes you think it was not a practical joke?"

"Because the house was burgled while we were at the dance. We got home to find the house upside down, as it were, the furniture moved about, drawers opened, the beds turned up. Strangely enough, Mrs Loftus could find nothing missing, and what the burglars hoped to find she cannot imagine. They were still prowling about after we reached home.

"Mrs Loftus and Miss Waldron slept together because they were so upset, and I determined to sit up on a kind of guard. After pretending to go to bed I got my rifle and sat just outside the door of my tent. Sure enough, half an hour after, I saw a man sneaking across to the house from the cart shed. I fired a shot at him, but in the dark only winged him, and he got away."

"Looks to me like a police job," Bony said quietly. To which Landon countered with:

"Well, it is and it isn't. Since George Loftus cleared out I've almost run the place for Mrs Loftus. She has come to rely on me to a great extent. She thinks, and I agree with her, that it is no ordinary burglary. We think that it was Loftus who came back—knowing that we all would be at the dance—to get something important, although Mrs Loftus can't think what it is he wanted. Not being able to get it, or being disturbed by our return, he hung about waiting for a second chance.

"Mrs Loftus is dead frightened, but she doesn't want to go to the police about it. I remembered hearing that you are good at tracking, and we thought it best, in order to create no more scandal, to ask you to pick up his tracks and find out where he came from and has gone to."

At this point Bony turned round from the mirror before which he was brushing his fine black hair, to say tentatively:

"Suppose the burglar's wound is serious? Suppose he has perished through loss of blood and I find him? That would have to be reported to the police. It would be a police matter."

"If you saw him run, as I did, you would know that he wasn't seriously wounded," Landon said. "I am not nervous on that score. What we want to do is to find out what his game is. There is someone in it with him, too. He must have had someone to help him, because one man couldn't have run the trail and burgled the place."

Dressed now, Bony sat on the edge of the table and rolled his second cigarette. Regarding Mick Landon, he could not but admire the man's capacity for cool lying. Without the slightest betrayal he had stated that the burglar had upset the furniture when Bony had done nothing of the kind, and he had said he had shot the prowler with a rifle when Bony knew he had fired a revolver.

It occurred to him then to proceed slowly. Believing Landon to be a dangerous man, knowing that a man will commit a crime to cover a crime already committed, he wondered if this invitation to the farm was to be the prelude to a regrettable accident. Or were they genuinely anxious to have the affair cleared up, desirous to know if really it was George Loftus that Mick Landon had shot?

"If you argue that it was George Loftus who burgled the place," Bony said slowly, "then I have found a flaw in it. If it had been Loftus it would not have been necessary for him to decoy away the dogs, because he knew them, and they would know him."

"Then who the hell was it?" Landon demanded with sudden heat.

"Not I. I can assure you that I'm not wounded."

"Of course it wasn't you. What would you want to burgle the place for?

It must have been Loftus, or it might have been someone he sent. He could have sent someone, couldn't he? Any old burglar would have pinched the several silver photo frames and some jewellery Mrs Loftus left in a drawer." Bony wondered which drawer. "Anyway, let's go. You might be able to pick up tracks. Mrs Loftus will be glad to give you dinner."

"Very well," Bony agreed. "Drive along to Mrs Poole's place. I must tell her I shall not be in for dinner. We can have a look at the empty garage, too."

Landon made no bones about consenting to this procedure. When he stopped the car outside the boarding-house they found Mrs Poole at the shop entrance and Mr Poole seated on a fruit case below the shop-window. Farther along the street a number of men and a small crowd of children were gathered outside the empty garage, shouting with laughter at two horses and several cows walking up and down the road sniffing at the trail. Mr Poole was most cheerful. The eternal cigarette drooped from beneath his drooping moustache.

"The missus says I played that joke," he said in his tired voice. "What I wants to know is, how could I?"

"Joe!" Mrs Poole snapped. "You're getting a bigger liar every day. I said nothing of the sort."

"Perhaps not. But you thought it."

"I'll tell you what I am thinking, if you like."

"I like," stated Mr Poole submissively.

"I think it's about time you chopped some wood."

"Wood! If it ain't wood, it's the cow; and if it ain't the cow, it's Mrs Black," sneered Mr Poole, brazenly winking at Bony. "Why don't you think of nice-sounding words like love and moonlight and—and beer? If it wasn't the blank wood, or the blanker cow, or the blankest Mrs Black, it would be the treble blank fowl that's got to be plucked."

Bony laughed delightedly. Even Landon laughed before saying: "Well, we must be getting on."

"Yes, I just wanted to tell you, Mrs Poole, that I shall not be home for dinner," the detective explained.

Mr Poole pulled himself to his feet by clawing at the shop-window frame. He said, almost wailing: "Well, for 'eaven's sake, be home for tea. We got to down the monotony somehow."

Bony chuckled again as they slid away, leaving husband and wife

144

laughing at them and contradicting the cat-and-dog life that their constant bickering would induce one to suppose that they led.

The crowd at the garage cheered when Mick Landon almost collided with a cow which refused to be driven away by a red-faced stout woman whom Bony knew to be Mrs Black. Along the wide, straight road leading to the old York Road were two horses, a dog, several cows, and a number of rabbits, all sniffing at the trail which there ran along the centre of the road. From the turn to the rabbit fence gate they met a horse and passed several dogs.

"Have your farm dogs gone home?" Bony asked.

"They went back along the trail when they were let out of the garage. Got home when I was about to leave, so I tied them up. Just in time, too, to shut the gate on three cows. If it wasn't for the cursed burglary, I'd appreciate the joke of that trailed decoy. The bird who put it down knew his onions."

"Too right," Bony agreed colloquially. "The fellows in Queensland scooped every dog and cat out of town and kept them prisoners in an old house two miles away. They undertook to find the lost animals at sixpence apiece."

"You in Queensland long?"

"Born there. Went to school in Brisbane."

"How did you come to be working in Western Australia?"

"I made a good cheque on a horsebreaking contract and took the opportunity I long wanted to see the West. I came to Adelaide by train and them took the mail plane. Foolishly I didn't book my return passage when I had the money. I went broke. Got tight one night, and someone relieved me of my last two tenners."

"So you got a job with the Rabbits."

"Yes. Met a fellow who said I might get a job with the Rabbit Department. After a little trouble I found the office and the chief. Asked for a job and was sent up here that night."

"Wonderful!"

"What is?" asked Bony blandly.

"You getting a job like that. You don't appear to know your luck."

"Well, I suppose I was lucky in a way."

"In a way!" Landon echoed. "It was only a few months ago that they put off three-quarters of the staff on account of the depression. There are two of the old hands doing nothing in Burra today."

"Well, well," Bony said smoothly. "One of them will have a chance soon. I've almost saved my fare to Brisbane."

Arriving at the farm gate, Bony got down and opened it, closing it again after the car had passed through. When they pulled up in front of the house Mrs Loftus came out to meet them.

"I am so glad you have come, Mr Bony," she said sweetly, offering him her hand. "Please come in. We are just going to sit down to a late breakfast."

Gone was Mrs Loftus's cynical aloofness. She accepted Bony on full equality, inviting him to enter her home with a nervous little laugh and many apologies for the untidiness of the living-room caused by the burglar. Turning from the stove with a dish of bacon and eggs in her hands, Miss Waldron smiled brightly and expressed the hope that he had not eaten breakfast.

Bony could see no alteration of the furniture, the heavy articles occupying the same positions they had done when he had paid his secret visit. Door and windows were opened wide, the window blinds drawn to minimize the glare. Above the conversation rose the hum of the curious blowflies attracted by the scents of the meal.

"You had quite an adventure last night," the detective said when all were seated at the table.

"Yes. We were so frightened," Mrs Loftus told him with a wan smile. "We were thankful enough when day dawned. I feel horribly tired, having had barely four hours' sleep."

"I am sure I shall sleep well tonight," Miss Waldron said in more cheerful tones.

"Tonight you need not be nervous, for that man won't come back again," Landon assured them with laughter.

Miss Waldron shivered. "I hope not," she said, adding when she turned to the detective: "Do you think you will be able to track the wretch?"

"I have no fear of failure," he replied egotistically, and then proceeded to lie with the calm assurance of Landon. "My mother was wonderfully adept in the art of tracking, and she trained my gift of observation, inherited from her." Bony could not remember seeing his mother at any time in his life. "To see marks on the ground of the passage of some living thing that no white man can see does not depend entirely on vision. A blackfellow will see a

146

track which the white man wouldn't see through a telescope, because he does not understand what his unaided eyes show him. The lubras are better trackers than the men, for the men are less energetic as food foragers, and, therefore, less practised."

"Is it correct that you have worked for the police?" inquired Mrs Loftus.

"On several occasions," he replied frankly, his teeth flashing in a smile. "Yet they are hard masters, although the pay is good. I don't like working for them. They are too suspicious. Because they cannot see so well the little tale-telling marks, they think, when a tracker faults, that he is lazy or is playing a game of his own."

"Tell us one of your tracking adventures, Mr Bony, will you?" Mrs Loftus entreated. "Let me fill your cup first."

"Thank you. Your coffee is delicious. If I bore you, tell me to stop." Bony leaned back in his chair, idly stirring his coffee. "The most remunerative work given me by the police was related to the Metters case. You might remember it. No? Well, in nineteen twenty-four a little girl was horribly murdered on a farm fifty miles west of Toowoomba, Queensland. I happened, at the time, to be in Brisbane, and quite by accident a detective officer met me in Queen Street. To shorten my story, I set off when the price of my services was fixed at sixty- five pounds and expenses paid, because they get all the praise for the work a black tracker does for them.

"I reached the scene of the crime three days after it had been committed. The child had been murdered in a small block of uncleared timber. She was returning from school, following a path through the timber as she had done for several years, and it was obvious that the killer waited hidden there. It was a most shocking affair altogether, and, apart from the money, I determined to get him.

"I can understand and have a little sympathy for the man who kills whilst influenced by alcohol or passionate anger, but I have none—and no normal person could have any—for a person who cold-bloodedly plans such a crime against an innocent girl. The murderer in this instance made no effort to conceal his tracks till he reached a main road two miles away. Once there he kept close to the crown of the road, where the wheels of passing traffic would obliterate his tracks.

"I had to examine every foot of eleven miles of one side of the road and seven miles of the other side before I found where he had left the road in his socked feet. In his socks he walked fifteen miles, taking every advantage of hard surfaces and several watercourses. It was ten o'clock in the morning when I started, in company with three mounted policemen, and it was six o'clock that evening when I pointed out to them the murderer's hiding place."

"Where was he hiding?" simultaneously demanded the women.

Bony, looking from one to the other, laughed softly, a little triumphantly, for he had captured their interest. His gaze fell to his plate, on which he began to butter a piece of bread.

"When Metters saw us crossing his paddocks he barred himself into his house, which, like this one, had only one door. He was armed with two rifles, and not only refused to surrender, but threatened to shoot anyone who went in to arrest him.

"Many of the neighbours came in their cars. A cordon was drawn round the house which at night was illuminated by the headlights of motor-cars. The fifth day Metters rushed out, firing a rifle and killing one man before he was shot dead."

"How dreadful!" exclaimed Mrs Loftus. "Didn't the police give the man a chance so that he might stand this trial?"

"I think it was as well he was shot dead," Bony said quietly. "At the time he came out there were more than two hundred very angry men, and only seven policemen, surrounding the small house. Police reinforcements were on their way. The crowd knew that. They wanted to fire the house. Metters knew it was but a matter of time before the crowd would burn his place down, and that when he did run out and was not killed the crowd would throw him back into the flames. When he was killed the police were hustled away until it was established that he was really dead. It would be impossible to imagine a more disappointed crowd."

"Dreadful!" murmured Mrs Loftus.

"It was a pity they shot him dead," her sister said fiercely.

Turning to her, Bony said:

"I believe that the utmost penalty the fool law inflicts on the killers of little children is ridiculously disproportionate to the enormity of the crime. Not being a Christian, I am not swayed by sickly sentiment. However, I have read your Bible and believe in the Old Testament's statement of justice so aptly condensed into the phrase, 'An eye for an eye.' To accompany the painless death of such a monster with legal and religious ceremonial is but to mock the little victim's cries for justice and vengeance. I am uncertain that vengeance belongs wholly to God. The torturers of little children should be pegged down on an ants' nest."

"Oh!" whispered Mrs Loftus, her face white, her eyes staring.

"So they should," Miss Waldron said with emphatic agreement.

"Cruelty will be stamped out only by cruelty," was Bony's opinion.

"And yet the cruelty of the Middle Ages did not prevent crime," Landon pointed out.

"Soft-hearted leniency hasn't diminished crime," Bony returned swiftly. "The tortures of the Middle Ages were crude, and men were then better able to stand pain than they are today. The discovery of anaesthetics has made us increasingly sensitive to pain. Man, a few years ahead, will faint when he cuts his finger." Bony was quite calm when he made these statements. Pushing back his chair, he got to his feet, when he said: "If you will excuse me, I will run over your burglar's tracks. I would like you ladies to remain in the house so that you will not confuse them. If you accompany me, Landon, please keep behind me always."

Outside the house he asked:

"Can you tell me precisely where you stood when you fired at the man?"

"Yes," Landon assented. "I was about four yards west of that broken-down grindstone. I fell over it when I was running after him."

"Good! Now, please, don't talk."

Walking to the grindstone, the half-caste saw the tracks left by Landon wearing slippers. He saw, east of the grindstone, the tracks of a man coming from the cart shed, turning abruptly eastward, where he staggered, saving himself with his hands, and then turning to the edge of the stubble paddock. The prowler had come from the direction of the main road and had returned to it after he was shot.

Without speaking, Bony proceeded to investigate on behalf of John Muir. Pretending to follow a track, he circled the cart shed before crossing the short distance to Landon's camp, which he also circled.

"Missed anything?" he asked the hired man.

"No. Did he go into my tent?"

"If he did, it was while you were at the dance. Your constant passage through the entrance has wiped out any tracks he might have left. But I think

149

he did go into your tent."

Slowly then the tracker walked to the dam, to find between the mullock banks a thirty-foot square of water fenced from the stock. A windmill raised water to a galvanized-iron tank on tall supports, from which it gravitated through pipes to the trough behind the stables and to the house.

Now southward walked Bony, passing the snarling dogs chained securely to their kennels of case boards, to a small shed containing superphosphate bags and other lumber. Fowls scratched in the shade. From that place he went on to the long haystack, and for the first time Landon offered a question.

"Did he come here?" he asked.

"He did," Bony replied cheerfully. Bending forward, he pointed to the straw-strewn ground. "There is the mark of his right foot. Can't you see it?"

"Be damned if I can!"

When he stood up Bony was smiling. Walking along one side of the stack, he noted the holes at its base where the dogs had scratched in the ground in search of coolness and the fowls had scratched to clean themselves. At the south end of the stack the shadow was longest, for the sun then was at the zenith. Here the detective paused to stand pinching his bottom lip.

"Did the fellow come here?" Landon demanded.

With his index finger Bony pointed at the ground.

"He passed along there," he said, impatient at the other's doubt; then impassive for a moment, a man sorely puzzled. A cockbird, perched on a pole leaning against the stack, crowed vigorously. The blowflies hummed like a harvester machine in a far paddock, anxious to remain in the deep shadow, swarming in the crevices among the straw.

Bony's vacant stare became focused upon Landon. Landon's mouth was a straight line, the lips drawn inward. His peculiar blue eyes were wide, expressionless, their gaze fixed on Bony's face. Not a muscle of his face moved. It seemed almost that he waited. Bony said:

"I cannot understand the interest your burglar took in the dam, your tent, the superphosphate shed, and in this haystack. You know, it does seem that Loftus, if it were he, hoped to discover an object which might be outside as well as inside the house."

Abruptly the detective moved away, walking direct to the house, where he was met by the anxious and curious women. He told them that the burglar had first visited the house and then had wandered about the homestead until he was shot.

Once again at the broken grindstone he followed the man's real tracks to the edge of the stubble and at once began to zigzag across it. Seven times he pointed out to the interested Landon a drop of blood on yellow straw. Unable longer to see footprints on the broken and matted straw, the drops of blood few white men would have seen blazed the trail for Bony.

On the far headland of the paddock he again saw tracks, now crossing a narrow, iron-hard ribbon inside the rabbit fence, and now beyond the fence crossing the wider and grassier ribbon between farm fence and road. The tracks turned south along the main road, but Bony turned northward, walking up the long sand slope till he was about midway to the summit, when he stopped and turned to Landon, saying:

"Here your man climbed into a car. His tracks go no farther. He wore several pairs of socks over his boots. His size in boots is either seven or eight. He would weigh about eleven stone. It might have been Loftus had not the dogs been lured away."

"It was George Loftus. He takes an eight boot."

Bony laughed. "Have it your own way," he said lightly.

"It must be Loftus. Who the devil else would come poking about and take nothing that we know? Anyway, Mrs Loftus will appreciate what you have done for her. Let's go back for a cup of tea, and then I'll take you to Burra in the car."

"I will not put you to that trouble, Mick, thank you all the same. I'll leave you here and walk back. I shall enjoy the walk. Convey my compliments to Mrs Loftus and to Miss Waldron, and thank them for me for that excellent breakfast."

"Getting the car will be no trouble."

"Really, I would prefer to walk," Bony said with smiling finality. "I hope to meet you all someday soon. Perhaps at a dance. *Au revoir.*"

They smiled at each other at parting as two dogs undecided whether to be friends or not. Bony, walking down the north slope to the old York Road, wondered about many things. He wondered why Mrs Loftus and her paramour were so perturbed by the theft of a candle; why they were so anxious to know who it was whom Landon had shot; why Landon had shot instead of first tackling the prowler; why he said he shot him with a rifle, and why he had not produced the rifle to back his statement.

Chapter Nineteen

Mr Jelly Is Shot

Eric Hurley was three days late returning to Burracoppin. With strange thoughtlessness, probably due to inexperience of sandy country, the Rabbit Department had permitted the farmers south of Burracoppin to clear the land to within one chain of the fence on its west side, subsequent stubble fires burning off the low bushes which are the natural protection against wind-driven sand.

When Inspector Gray returned from his north trip of four hundred and twenty-one miles, Bony inquired of him the whereabouts of Eric Hurley. Gray explained the reason of Hurley's delay—sand against the fence—and on hearing that the detective wished to interview his subordinate he offered the loan of the government truck for the afternoon.

Bony found the boundary rider shovelling sand from the fence at the fifteen-mile peg. It was a sweltering hot day, certainly not a day suitable for sand shovelling. The place where Hurley was working was on high ground at the southern edge of a wide belt of wheat country, a district which bore the name of a State governor. The land fell away east and west of the straight fence and adjacent road, tree- and bush- cleared land with the horizon flung back for a dozen miles, thousands of acres of ripe wheat and thousands of acres of fallow roughly forming a vast chessboard. Here and there the giant sloths devoured the wheat with a thin, purring whine of pleasure and a halo of dust. Along a distant road the leaping dust clouds indicated the speeding trucks and the slower, lumbering, horse-drawn wagons. The granite rocks, lying along the horizon like recumbent reptilian monsters, breathed and lived in the fierce heat haze which caused the wheatears on the near rises to a dance as the chorus in a superpastoral play. To emerge on that wheat belt from the bordering bush was as though one stepped out from a church.

"Hullo, Bony! Got the inspector's job?" exclaimed Hurley, leaning on his shovel, which a second later he dropped. Then vaulting the fence with the ease of long practice, he came round to the off side of the truck and sat down on the running board in the shade.

"Which inspector's job do you mean?" Bony asked mildly.

"Gray's, of course."

"I am informed that you know I am a police inspector," Bony said a little sternly.

"Oh! Who told you?"

"Sunflower."

"Then you know that I learned about you by accident. The boss was careless about that letter, but I've told no one. Lucy made me promise."

For a little while the detective stared down into the strong, lean face. That Hurley had kept a promise delighted him.

"I am glad to hear you say that, my dear Eric," he said. "A man who can successfully guard his tongue will never want for friends. Let us go along to your temporary camp and boil the billy for tea. It's too hot to shovel sand just now, and I'll make up your lost time by working for an hour with you this evening."

And then, while they sipped tea from enamel pannikins:

"You must have thought a lot about Mr Jelly's mysterious absences. Have you any idea of the reason behind them?"

"The old feller's all right," Hurley said without hesitation. "A bit strait-laced, and a crank on one thing. If he'd give up collecting murders, Lucy and Sunflower would be a lot happier."

"You would, of course, like to have those girls more happy?"

"Naturally. But there's nothing crook about the old man," Eric loyally maintained. "Some reckons he goes after a woman, being a widower, and others say he goes away on a bender. Well, a man is entitled to do both—within limits. A man who indulges in either near his family is a blackguard, which old Jelly is not. I don't think it's either women or wine, because the old chap always comes home richer than when he went away."

"He has gone away again. He was not home when Lucy got up on Sunday morning," Bony stated.

"It's a pity he can't stay home for the harvest. It leaves old Middleton shorthanded, and he's not as young as he used to be. Lucy will be worried again."

"She is doubly worried this time, because her father was wounded when he went away early Sunday morning."

"Wounded!" Hurley echoed.

154

"Yes. He was prowling about the Loftus farm and Mick Landon shot him."

"What the devil was the old feller doing messing about the Loftus farm?"

"That I do not know. He was shot about a quarter past three in the morning. He went home wounded. I tracked him Sunday evening. Lucy told me that one of his bed sheets was torn up, presumably for bandages, and there was a tinge of blood in the wash-basin."

"But what was he doing on the Loftus farm at that hour?"

"We do not know."

"What does Mick Landon think about it? Why did he shoot?"

"Landon does not know that it was Mr Jelly he shot. No one knows that Mr Jelly was shot, other than Lucy and myself, and now you."

"Then how did you know? How did you come to track him?"

"Because I saw him shot."

"Then what were you doing on the Loftus farm?"

"Having a look round."

"I give in," Hurley announced resignedly. "You're like a stonewalling batsman. You'll answer a hundred questions and yet give away no information."

The detective looked down from the cigarette he was making.

"Because it is proved that you have a silver tongue, because you are in love with Lucy Jelly, and because I need your assistance, I will take you into my confidence," Bony said slowly. Whereupon Hurley learned many things which had occurred after the dance at the Jilbadgie Hall.

"I cannot but think, Eric, that the disappearance of George Loftus is connected in some way with the occasional absences of your prospective father-in-law," Bony said when the fence- rider ceased to chuckle at the story of the aniseed trail. "Strictly between ourselves, I have promised to reveal to your young lady the reason or cause of her father's going away. She asked me to help her know so that she could help her father if he was practising some habit which love could help him conquer."

"What makes you think the two mysteries are connected?" was Hurley's reasonable question.

"George Loftus and Mr Jelly were great friends. They were neighbours, assisted each other over any difficulty. When the majority of farmers in this district are broke Mr Jelly goes off and brings back money, and Loftus had one hundred pounds on his person when he left Perth of the hundred and seventy-odd pounds he had hidden away in a private bank."

"Someone told me that they had found Loftus at Leonora," Hurley said interrogatively.

"Of the suspect at Leonora they took photographs, and the Merredin police got them quickly through a motorist who happened to be leaving the northern goldfields. The man at Leonora is not Loftus. At no time did I really believe that he was. I know where George Loftus is today."

"Oh! Where?"

"All in good time, Eric," Bony replied, smiling blandly. "I am not going to reveal one mystery until I have progressed further with that surrounding Mr Jelly. I am now afraid to finalize the Loftus affair for fear of wiping out the thin, faint trail leading to the Jelly affair. Do you think Mr Jelly suffers fits of insanity?"

"No. He's sane enough."

"That is what I think, but I am not an expert analyst."

Neither spoke again for a little while. Bony gazed idly along the fence at Hurley's horse, in hobbles, placidly grazing on the sun-killed herbage. The humming harvester machines vied with the humming blowflies at which now and then Ginger languidly snapped. The fence road was little used along that particular section since the main road to Burracoppin passed through it at the Fourteen-mile Gate. They could hear the roaring trucks on that road, drops of the stream which carried the flood of wheat to the railway siding as the wheat was poured into Pharaoh's granaries during the seven good years.

"Do you know if Mr Jelly has any friends in Merredin?" Bony next asked.

"Don't think. Never heard him or Lucy say so."

"Tell me. Why should the Loftus people stack hay when there are no horses and only two cows on the farm?"

"There's nothing funny about that, Bony. Many farmers cut wheat for hay, especially when the straw is long, as it is in a good year. Almost any year it pays to cut hay for chaff, because if the price is low in a good year it is bound to be high in a bad year, and hay will keep several years."

"I thought that might be the reason. Whilst studying the produce market reports I have been thinking that it would be an excellent money gamble to buy hay now, and have it cut into chaff by a contractor, and stored until a

156

bad harvest comes, when, as you say, the price is bound to be high."

Hurley laughed.

"You must have a lot of money," he said.

"I haven't much."

"Then I wouldn't risk what you've got," was the advice instantly given. "If you are going to gamble on hay, don't cut it into chaff until you are going to put it on the market; otherwise storage costs will more than wipe out any profit—if there is any profit."

"I am inclined to accept the risk. Do you know any farmers who would sell me their haystack?"

"No, I don't."

"What would be a fair price to offer for hay in the stack, do you think?"

"Dunno. Chaff is three pounds fifteen a ton."

"Do you think I could buy for two pounds a ton?" Bony persisted.

"What the devil are you coming at?"

"Hay, my dear Hurley, hay. I am keenly interested in the hay and chaff market. I want a gamble in chaff. Would you be my buyer, say at a commission of one per cent of the purchase price?"

"Well, yes, I suppose so, if you have made up your mind to chuck your money away. I could ask some of the cockies when I go south next trip."

"Excellent! I want to buy the haystack on George Loftus's farm. It contains about sixty-four tons. It is magnificent hay. I would be satisfied with that stack for the present. As a matter of fact, I want to buy that stack very much."

"That particular stack?"

"That particular stack," Bony repeated with emphasis. The rider searched the detective's smiling features.

"You make a good third for a mystery," he said with conviction. "Now why do you want to buy that haystack?"

"Because it is built with such perfect symmetry that it pleases my artistic eye," Bony replied without smiling. "I desire that stack, and I have the money to buy it at two pounds per ton. I want you to do me the favour of acting as my buying agent. Forget that I am a crime investigator. You say that you will reach Burracoppin tomorrow. Arrive early in the afternoon. I have spoken to Inspector Gray, and he will have both eyes shut if you get in about three o'clock. You will then be able to set off for the Jelly farm about four o'clock. You will find that Lucy is anxious to see you. Convey to her and Sunflower my regards. On your way call on Mrs Loftus and say that a farmer, who shall be nameless, wishes to buy a whole stack of hay. Ask her if she would sell her stack, as she has no horses to feed. Is that clear?"

"It is, but I don't know what you're getting at. I'll do as you ask, and thank you for working that early arrival at Burracoppin. What are you going to do with the blasted hay when you get it?"

Bony now smiled a little grimly. His eyes were almost invisible behind the puckered lids when he replied:

"Have no fear. I shall not get the sack. Mrs Loftus will not sell."

Chapter Twenty

The Return of John Muir

Colonel Spender's reply telegram, a letter from Marie Bonaparte, and Detective-Sergeant Muir all arrived at Burracoppin the next day, Wednesday, 6th December. The telegram and the letter Bony received at nine o'clock, when the post office opened for business. It was the letter Bony opened first. It read:

DEAREST BONY

You must come home, really you must. They are very angry at the office because John Muir introduced you to a case in Western Australia, which they fear will delay you reporting for duty at the end of your leave. By what you tell me of it in your letter, just received, it is the kind of case which will hold you until you clear it up. I sigh, because I know that you will not give it up till you finalize it. I think you will never forget how you failed at Windee.

Inspector Todd came out this morning especially to ask me to urge you to return in haste, as there is a particular case they want you to investigate. They are relying on you because there are aborigines mixed up in it and because the victim of a brutal murder is related to the Premier. He is now blaming Colonel Spender and his officers for incompetence.

And, aside from this, dear Bony, your leave is quite long enough, taken away from us, for your absence to be prolonged. I am getting worried about Bob. He has not written for some time. Ed is well and sends you his love. And Charles has passed his examinations even better than he hoped. I am so glad and proud, and know how proud and glad you will be, too.

Wire me to say that you are coming home. You owe a lot to Colonel Spender, and he wants you now so badly.

Ever your loving wife,

MARIE

P.S. — I gave John Muir a good talking-to for being so silly as to interest you in the wheat-belt case.

P.P.S. — He has not altered a bit. Rushed in yesterday to tell me that he had got his prisoner to Brisbane and was leaving with him the next morning. Danced me round the kitchen and then insisted on making afternoon tea.

Bony read Marie's letter a second time. He felt proud of her and very proud of his oldest son, Charles. He was conscious of the position to which his achievement had raised him, feeling warmly satisfied that he, a half-caste, was urgently wanted not only by his adored wife, but by a Chief Commissioner of Police. The telegram he opened with a wry smile. It was short — and to the point.

NO EXTENSION OF LEAVE CAN BE GRANTED. REPORT FOR DUTY AT ONCE.

G. H. SPENDER

Such a message would have made many men downcast with disappointment, but Bony chuckled, for he could so easily visualize the Colonel whilst he dictated the telegram. With red face and stuttering speech, he would have raised himself and his chair and banged the chair on the floor at least six times. Bony should have reported for duty before that day, and even if he left Burracoppin that night for the eastern States he would have overstayed his leave by ten days. He foresaw the inevitable "sack" then on its way to him through the mails and tentatively considered an original method of gaining reinstatement.

After dinner this evening Mr Poole and he sat on fruit cases outside the boarding-house shop, when the western sky was like a celestial slaughterhouse and the air was coloured like old port. A long goods train drawn by two engines was then halted at the station, while the engines took on water from the huge iron tank high up on supporting staging. Steam escaping from one engine, with a low roar beneath the hissing, beat on their ears so that when eventually the escape was shut off the drooping Mr Poole sighed his relief.

"The old 'un is a bit waxy tonight," he said whilst engaged in fashioning one of his long, drooping cigarettes. Mrs Black riles her a deal. The blanky cow was dry again this mornin' when I went to milk her."

"Why not keep the cow tied up all night?" Bony suggested.

"That's my idea, but the missus won't 'ave it," Mr Poole said, going on to talk as a sage of ancient times. "You know there's been wiser coves than me wot's tried to understand a woman and give it up as hopeless. To take my missus. I suppose she's just average woman. Sometimes she's lovin' and soft, and at others she's like one of them railway engines, ready to bust if the steam ain't let out. But wot raises the steam no man yet, or a woman either, can say. Now a man's about the same all through the piece. You and me can count on bein' tomorrer night just wot we are tonight, but there's no telling what a woman will be like one hour ahead.

"If it was me I'd beat Mrs Black by havin' the cow tied up all night, as you said, but the missus will let the cow loose before we go to bed. Why? I'll tell you. Because she likes arguin' with Mrs Black, and the blanky cow gives her a good excuse. She would be real unhappy if Mrs Black gave up milkin' our cow. Here comes old Thorn. Look—he's gettin' rounder every day."

"You seen the old woman?" demanded the Water Rat of another and a Rabbitoh.

"Nope. You chasm' her?"

"No fear. Only I'm goin' along to 'ave one, and I didn't want to run into 'er. Comin' down to the pub for a snifter?"

Mr Poole glanced sharply back into the shop before saying:

"All right. Comin', Bony?"

"Well, yes," assented the detective hesitatingly. "I will not stay with you long, as I have letters to write which should have been written a week ago."

For the third time during his stay there Bony found himself in the bar of the Burracoppin Hotel. Mr Wallace waited upon some dozen customers unsupported by his wife. The general conversation was held in a loud tone, but as yet the evening was too young for hilarity.

"Good night, Leonard?" inquired Mr Thorn when he came to rest against the bar counter with a seraphic smile. The red face was beaming. His manner was affable as he openly nudged Bony.

"None the better for you asking," replied Mr Wallace with a snarl of temper.

"Oh! Fightin' the missus again? Give up, Leonard," advised Mr. Poole. "You're old enough to know that you ain't got a hope of besting a woman on a wet wicket."

The publican leaned over the bar counter the better to get his mouth closer to his customer's ear. He said:

"She makes me sick. Locked me out again last night after telling everyone I'd murdered George Loftus. If only I could get hold of a gun them times."

Mr Thorn laughed wheezily and added his advice to that given by Mr Poole.

"Give in, Leonard," he said. "Be like me. Take no notice. Make out you're taking it lying down, but chalk up a mark on the quiet, and don't wipe out the mark until you get your own back in your own little quiet way. Use your brains. You can always beat a woman with brains."

"I'll use a gun one of these nights," Wallace said darkly, and turned then to attend an impatient customer.

"I overheard him trying to borrow Inspector Gray's gun not long ago," Bony remarked softly. That made his companions chuckle.

"Everyone in Burra knows these two," Poole explained. "And, of course, when either of 'em wants to borrow a gun everyone says their gun is out at the farm or away bein' repaired. You see, they do get terrible narked with each other on occasions, and they might use a gun then, but neither of 'em in cool moments ever dreams of buyin' a gun. Poor old Wallace! He—"

"Good evening, people! Mrs Wallace said gaily when she appeared dressed in her usual black silk. She smiled at every customer in turn, but when finally she noticed her husband the smile vanished. "Go and get your tea. Do you think the maid is going to wait all night for you? Don't stand there like a stuck ninny. Go … and … get … your … tea."

She was then facing the main door, and her frown of displeasure became magically replaced by a radiant smile of welcome. The general hum of conversation ceased. A man's laughter was cut short. For the second time that night Mr Thorn nudged Bony, and the detective, turning towards the main entrance, observed the well-built military figure of John Muir standing against the bar counter. Mrs Wallace's carefully attuned voice was one degree higher than it should have been. "Hullo, Mr Muir! You're quite a stranger. I do hope you are not going to ask me any more questions about my dear husband and poor Mr Loftus."

"I am going to ask you one serious question, Mrs Wallace," Muir said with affected grimness.

"Very well. Only one, then."

"Is the beer cold?"

"Oh! It is, I assure you. Why, you frightened me. Yes, it is ice cold. Will you take a pot?"

John Muir overlooked the customers, including Bony. Between them no sign of recognition passed. Not a few there eyed the sergeant in a furtive manner. Mr Wallace disappeared towards the dining-room, and his wife again laughed gaily and chatted with the new arrival as though her life was

162

one long dream of domestic bliss.

John Muir's appearance acted like a refrigerator with warm meat. His presence froze the conviviality of perfectly law-abiding men, a manifestation of crowd psychology which Bony often before had observed. It was the main reason why he always worked incognito, a circumstance to which most of his successes were due.

It was not now letters he wished to write, but to talk with John Muir, and, when able, he left Mr Thorn and Mr Poole and crossed to his room at the Rabbit Depot. Twenty minutes later the sergeant joined him.

"Good night, Bony," he said with restrained quietness when he had carefully closed the door. "How goes it?"

"Excellent, John. Your trip, I hope, was successful?"

"Yep. I landed Andrew Andrews without any trouble. He proved to be one of those birds who give up when caught, and now he's due for fifteen of the best. The Chief was mighty pleased with me, but he seemed a little disappointed with you. Can't understand why you haven't reported progress."

"That is as I wished. I wanted you to get the credit for the location and arrest of Andrews. I am glad that you have got it. I want you to get the credit for this Burracoppin case, and you will get it if you obey my instructions. As you know, I am indifferent to authority. Unlike you and your colleagues, I do not dream of promotion. The excitement of the chase is all that I desire. You saw Marie?"

"I went to see her, of course. She gave me afternoon tea."

"And you boiled the kettle and danced her round the kitchen to stop her speaking her mind to you for interesting me in this case."

"You've had a letter from her?"

"This morning. And how did you find Colonel Spender?"

Only with an effort did John Muir refrain from laughter. Then:

"I had to report to the old boy. Like a fool I let the cat out of the bag when I told him about the Loftus case and you taking hold of it. He didn't look too healthy then. He kept on calling me 'sir'; that is, when he got his breath. He said: 'You're a damned scoundrel, sir. I'll have you broken, sir. I'll raise hell, sir.' You go back, Bony, by the quickest and shortest route."

"It is now too late, John. The 'sack' will be on its way through the post. I shall have to think out a quite original method to gain reinstatement, and I am almost run out of ideas."

"I've a letter for you from Inspector Todd. He's much worried. He said all the things the Colonel said, bar adding the 'sir'."

Smiling, Bony took the proffered envelope, tore it open, and extracted the contents. Before reading it he said:

"Go outside, please. Look at the sky east of north. Look for a red glare in the sky."

"Eh!"

"Please, John."

Bony's voice had suddenly become hard. It was not the hardness of a superior so much as the steel hardness of the master displeased by a pupil's rebellion. The sergeant went out. Bony read Todd's long letter, which described a case beyond Cunnamulla made extraordinary by features of aboriginal participation in it. Reading between the lines, the detective saw Colonel Spender's plea for immediate help on account of the victim's relationship to the most powerful politician in office. Presently he glanced up at John Muir, who had come in to report.

"I can't see any glare in the sky. Is it a joke, Bony?"

"No. I am expecting developments in this Loftus case."

"How far have you got? What have you discovered? Was Loftus murdered? Do you know who murdered him? When are you going to effect an arrest? How—"

"For heaven's sake, cease your machine-gun questions."

"By the Great Wind! I'm not a Doctor Watson. I tell you I'm not," Muir declared with sudden passion.

"You are," Bony said definitely. "You will remain a Doctor Watson for a further period of four days, five days at the most. You will retire to Merredin, where you will do nothing but pretend to be making inquiries. You will report to your chief that you are about to finalize this matter, having received a lead from me. Patience will win you promotion."

Into John Muir's wide, fearless grey eyes flashed an appealing look. His red hair was tousled by the freckled fingers which tore through it like horse combs.

"Be a sport now," he entreated. "Tell the tale. Was Loftus murdered?"

"He was."

"Who killed him?"

"Cock Robin."

"A man ought to pick you up and shake you. You're the most aggravating cuss I know.

Bony sighed deeply. "Your only hope, John, is in the cultivation of patience. Age might change you. For your sake I hope it does. I will give you your bird in the near future. There is plenty of time for that. Now tell me what Todd told you about the case which has them bluffed. Relate the details to me slowly and carefully. Omit nothing, nothing. Banish from your mind any thought of Andrews and of Loftus."

And so for more than two hours they discussed the Queensland case. They read copies of statements and reports. They studied roughly drawn maps and many enlarged photographs of aborigines, tracks, blackfellows' signs, or what might be signs, and pictures of station scenes.

"To me everything now is quite plain," Bony said at last. "That is a blackfellow's sign, although the ignorant would not think so.

"It describes a violent death, a death of vengeance, carried out by an aboriginal. The emu feathers stuck among the fan-arranged sticks at the bottom of a steer's leg bone denotes the totem of the killer. The murdered man seduced a gin, and the gin's husband or lover slew him.

"Yes, despite all this, the killer was not a black. He was a white man, devilish clever, who, however, made the one inevitable mistake. Clever as he was in forging the sign, he forgot to add the hair of a black woman, which a black killer would have placed just below the emu feathers. The murder was committed by the only white man who could possibly have done it. In the morning, John, I will telegraph Todd to arrest Riley. You see, I can successfully conduct a case through the post. Easy isn't it?"

"Easy! By the Great Wind! If only I had one-tenth of your gumption, Bony."

"Patience will give you just as much gumption. You must learn to proceed slowly. Now go. I will accompany you to your hired car. Remain in Merredin as I said. You will hear from me soon." At the Depot gate Bony gazed long and earnestly towards the south-east.

"What the dickens are you looking for?" demanded John Muir.

"Even at your departure you must ask a question. I shall have to arrange a scale of fines for your questions according to their degree of pertinence. Your last question of tonight, John, I will answer. I am looking for the reflection in the sky of a burning haystack. Now, good night! Good night!"

Chapter Twenty-One

Needlework

As Bony expected, Mrs Loftus definitely refused to sell her hay. Yet by no means did her refusal indicate any guilty knowledge of the whereabouts of her husband, for the stack might well be the property of the Agricultural Bank; or she might think that the run of good harvests would not continue beyond this year, when certainly the price of chaff would rise.

Still, the detective regarded both Mrs Loftus and the hired man suspect. He had cast his net and had landed his catch. He had examined fish after fish until but two remained which bore the outlines of that terrible marine monster, the stingray.

Contrary to his emphatic assertion to Hurley that he knew just where George Loftus was, he was not positively sure that the body was where he suspected it to be, and he was sure only that Loftus was dead from that sense of intuition which had stood to him in the past. Had it not been for his rash promise to Lucy Jelly, had not her father interested himself so much in the Loftus case, Bony might at this stage have handed the case over to John Muir, confident in the sergeant's ability to finalize it, and himself have returned to Brisbane.

But he had given that promise to Lucy Jelly. In winding up the case Muir would not separate the two cases as Bony hoped to do in order to keep Lucy's father out of it if possible. And now, in keeping his promise to her, he would complete the case against the two suspects in his own peculiar way. He was the relentless nemesis, the king of Australian trackers well forward on an easy trail.

In his possession was a duplicate of the key guarded by the secret of the table leg. That morning experts in Perth had reported on the three hairs submitted to them: that long hair which Bony had taken from Mrs Loftus's hairbrush, the short hair he had found in the lace of Mrs Loftus's pillow, and the second short hair he had secured from Mick Landon's hair- comb. The experts stated that the two short hairs originally grew on the head of the same man. It was, therefore, proved that Landon had slept in Mrs Loftus's bed the night or one of the nights previous to the Jilbadgie dance. And if Bony's belief in the position of Loftus's body was correct, then it was more than likely that, as Mr Jelly had surmised, Landon had not been in his right bed the night the farmer had reached home.

The detective had arrived at that most interesting point in any criminal case, the point where surmises and theories are proving to be correct. In the one circumstance of the urgency of his return to his native State he would have relinquished his investigations to John Muir, but it was the circumstance of Mr Jelly which kept him back from such action. Normally the case was not rightfully his, but since he had decided to carry on in order to fulfil his promise to Lucy Jelly, he delayed action against the suspects until he had discovered the receptacle fitted by the secret key and had laid bare the secret of Mrs Loftus's mattress.

Doubtless he would not have appeased any other officer so easily as he had appeased John Muir. The Western Australian knew Bony, knew his methods, had experienced the iron of his will. Bony had said, "Go away for from three to five days. I will send for you", and Muir had gone, knowing that Bony would send for him, would hand over to him the completed case, would allow him all the credit before departing for Brisbane satisfied with the knowledge of his triumph.

Early in the morning, after John Muir returned to Burracoppin, Hurley related to Bony what had transpired during his visit to the Loftus farm. Mrs Loftus had received him alone: Landon was out on the harvester machine and Miss Waldron had driven herself to Merredin. At Hurley's casual inquiry regarding the sale of her haystack Mrs Loftus had become momentarily agitated, had regained control of her features in an instant, and then had said that she had no intention of selling.

She wished to know the name of the prospective buyer, and, this information not being obtained, she was made easier when Hurley said he would apply to a farmer farther south who had two stacks of last year's hay, one of which he might sell. Then she made one slip. She revealed her true thoughts of Bony; revealed the lie she had acted the Sunday he had visited the farm when she was so friendly, by saying to Hurley in a parting shot:

"Take my advice, Eric, and don't introduce your friends to your best girl. One of them has been paying Lucy a lot of attention, and a fence-rider cannot stand that, because he is away for such long periods."

"The old man is still away," Eric said with a grin which wiped away the possibility that Mrs Loftus's poison had had any effect on his mind. "So I can court Lucy as she should be courted. I am to tell you that she and Sunflower expect us both for tea at six o'clock this evening."

"That is delightful of them," cried Bony. "I shall be most pleased to accept."

"Good-oh! I'm going out there for the day—I've got three Sundays to take out—and I'll come for you about five o'clock. Try and knock off on time tonight."

Bony smiled generously, saying, "Permit me to remind you that I haven't any Sundays to take out, that I am working for the Rabbit Department, and that I shall be late for work if I do not go along for my breakfast at once."

Hurley sighed.

"I wish I had the gift of the gab," he said. "I wish I could talk like a book. Tell Ma Poole that I'll be up for brek at eight."

Leaving the Depot, Bony walked rapidly along the main street. Beyond the station, already eight or nine wheat trucks awaited admission to the wheat stack now daily growing steadily higher. A large sheet of white paper bearing roughly printed letters in red ink, pinned to the notice board outside the post office, attracted the detective's attention, and, reading it, he was informed that the officers of the local branch of the Wheat Farmers' Protection Association desired the attendance of every member at the meeting to be held at the Burracoppin Hall the following Saturday evening. Mick Landon's neat signature was appended as the secretary.

Now a little less hurriedly, Bony went on his way, his gaze fixed reflectively upon the ground. Next Saturday night Landon would be in Burracoppin at that meeting. Would Mrs Loftus accompany him? Mrs Loftus was a member of the Association, Bony knew. She would have a vote. Probably she *would* accompany Landon. And if Mrs Loftus and Landon attended the meeting it seemed certain that Miss Waldron would go with them, for Miss Waldron would be nervous of remaining alone at the farm after what had occurred there.

"You are quite an expert needlewoman, Miss Jelly," Bony said when, after tea, Lucy and he were sitting on the veranda and Hurley was helping Sunflower with the washing-up in the kitchen.

"Yes. I am supposed to be very good," Lucy admitted with low laughter.

"Do you like this?"

Bony's gaze travelled swiftly from the ample figure of Mrs Saunders, then gallantly watering a single rose-tree with water ladled from a petrol-tin bucket, to the silk-worked table centre, almost finished, which lay spread over the girl's lap. The sun was about to set. The still air throbbed with the incessant hum of the tireless harvester machines.

"It is certainly very beautifully done," he told her with an engaging smile. "It must take long and constant practice to be able to do it so well."

"I have almost finished it. Would you like to guess for whom it is intended for a gift?"

"For Eric?"

"Oh no! One does not give a man a table centre."

"Then it must be for Mrs Saunders. If not she, then I give up."

"It is not for dear Mrs Saunders, either. I'll tell you. I am making it for your wife."

"For Marie?"

"Yes. Will she not like it?"

"Like it!" he echoed. "Why, of course she will like it. We have nothing so beautiful as that in our home, because one could not buy such exquisite work in a factory-filled shop. Like it! My wife will adore it. Indeed, it is very kind of you."

Bony's blue eyes were lit by the bright flame of his mind. He was glad that he had promised this young woman to remove the shadow over her life, and his sentimental heart beat at its nearness to her sweet presence.

"I am glad you think she will like it. I wanted to show my appreciation of your kindness to us, and this centre will remind you of us when you are at home in Queensland. Will that be soon?"

"It will, I think, be soon."

Pensively he stared out over the vast extent of cleared flat country to the far-distant mottled-green sand rise with the clumps of ragged trees along its summit. The proposed gift touched him as nothing ever had done. She was saying:

"May I ask when you expect to leave? You see, I would like to know so that I can finish this for you to take with you."

"I shall be staying in Burracoppin until I have learned the reason of your father's strange absences, and that will be shortly after he receives the next

170

telegram calling him away. Meanwhile, would you like to join me in a little adventure?"

Lucy Jelly regarded him with wide, steady eyes. "Tell me about it," she said invitingly.

"I am badly in need of the services of a good needleworker," he began slowly. "Unfortunately, I can use a needle only in a crude way. You remember I told you how your father was shot, and I know you have been wondering what I was doing near the Loftus homestead to see it done. Actually, long before the Loftus people returned from the dance, I thoroughly examined the interior of the house. There I found several most interesting things and came across a little mystery which has been bothering me. I found that a small opening had been made in the flock mattress of Mrs Loftus's bed, an object pushed among the flock, and the opening most neatly sewed up again. "Badly as I wanted to know what the mattress concealed, I dared not cut the stitches because I knew that I never could sew up the slit precisely as Mrs Loftus had done. Of course I could not make another opening, for she would discover it, and it was important that she did not know I had been there. "Later I thought of you. You could sew the slit again exactly as Mrs Loftus had done after I had cut her stitches and found what she had hidden there."

"But whatever would she say?" asked Lucy.

"She would not know. We would go there next Saturday night if she and her sister and Mick Landon go to the farmers' meeting at Burracoppin, which I think most likely. They should be away at least three hours, so that we would have plenty of time."

"Is it important that you should know what she has hidden?"

"Were it not I would not dream of asking you to assist me."

"Of course you wouldn't. I am sorry I asked you that." For three seconds she paused, biting her nether lip. Then, with sudden resolution, she added: "I'll help you. What number cotton did she use? Was it white cotton?"

"What number?"

"Yes. Sewing cotton is numbered according to its size and strength. Very likely, as the mattress is of strong material, she would have used a forty cotton. It was cotton, wasn't it? It was not white thread?"

"Inside a lady's room I am an utter fool. Still, I believe Mrs Loftus used white cotton and not thread. But the number of the cotton ..."

"In that case I will take several different cottons, several sizes of needles, and some white thread because some thread is very like cotton."

"But surely Mrs Loftus would not note a change in the number of the cotton she used?" Bony asked, aghast at his exposure of his lack of knowledge.

"It would be quite likely for a clever woman to do so, and Mrs Loftus is a very clever woman. If you want her work copied, let us make a good copy. What time shall we go?"

"You would really like to accompany me?"

"I know now that I would. Tell me, do you suspect Mrs Loftus of anything? I shall not repeat what you tell me, Mr Bony."

"I think she has *le mot d'énigma.*"

"Meaning that she holds the key to the mystery," Lucy said, laughing. "You see, I haven't forgotten all my French."

"Nor have you forgotten anything about cotton," he added, laughing with her.

Bony was coming to respect Lucy Jelly for her mental qualities. She was so feminine, yet so sure of herself. She was entirely without the frivolity and shallowness of many young girls, so very worthy to receive his confidences. So he said:

"I think I know where Loftus is, and I believe that Mrs Loftus, too, knows where her husband is."

"Do you?" She was staring at him when she added: "And do you think Father knows?"

"Frankly, I cannot say 'yes' to that. Precisely what is the mainspring of his interest in the disappearance of George Loftus I have no idea, unless he is engaged in a little private detective work, thinking that the police have given up the case. Of course there may be something inside the Loftus house which he badly wants, which would explain his visit there the other night. Much concerning him will be made clear when he receives the next telegram, because I shall then know who sent it, and, knowing, can trace the reason of it all.

"I'll have a quiet talk to Eric about our going to the place on Saturday. We shall want his assistance. Yes, that is a very lovely centre. Hullo, Sunflower! Have you and Eric finished already?"

"It doesn't take him and me long to wash up. We can talk and work.

Lucy and Mrs Saunders can't talk and work, Mr Bony," the maid explained, adding when she saw that her sister was about to offer objection: "Look! What did I say? Lucy has put in only five threads since you have been out here together. I said that she couldn't talk and work at the same time."

"You have sharp eyes," Bony said with admiration.

"Have I? I wish they were as sharp as yours."

"They are, every bit, Sunflower. Eyes become sharp with practice. It is a great asset to be able to use one's eyes, and that is done only by making observation a habit. What were you both doing down at the dam this afternoon?"

With a pretty blush Sunflower said: "How did you know?"

"Well, as both you and Miss Lucy went to the dam this afternoon, I assume that you went in for a bathe. There are faint smears of clay on your shoes. The clay is identical with that surrounding the dam."

When the laughter had subsided, in which Mrs Saunders and Eric were able to join. Sunflower suggested with wonderful tact that Bony might like to play a game of euchre. Quick to see what lay behind this suggestion, he instantly agreed and followed the maid and Mrs Saunders into the living-room-kitchen, leaving Lucy and her lover to stroll away through the fast-falling dusk.

The three played euchre with much concentration for over an hour, when the dogs barked, and a moment later steps sounded on the veranda boards. From the open doorway Mick Landon said pleasantly:

"Good evening, everyone! May I come in?"

"Certainly, Mr Landon. Will you take a hand at euchre?" Sunflower asked politely but not warmly.

When Landon stepped into the lamplight they saw that he was dressed in a well-pressed pair of gabardine trousers, a white shirt with collar laid back and sleeves rolled to the elbows, and white tennis shoes. As usual, he was shaved. Seating himself at the table, he said:

"Really I came over for a word with Eric. Is he out?"

"Yes, but they'll be back for supper shortly," Mrs Saunders told him, holding the pack of cards ready to deal.

"If I may, I'll wait. Please deal me a hand too."

Coolly sure of himself, Landon picked up the cards dealt him, smiled at Sunflower, and nodded genially at Bony. He asked Mrs Saunders how she was weathering the heat, and of Sunflower how she enjoyed the dance at the Jilbadgie Hall.

"We shall not be having another dance till March," he said regretfully. "It's too hot during the summer to have dances, don't you think?"

"Yes, it is" Mrs Saunders agreed. "And besides, people are too tired to go off to dances after a long harvesting day. There's the dogs barking again. That'll be Lucy and her boy coming back."

The lovers entered a few moments later.

"Here is Mr Landon waiting to see you, Eric," announced Sunflower, when the two halted just inside the door.

"Evening, Miss Jelly. Hullo, Eric!"

"What do you want to see me about?" Hurley asked, unfortunately, so Bony thought, glancing quickly at him.

Laying down his cards, Landon swung round to face the fence-rider.

"Mrs Loftus was saying that you called yesterday to make an offer for her haystack. We saw you pass with Bony this evening, and she asked me to come over to find out if you have found a seller yet."

"Well, no, I haven't."

"You offered two pounds, didn't you?"

"I did," Hurley replied stiffly.

"Do you think that your man would go a bit higher?"

Bony's eyes were engaged with the task of making a cigarette, yet he sensed that once again Hurley glanced at him sharply. All his nerves felt as though tautened by one string, as a violin string is tightened by a musician.

"He might go a little higher," Hurley admitted after that revealing glance. "What would Mrs Loftus take?"

When Landon next spoke Bony knew that he was bluffing.

"Well, really it is not for her to say what she would take, but rather what your man is prepared to give. She is not at all anxious to sell, but, being a businesswoman, she would feel bound to accept a good offer." The man paused, then added: "Say three pounds a ton."

Hurley did not now need silently to refer to Bony. Three pounds per ton for hay in the stack was absurdly high. He did not see, as did Bony, that the sum was set high purposefully.

"A man would be a fool to pay three pounds, Mick."

"Of course he would," Landon agreed instantly. "As I said, Mrs Loftus doesn't want to sell, but she will sell for a really good price. Who's the man who wants to buy?"

"I was asked not to say."

"Perhaps I could guess?"

"I don't think so."

"Was it George Loftus?"

The detective noted how Landon's peculiar slate-blue eyes were blazing at Hurley. Instead of prevaricating, as Bony would have done by asking a cross question, Hurley answered Landon's question in the negative.

"Was it Mr Jelly?"

Bony learned afterwards that at this point Hurley feared that Landon would find out what he wanted to know by a process of elimination. The fence-rider suddenly retrieved his former mistakes by saying in a hesitating manner:

"Er—oh no! It wasn't Mr Jelly. It's no use keeping on, Mick. I shall not tell you who asked me to buy hay. Anyway, if Mrs Loftus won't sell at two pounds, I'm sure I'll find someone else who will."

Landon capitulated with a smile. Getting to his feet, he said:

"Very well, if you won't say."

Bony could have patted Hurley's back with approbation, for his hesitant reply removed Landon's suspicions that the buyer was Bony and centred them on the absent Mr Jelly.

"Your father away again just now?" he said to Lucy Jelly with the calculating eyes of a sensualist. It made Hurley fidget. Bony felt a surge of blood at the temples.

"Yes. He went on Sunday," Lucy replied coldly.

"What time Sunday?"

"I think Mrs Loftus will be waiting to know about the hay, Mr Landon."

Once again came Landon's easy laughter. It was as though he knew his power over women, knew that he had but to exert himself to conquer Lucy Jelly.

"I seem crammed full of questions, don't I?" he said. "Mr Jelly is a strange man. One of these times when he goes away he will never come back. If you rear a parrot in parrot country, directly the young bird can fly it will go away with the wild ones for ever-lengthening periods until the time comes when it will stay with the wild ones for good. I'll be going. Good night, everyone!"

Still smiling, he walked out of the house, followed by Bony, who really wanted to make sure that the fellow actually did return at least as far as the rabbit fence. Outside in the silent night he said:

"Seen any more prowlers?"

"No. I think old Loftus is satisfied with what he got."

"You still think it was Loftus?"

"I am more sure it was since we heard that it wasn't Loftus at Leonora. By the way, do you know who it is who wants to buy hay?"

"I do not." Bony replied distinctly.

"Would you like to earn a tenner?"

"I'd do a lot of trying," Bony admitted. "I'm sick of Western Australia. I want to get back to Queensland."

Landon caught at Bony's arm.

"I'll give you a tenner," he said, "if you find out who it is who wants to buy Mrs Loftus's hay. Will you have a go?"

"I certainly will," the detective agreed fervently. "That will be an easy ten pounds for me."

Chapter Twenty-Two

Lucy Jelly's Adventure

The farmers' meeting at the Burracoppin Hall was advertised to start at eight-thirty. At eight o'clock Bony had made his dispositions for his second attack on the secrets of the Loftus homestead.

Behind his offer to purchase Mrs Loftus's hay was his conviction that buried in the haystack was the body of the missing farmer, and if this were actual fact he considered it likely that immediately Mrs Loftus heard of some person's interest in it she would have it fired.

If the body of Loftus was buried in the stack, its position most assuredly would be somewhere along its line of centre, as far as possible from either wall, so that the smell it cast off would not penetrate to the outside to be noticeable to the chance passer-by. And, too, it would lie near the ground, because when Loftus disappeared the haystack was only beginning to be built. To remove it would necessitate pulling away from the stack tons of hay in sheaves, sheaves to be piled in great heaps to arouse the curiosity and suspicions of more than one visitor to the homestead. The only practical method of removal was to fire the stack, and, when the ashes were cool, to remove the remains and dispose of them finally elsewhere. It was this procedure, Bony was confident, Mrs Loftus and Landon would carry out when satisfied that the search for Loftus was long given up, and he had hoped that his offer for the hay would expedite the date.

Yet Landon and his mistress had made no such move after Hurley had made the offer for the stack. Nor had they done so when the fence-rider had brilliantly insinuated that Mr Jelly was the prospective buyer. This, in consequence, had made Bony one degree less sure that the body was in the haystack.

What he wanted, and hoped to obtain, was further evidence against the suspects. Previously dissatisfied with his examination of the kitchen, he counted on the possibility of there finding the box to the lock of which fitted the key he had found in the table leg. If not in the kitchen, it might be found beneath the earth floor of Mick Landon's tent.

At eight o'clock all that was left of the day was the shaded purple ribbon lying along the western horizon. Far to the north-west and north lightning flickered about massed clouds, lighting up their snowy virgin hearts coyly hid by the falling veils of rain. The muttering thunder held no menace, so distant was it.

Hurley and the detective sat at the edge of the main south road, ready to take cover among the close-growing bushes massed on either side and covering the summit of that long sweep of sand rise between the Loftus farm and the old York Road. They could see light shining from the window of the Loftus farmhouse and could judge with fair accuracy the position of the farm gate down the long, straight road fading into the ever-mysterious gloom of early night.

Beyond the rabbit fence, beyond the government's private road, hidden among the scrub, was Hurley's motor-cycle.

To avoid the probability of anyone on the Loftus farm hearing the machine stop at this place at this time, the two men had brought the machine from the town that morning in the fence-rider's cart. The canvas drop sides of the hooded vehicle adequately masked the operation of withdrawing the machine from the cart and carrying it into the dense bush. Most carefully Bony had obliterated their own tracks, and they then had renewed three posts in the fence to account for their halt there. Everything possible had been done to prevent suspicion, which, once aroused, might decide Mrs Loftus not to attend the meeting with Landon, whose secretaryship commanded his attendance.

They now waited the passing of the Loftus car, and at twenty minutes past eight first observed its headlights flash out near the house and later watched them whilst the car was being driven slowly over the bumpy track to the gate. Bony walked across the road and took concealment amongst the bush, leaving Hurley on the fence side, so that their observations of the passengers in the oncoming car might be checked.

"It was Landon driving, all right," Hurley said after the car had passed and they were watching its red tail-light dwindling to the glow of a cigar end. "The two women were on the front seat with him. There was no one in the back seat."

"Your report coincides with my own, save that from my position I could not identify the driver," Bony said. "We will give them a quarter of an hour."

Actually the detective allowed twenty-five minutes to pass before he and Hurley brought out of the bush the latter's machine to the government track.

"You carry on, Eric. I'll await you at the farm gate."

When Hurley had set off to pick up Lucy Jelly, waiting opposite her father's house, Bony picked up two sugar sacks, shouldered them, and walked down the rise to the meeting place. Three cars passed, travelling with speed towards Burracoppin and, presumably, the farmers' meeting. By his watch it was five minutes to nine when Lucy and her cavalier reached him.

"You are still willing to help me, Miss Jelly?" Bony asked her when he had assisted her to alight from the pillion seat.

"Yes. I've brought cottons and needles and a pair of scissors."

"It should not take us long. Now, please, permit Eric to lift you over the fence. I will go first, because the barbed wires are dangerous."

Now on the west side of the rabbit fence, he led them to the Loftus farm gate, wide open, and halted them several yards from it, where low bushes gave adequate concealment. Here he emptied the contents of one of the sugar bags, which proved to be three balls of binder twine. From one of the balls he secured the running end, made a loop, and gave it to Hurley with instructions to fasten it to his wrist, for it was his intention to lay a line signal to the homestead. He said:

"When I am ready I will pull on the twine till it is fairly taut. I will then tug three times as a signal, and you will tug three times, signalling all clear. Whereupon you, Miss Lucy, will at once come to me, keeping to the stubble and wearing those elegant sheepskin shoes I made for you. Should anyone pass through the gate towards the homestead, you will warn me by pulling in all the twine, replacing it in the bag, and then stand by for a possible quick retreat. Now is that all thoroughly understood?"

Having their assurance that it was, he set off with the remaining sugar sack and the two balls of twine, allowing the twine of the third ball to run out after him until, reaching its length, he paused to secure its end to the new end of the second ball. In this way half of the third ball was laid down when he came to the edge of the stubble paddock facing the front of the homestead.

The three dogs were barking viciously, chained to their kennels. They presented to him the greatest problem, as he had expected they would be after the laying of the aniseed trail, and, short of poisoning them, the only method left him to silence them was the tempting offer of many beef bones

179

within the second sugar sack.

Leaving the half-used ball of twine near the only door of the house, he strode swiftly and unfurtively towards the dogs, crying in a loud, stern voice for them to cease. Two obeyed, but the third was loath to stop, crouching and alternately barking and snarling. This was the one ferocious animal among them. He could see it dimly, crouched. When the others seized upon the bones this dog spurned his share, and without waste of time the detective found a stick and masterfully proceeded to thrash it till it slunk into its kennel. After that they all remained quiet.

He spent five valuable minutes closely examining the haystack, becoming satisfied that no attempt had been made to remove anything from its interior. His next move was to the house. He discovered that a Yale lock had been fitted to the door. A close scrutiny of the two windows revealed that someone, probably Landon, had increased the efficiency of the clasps by the addition of two extra to each window, but these catches being far more simple than the Yale lock, it was but a matter of half a minute before he was in the house, searching the two rooms with his electric torch. The house, as he had expected, was empty of human beings.

Able to open the door from the inside, he passed out, picked up the binder twine, pulled it taut, and tugged three times. The answering three tugs immediately came back. He cut the twine, made a loop of the line end, and dropped this over the handle of a tin washing dish he balanced against a leg of the washing bench on the narrow east veranda. When Hurley pulled the twine the dish would be upset with a clatter and the loop end freed for Hurley to pull back, hand over hand, to the farm fence.

With much satisfaction, Bony waited for Lucy Jelly to join him.

"Are you quite steady?" he asked when she did join him.

"Yes, Mr Bony," she whispered, which made him say:

"You may talk normally. There is no one here. There is not the slightest need to be nervous, and Eric will warn us in ample time if they do return early from the meeting. Come along."

Conducting her into the house, he closed the door but left open the kitchen window through which he had gained access. They could not fail to hear the wash-basin fall over should Hurley pull on the binder twine. When in the bedroom the detective lowered the blind, and then, to save time, he gave the torch to the girl and began searching for the repaired slit at the foot of the mattress.

"What do you think of that, Miss Jelly?" he asked when he had carefully laid back the bedclothes and had arranged the mattress for her easy inspection of Mrs Loftus's sewing.

"Bring the lamp nearer, please," she requested, adding when he obeyed: "She used number forty in cotton. It is well that you did not cut the stitches. I doubt that I can do it good enough to deceive her. See! She has featherstitched it after herringboning it almost exactly in line with the overcasting. Why, it will take me more than half an hour to do it like she has done it. Hold the light still closer."

Swiftly Bony glanced at his watch to note that the time was eighteen minutes past nine o'clock. For forty minutes the farmer's meeting had been in progress, and much could be said and decided in forty minutes.

"Cut the stitches and go ahead," he told her with unwonted sharpness. "Do it as well as you can. Make a good imitation. Let me assist, if possible."

"Then fix the lamp so that you can hold things."

With string he tied the lamp to the bedrail, drawing no knots, permitting the brilliant shaft of lift to fall directly on the work to be done. He was told to pocket several reels of cotton and to hold one particular reel of cotton, the number forty, and a packet of needles. The scissors flashed in the light as they snipped, snipped, snipped at the intricate stitching. Care and time were expended in gathering the extremely short pieces of snipped cotton, and it was after a lapse of five minutes before Bony gently inserted his hand into the opening and his fingers began to grope for the secret of the mattress. When, with care not to bring out any of the flock, he withdrew his hand, he held a small flat package wrapped in white paper.

The package was tied with white cotton. Holding it to Lucy, he told her to cut the cotton with her scissors. His long, brown, pink-nailed fingers quickly removed the wrapping paper and revealed a folded wad of treasury notes, which further examination proved to be of one-pound denomination. In the middle of the fold lay a man's gold safety pin with a single small moonstone in its centre. The tie or collar pin Bony fastened to the lapel of his coat. He counted the notes. There were sixty. Their serial number was K/11. They were quite new. Their running numbers were within twenty of the numbers of the notes Mrs Loftus had paid to the garage-men.

Placing the notes safely in a pocket of his jacket, Bony carefully prepared with newspaper a dummy package which he wrapped in the white paper, and this he placed in the same position among the flock which the genuine package had occupied.

"Now, Miss Lucy, get to work. Make haste; try to replace those puzzling stitches. I may yet have to play Mrs Loftus a little longer," he said with triumph in his voice.

"Needles and that number forty cotton, please," she said with a calm efficiency which delighted him, even though he had met many calm and efficient women in the bush.

He fell to watching the slim fingers threading the needle, the eye of which would have daunted any man. He saw her first secure the lips of the seven-inch slit with what he afterwards learned was overcast stitching, the needle passing the cotton through the original holes. When she began the herringbone stitches he saw her difficulty in using the holes Mrs Loftus had made, yet marvelled at her dexterity. It was fifteen minutes to ten o'clock. She began the featherstitching.

"I can't see it! I can't do it!" she breathed.

"Never mind the original holes now. Make as good a copy as possible of her stitching."

The light gleamed on the now slower flashing needle. Across the darker bands of the mattress material the featherstitching made him realize how difficult was her task, hopeless of accomplishment to any but the most practised. Despite the necessity for haste, she made a splendid copy of Mrs Loftus's work, although Bony was unable to appreciate it properly. When it was done Lucy said:

"Unless she takes the mattress out into strong light I think she will not discover the trick."

He saw the paleness of her face when she stood up, even though her face was outside the light beam. Now that her work was done, the terrific excitement was becoming felt, threatening to overwhelm her. Gently he took her hands in his and said firmly:

"Thank you! You have behaved wonderfully. Remain calm. There is absolutely no cause for nervousness. There is yet plenty of time. Just wait two minutes."

Quickly he detached the string from about the lamp. Now its circle of light swept over hessian walls and moved across every floorboard. It gleamed on the polished surface of the table and flashed across the picture on the easel. Finally it halted on the floor at his feet.

"It is not here," he said.

"What is not here?"

"A small box having a lock fitted by a peculiarly shaped key. Stay there."

His voice, she noticed, had lost its soft inflexion. No longer was he the courteous acquaintance, the understanding friend. The guttural liquids of his aboriginal ancestry had crept into his voice, as their hunting stealth had crept into his limbs. When he walked into the kitchen his legs were like clock springs and his body rested on the extreme tips of his sheepskin boots.

Following him to the door of the bedroom, she stood to stare at his grotesque figure revealed by the quick-moving light which never once shone directly out of the window. She wondered why he did not lower the blind, as he had done in the room behind her. He was now examining the glass-fronted bookcase, now beginning the task of taking from the shelves every book to see if there might be one which really was a box fashioned like a book.

Standing on a chair, he examined the top of the bookcase. Lying on his chest, he searched the narrow space between the bottom of the bookcase and the floor. With the fluttering quickness of a butterfly he hunted for that little box, even removing the wood billets in the iron scuttle. Finally his lamp flickered about the fireplace.

It was a double fireplace, or rather a large open hearth with one-third of its space occupied by a cooking stove. At the time of the year the open wood fire would never be required, and now sheets of crimson tissue paper covered the brick flooring partly hidden by a hand-painted screen.

Stooping, appearing like a giant spider framed against the whitewash of the fire back, Bony removed the tissue paper and examined the floor of bricks. The bricks appeared solidly cemented together. Whitewash made level the crevices between them. And yet Bony tested every brick and found the central three loose.

It appeared that he had forgotten the watching girl, for he neither looked at nor spoke to her when he almost jumped to the painted dresser and took from a drawer two stout-bladed knives. With these he prised up one of the bricks sufficiently to grasp it with his fingers. The brick came up easily enough, and the two others were lifted out quickly. His light fell on the hole their removal made. It showed him a handle let flush into a japanned surface, and, when he lifted the handle and pulled, it required no exertion to lift out a square-shaped metal box. With it in his hands he was looking at the lock, preparatory to setting the box down and fitting the key, when the wash-basin outside topped over with a sharp crash. At once the light was switched out.

The noise of the overturned dish sent Lucy's fingers to her lips to prevent the threatened scream. Someone must have come in through the farm gate, for Hurley had signalled. To Lucy the silence was dreadful. She could not hear the near approach of a car, so that they were not coming in a car. Bony was at the window. She could distinguish the silhouette of his head and shoulders against the dark grey opaqueness of the window oblong. Thirty seconds passed, thirty hours to the girl, and then Bony's head and shoulders vanished. She was alone, she thought, and they were coming, those people whom she guessed were evil.

As though a snake menaced her she shrank back against the bedroom door-frame when flesh touched the flesh of her forearm. She wanted to scream, but was unable to open her mouth. Something brushed her hair, her cheek. Warm breath beat against her left ear, and, as though from the distant ages, soundless words came drifting to the electrical present. She heard Bony's whispered sentences: "There is someone outside. He tripped up the binder twine and set off the alarm. Do not move or make any sound. Have no fear. I am with you."

They were both gazing at the open window, the oblong of dark grey. To the right of it was the door, now shut, fastened by the Yale lock. The silence pressed on their ear-drums, causing mental pain which was almost physical. From another world, millions and millions of miles away, came to them the faint hum of a motor engine.

Bony thought of the moon being eclipsed by the earth's shadow when slowly, low down on the left edge of the window oblong, the edge of a large disc grew outward from the window frame. It was one quarter of a sphere before movement ceased.

Turned to stone, Lucy looked at this strange object with wide-open eyes and parted lips. After what appeared to her to be an eternity she saw that the outer edge of the disc seemed to dissolve, and then outward from it there appeared a nose, lips, and chin. Only for a moment, and then the disc vanished. A man was outside that window listening.

The dogs had never barked. Save from the falling dish, no sound had come to them of his approach to and presence there. Was that man George Loftus? Or Mick Landon? Bony shivered. He had been so sure that the body of Loftus was buried in the haystack.

Chapter Twenty-Three

Trapped

Don't move — an inch," Bony whispered, his mouth close to the girl's ear.

With the silent movements of a stalking tiger cat he reached a position directly opposite the window and two yards from it. He could see the stars and a single deep black thundercloud east of meridian. He could see the faint whiteness of the stubble paddock, but not across to its farther side bordering the main road. Infinitely cautious, he drew nearer to the open window, its oblong frame giving him a growing view with every step he took.

Four feet from the window, now three feet, and now but one foot. He could distinguish the edge of the stubble where it met the hard ground in front of the house. There were no car lights on the farm track, nor were any to be seen on the highway beyond the gate. He could not now hear the car engine he and Lucy had recently heard, and that car, he suspected, had been travelling on another road. The silence beyond the window was no less profound than in the house.

And yet outside the house was a man.

And still the dogs remained silent.

The fact that the dogs had not barked once since Bony had thrashed the recalcitrant one was peculiar, to say the least. The arrival of the unknown at the homestead surely must have aroused them to angry barking, yet they were as silent as though they were dead.

Standing there at the window, he was weighted with one regret. He had not brought the automatic pistol then locked away in his grip. Only in exceptional circumstances did he ever carry a weapon, relying on his wit and his extraordinary native hunting gifts to secure escape from awkward situations. Now he regretted his defencelessness wholly on account of having Lucy Jelly with him, and, therefore, being responsible for her safety. He had more than once assured her that she was safe and had taken adequate measures to receive warning of anyone approaching the house. Now he was mentally flogging himself for his sin of omission.

With quick resolution he took the last step to reach the window, but with resumed caution leaned forward over the sill, inch by inch, until his eyes were just beyond the outer edge of the frame. To his left, to his right, and downward he looked, to see that no one was crouched against that side of the house.

Black against the lighter side of the distant stubble were the grotesque outlines of the cart shed, and, as though it were an optical illusion he then believed it to be, he saw for just a fraction of a second a tall shadow move beyond its eastward edge. For several seconds he gazed hard at that place and so saw instantly the night-shrouded figure of a man edging round the right angle of the house wall.

Inch by inch, so slowly that movement could not be detected in that darkness, Bony drew back from the window, backed till he came against the dining table, where he remained and waited, hoping and praying that the girl, crouched against the bedroom doorpost, would not speak or cry out!

Oh, for that automatic in his right hand! He remembered that on the table against which he pressed was a large china vase filled with flowers, and his hands swiftly groped for it, found it, plucked from the water the flowers, took it up with its water content intact, and faced the window again with the base held before him.

The window frame remained vacant for an apparently long period of time before Bony first saw a man's hand, and then the forearm which the hand joined, silhouetted in the window oblong. The hand moved inwards, the fingers outstretched. Then both hand and arm vanished. The stalker had ascertained that the window was wide open. Still Bony waited. With wonderful courage Lucy, who had seen the groping hand, barred back the cry of terror with her teeth.

The weight of everlasting silence was lifted from their eardrums by the quick insertion of a key into the Yale lock of the house door. The door was flung inwards. It banged jarringly against a chair set near the wall between its frame and the window.

"Jelly—come out!" ordered Mick Landon.

With all his will power Bony commanded the girl to remain both silent and motionless. He himself moved from the table edge to a position opposite the door without sound, the water-filled vase now resting on his head and held by both hands.

"Do you hear me, Mr Jelly? Come out!" Landon again ordered, with raised voice which held chilling menace. Standing to one side of the door, he was invisible to Bony.

Again, one of many periods this night, the seconds slowly dragged away. Not a tiniest sound came from Lucy or from Bony, standing as a statue of an Indian water-carrier. Bony could not hear the girl's breathing, not knowing that she had stuffed her mouth with her handkerchief. Bitterly now was he blaming himself for having brought her to this position of danger, when almost sure of the kind of man Landon was, merely to serve his vanity to complete this case with irrefutable evidence before handing it over to John Muir; when by the bold move of having the suspects arrested he could have secured the evidence without let or hindrance afterwards.

With abrupt swiftness Mick Landon stood squarely in the open doorway. Before the match he struck broke into the full volume of its flame the spluttering light revealed to the detective the long-barrelled revolver in the hand which held the match. Almost at the precise instant that the vase left his hands, when he hurled it at Landon's face, he launched himself across the short space between them, his hands flung forward to grip the wrist of that hand holding the revolver. So quick was his leap that the water cascaded over him as well as Landon, and the vase was crushed between their meeting bodies.

With a shattering report the revolver exploded. The report deafened him, for when the cartridge was discharged the weapon almost was touching his ear. He heard Lucy Jelly cry out at the instant that he gripped Landon's right arm, then to endeavour to bring it across his own in a bone-breaking arm lock.

But Mick Landon had not forgotten the lessons taught him in the Police Barracks during his training as a recruit. A younger and much stronger man than Bony, he tore free his arm, jabbed at Bony's face with his left elbow, swung round, and pressed the muzzle of his weapon into Bony's stomach.

"I've got you," he said with a short, hard laugh. "Put your hands above your head quick—quicker."

"Mr Bony! Oh, Mr Bony, I'm hurt!" Lucy cried with a low wail of anguish.

"Who's that in there?" Landon demanded, startled by the voice within the house. Then he said, as surprise swamped surprise: "So it's you, is it, you black sneak? What's your game? What are you after?"

The whites of Landon's eyes were clearly revealed to Bony, so wide and staring were they. Believing that the man had killed a human being in the person of George Loftus, Bony now believed that Landon would not hesitate to kill to cover the first murder. To prevaricate would not do; the truth only would so astound Landon as to present to Bony a possible chance to get by the steadily held revolver.

"I'm after you, Landon, and the woman who is the moral co-sinner with you," he said, watching the other like a hawk.

"You seem to know a lot. Why do you want me? Speak up quick."

"I want you, of course, for murder—you and Mrs Loftus. I have you both in my——"

"Oh, Mr Bony! I'm wet with blood. Come quickly. I— don't you hear me? It is so dark. I—I—I—can't see the window."

"Who's that in there? I've asked you once before."

"It is Miss Jelly, Landon. You hear; she is hurt. She must have been shot when your weapon was discharged. Let us go to——"

And the detective risked almost certain death. With panther quickness, knowing that the space of time Landon had held him rigid with the threat of his weapon inevitably would have worn away a little of his vigilance, his raised hands flashed downward, knocked the revolver to the left as he leaped to the right, reached upward as his now doubled body lurched towards the man's ankles. Landon felt his legs swept from under him. His revolver shattered the night stillness. From the ground he fired again at the hurtling figure of the detective, missed, was paralysed for a split second to see one rushing shadow coming from the cart shed and a second speeding across the stubble, rolled away from Bony's groping hands, sprang to his feet, and raced round the south vine-clad veranda of the house. Overwhelming panic fell upon him as a deluge of water. He thought of but two matters—the encircling police, and the coming to him in a cell of the public hangman.

Immediately Landon disappeared Bony forgot his first duty of giving pursuit, his mind at once becoming occupied with the plight of his brave assistant.

"Let him go," he cried to Hurley and the second man, now both close to him. "Come with me. Miss Jelly has been injured. Hurry!"

Rushing into the house, he produced matches from a pocket, struck several in a bunch, and lit the lamp on the table. When the wick had caught fire, when he had replaced the glass chimney, he turned to see Hurley just inside the door, and beyond him Mr Jelly.

The three saw Lucy Jelly lying across the bedroom doorway as though dead. Mr Jelly almost jumped the distance between the main door and his daughter, sweeping Hurley aside in the movement. Bony, picking up the lamp held it near the limp figure in Mr Jelly's arms. Mr Jelly's fingertips gently caressed the ashen face.

Her eyes opened in a flash of consciousness created by his touch. Her wandering gaze became held by her father's ruddy face beneath its halo of grey hair.

"Father! Father! Oh, it was so dark! That man, Landon, I think he shot me. The flash of the pistol! It was like—like— like a shooting star which hit me."

Mr Jelly's voice was tremulous.

"It is a time for courage," he said softly.

Bony watched with fearful heart the girl's lids flutter down over her eyes whilst he recalled that when Mr Jelly had returned from his last absence, and his attention had been drawn to little Sunflower suffering from a scalded foot, he had used the same expression: "It is a time for courage."

Blood, a dark mass of blood, was oozing through the silk of her blouse. Her father snatched up her own scissors which she had been holding when the bullet struck her. He began to cut the blouse downward from the neck. Above the snipping of the scissors Bony heard the distant hum of a car engine, and that sound appeared to melt the ice clogging his mind, yet had no affect on the ice freezing his heart.

"Eric, fetch that car," he ordered sharply.

He heard the fence-rider run out of the house but did not see him leave. He sprang up and to the fireplace where he had left the japanned box and the torch. With the light of the torch dispelling the shadows cast by the table and the kneeling figure of Mr Jelly, he found a large enamelled basin which he filled with rainwater from the galvanized tank outside. Without speaking, he set it down beside the working farmer, stepped over the girl's form into the bedroom. Counterpane and blankets he tore from the bed. The upper sheet he whipped away, and, at the bedroom door, began to tear it up into large squares and long strips for bandages.

"The swine! The shooting, murderous beast! I'll get him. I'll make sure that he drops," he actually snarled in so ferocious a tone that Mr Jelly looked sharply up at him, to wonder at the hate-convulsed brown face and the blazing blue eyes.

Bony spoke no more for a full half minute. Then he said as fiercely:

"Is she dying! Is she badly hurt?"

When the farmer replied it was as though he lifted a bag of cement from Bony's shoulders.

"No, thank God! The bullet has passed through her body high up on her right shoulder. I fear that it has shattered the blade, but I don't know for certain."

Whilst Mr Jelly saturated the squares of sheeting to wash the wound and to form cold compresses, the detective rolled the long strips into bandages. Bony was hunting for pins when the rapidly approaching car roared to a stop outside the house. There entered the Spirit of Australia in the van of two other men. "What's up, Bob?" he demanded in tones of unaccustomed softness.

"Landon shot her," Mr Jelly replied sharply.

"So Hurley told us. But why?"

"I'll answer no damn questions now," Mr Jelly said with equal sharpness. "We've got to get her home quickly. Mrs Saunders can look after her properly until we get a doctor. Come on! Give us a hand to get her into the car."

Bony found Eric beside him when they had passed the limp form into the waiting arms of her father, seated in the rear seat of the car. With but ill-restrained impatience he said:

"Eric, straddle that machine of yours. Go to Merredin as quickly as possible. Find Sergeant Westbury. Tell him to come out at once. Tell him to bring a doctor. Tell him to bring Sergeant Muir. Tell him we want Landon for the murder of George Loftus, and to organize search parties to stop him getting on the trains or escaping by somebody's car. You'll ride fast, won't you?"

"No one has seen me ride real fast yet."

Chapter Twenty-Four

Mrs Loftus Passes On

The car moved off with its burden and its passengers. The motor-cycle made off at racing speed along the east side of the rabbit fence. Bony ran out to the road. He stopped the first car which came along, explained the situation to the driver, who then consented to act on Bony's instructions. They speeded away on a tour of the country south, east, and north, rousing the farmers, getting guards on all main and subsidiary roads.

When at twenty minutes to eleven Mrs Loftus and her sister drove in through the farm gate the haystack was in flames.

Mrs Loftus drove the car to the back of the house, put the brakes hard on, and gazed with the fixed stare of the hypnotized at the stack of hay blazing at both ends.

A fire brigade then could have extinguished the flames within a few minutes, provided, of course, that the pumps were fed with water from hydrants. The fact that the stack was newly built must be taken into consideration to account for the rapidity with which the fire gained a mastering hold, for with an old stack the hay would have become compressed with the passage of time.

The ruddy glare lit up the house, the stables, the cart shed, and the dogs' kennels. The three dogs lay in recumbent attitudes, as though asleep. The gentle south wind had but little effect on the flame-lit smoke until it had risen two hundred feet in leaping, spark-streaked spirals which formed the huge column.

"How could it have got alight? Someone must have done it, sis!" Miss Waldron exclaimed indignantly.

"It looks like it," Mrs Loftus agreed absently. She was thinking how strange it was that she simply could not put from her mind a picture once she had seen of a Viking funeral pyre, even while she wondered why it was that Mick Landon did not come out of the house; for he was nowhere near the stack, and the lighted lamp indicated that he must be at home. In agreement with her, Landon had excused himself from his duties as secretary to the meeting early in the proceedings on the plea of indisposition. He had hired Fred, the garage- man, to drive him back, and at the old York Road fence gate he had got out of the car, telling Fred that he preferred to walk the rest of the way, hoping that the exercise would do him good. Landon then had kept to the main road until he reached the north-east corner of the farm. Cutting in as he did from the corner to the cart shed, Hurley, of course, could not possibly have seem him. At his arrival at the homestead the silence of the dogs had warned him.

Soul-shrivelling foreboding seized upon Mrs Loftus while she sat in the car. An imp perched on her shoulder and shrieked into her ear, "You fool! You fool! You fool!" She could see it all now, the stupidity of all that self-deception, the wilful creation of that illusion of happiness and security. "You fool! You fool! You fool!" She should have known that Time would wear away the covering she had so carefully woven about her skin.

The car engine had stopped, and without troubling to start it again—it meant cranking, since the self-starter was out of order—she got out and walked round the house to the door, closely followed by Miss Waldron.

"Hullo, Mick! Where are you?" she called when, at the doorway, she failed to see the hired man.

On the step of the door she stood. The shattered fragments of the china vase beneath her feet made her look down to observe them whitely gleaming against a background of water-veneered boarding. The lamp was set at the farthest end of the table. The big enamelled basin was still on the floor between the table and the bedroom door. At the same time both she and her sister saw the bloodstained swabs and the stained water in the basin.

Mrs Loftus was experiencing a slow invasion of cold which had no centre in any part of her body and yet seemed not to come from without. She heard her sister's cries of alarm but felt no affect from them. They sounded such futile, childish cries, now that the wonderful barriers she had built between herself and disaster had been apparently torn down.

Mick! Was that Mick's blood in the basin? Whom had he discovered here, and what had happened to him? Oh! These hammering questions! Never during all her life had she felt so icily calm.

Unable to have known, yet she did know that the secrets that the house contained were no longer there. For fully a minute she stood gazing down at the open hearth, stripped of its covering of crimson tissue paper, incuriously noting that one of the three lifted bricks rested on the other two, knowing that the japanned box had been taken without troubling to bring the lamp near to assure herself.

Heedless of her sister's questionings, she turned away from the fireplace, picked up the lamp, and carried it into the bedroom. The counterpane and the blankets cast on the floor, the remains of the torn sheet, were clues which, added to the bloody swabs and water, proclaimed plainly that someone had been badly injured. For the first time she felt fear, fear for the man she loved so passionately. Where was Mick Landon? Where was the man who had swept her into a world of delirious delight?

The mattress did not appear to have been disarranged. However, still holding the lamp, she raised the foot of the flock mattress and calmly scrutinized the opening she had cut and sewed together. She could not detect Lucy Jelly's work, but she must make sure, she must know the worst. And then? And then? Well, all along, in her inmost heart, she had known that she would have to take the last long journey. And now that this departure seemed imminent, she knew that the journey would have no terrors for her if her lover accompanied her. Suicide pact; yes. That is what people would call it.

As though she opened a door and stepped into a room, she came to hear the questions being fired at her by Miss Waldron. She realized now that her sister could no longer remain with her. She would have to leave at once, before they came to find, to find— —

"You see, we have had burglars," she said in a clear and steady voice. "They have gone now, after taking what they wanted and firing the haystack. The police will come and ask questions, and you must not be here then. I shall be all right, but I want to be alone. You cannot sleep in your veranda room tonight. You must go to the Kingstons."

"But—but—, sis—I can't leave you know," objected Miss Waldron loyally. Mrs Loftus melted for a second. Her sister saw a fleeting expression of wistful tenderness sweep into the marble-pale beautiful face. Mrs Loftus said:

"If you love me, you will go without arguing. I have made a mess of everything. Here you see the visible expression of the wreckage of my life. Drive yourself to the Kingstons in the car. Please, please don't stop to argue. Go—at once."

"But—but— —"

"Go!"

Miss Waldron shrank back from the look of blazing fury suddenly leaping in her sister's eyes. What she saw in them terrified her, and in backing to the door she wanted to scream when Mrs Loftus steadily followed her. The strain at last became unbearable. The mystery of this night, the suspicion that her sister held some awful knowledge, made her long to lean against someone stronger than herself; and her sister would not support her. She began to sob, no longer able to resist her sister's dominance. Helplessly she permitted herself to be hurried to the car and pushed into the driving seat. When Mrs Loftus had cranked the engine she came back to Miss Waldron to say:

"Good-bye! Go to the Kingstons. Tell them not to worry about me. Do not come back till tomorrow afternoon."

"All right, sis. Let me kiss you."

"Kiss me! My God, child! Go! Go at once. Do you hear?"

And so Miss Waldron drove off over the bumpy track to the farm gate, stunned by perplexity, horrified by her sister's strange mental condition. Mrs Loftus watched the red tail- light grow small, saw the sweep of the headlights turn southward when the car reached the main road. A vicelike hand gripped her arm.

"Where has she gone? Didn't you hear me shout?" Landon demanded sharply. "We had a chance with the car. Why did you let her take the car?"

"Mick! Mick! What does it all mean?" she said, quickly limp now that he was at her side to hold her with his love and protection.

"It means—come into the house. Is anyone there?"

His presence, his touch, melted that terrible frozen feeling which had kept her as stiff as a robot. She clung to him now as her sister had wished to cling to her. She was on the verge of hysteria, unable to realize that he was roughly dragging her into the house. He slammed the door shut behind them.

His eyes were bloodshot, the sinister slate-blue eyes unnaturally wide and fixed. He brought his handsome face close to hers, and she wanted to cry out when she knew that the action was not prompted by the old desire to kiss her. Never before had she seen his mouth with the lips drawn back.

"Means?" he said. "It means that the play is over. They must think that

Loftus is in the haystack. Anyway, I fired it when I saw Bony and the others leave. I found Bony here. There were two other men waiting to grab me, but I came too soon. Bony's a tracker all right. A police tracker he is. I've got to get away. You have to give me a chance. You can give me a chance if only you keep your mouth shut. I want that money. I want that box to take away and hide somewhere else."

"You wouldn't leave me, Mick?" she asked with stricken features.

"Of course I must leave you. You'd be a drag. I've got to keep going till I get out of the State. There's no sense in our both getting caught. I'll get the box; you get the money."

"The box has gone. You idiot! Firing the stack won't help us. Who was hurt?"

"They got the box!" For seconds Landon stared incredulously.

"Yes, they took the box," she said dully, despair seizing her when she saw him with the eyes of searching truth.

"Well, it only helps them to what they already know. I want that money. It can't help you. I've got to keep going; go before they come back. They've taken the girl home. I could hear them talking when they were putting her into the car, even though I was up on the rock."

"Girl! What girl?"

"Lucy Jelly. She was here with Bony. He charged me, and the gun went off. She was wounded."

Snatching up a carving knife from the dresser, Landon rushed into the bedroom. Mrs Loftus followed, carrying the lamp. In the act of putting it down on the pedestal table she began to laugh dreadfully.

"You're a fool, Mick. What chance have you got when they've got the black box?" Again she laughed, shrilly, mockingly, with the devilish notes of a kookaburra. "Lucy Jelly! Ah! Ah! Lucy Jelly! Get the money, Mick. You can have all of it. You may go and leave me to face it out alone, dear, foolish, stupid Mick."

"Stop it!" he shouted when she began to laugh again.

"I can't help it, Mick. You are just like a poor little bunny in a netted warren with a ferret."

With one long stroke he gashed the end of the mattress for a yard. He searched for and found the package, looked at it swiftly, placed it in his pocket. And yet again Mrs Loftus laughed.

"Look inside! Look inside! Don't you understand why Lucy Jelly was brought here?"

With his gaze fixed on her, Landon's hand went into his pocket and brought out the package. Now looking down at it, he slipped off the covering of white paper, unfolded the newspaper, turned it over, and then allowed it to slip from his fingers to the floor.

"Where is the money, you?" he snarled at her in a way which finally unmasked him, revealing himself to her as a broken reed, a clay idol, a weakling, a cur.

"Can't you see that they brought Lucy Jelly here to sew up the mattress after they had cut it and got out the notes?" she asked with withering scorn at his mental obtuseness. "It wasn't Jelly who came here the night of the Jilbadgie dance and took the candle. It was Bony. I remember now that he wasn't at the dance for hours. He came here and felt the package in the mattress and saw that he couldn't sew it up if he cut my stitching. He brought the girl here tonight to do that for him. But how he found out about putting George in the haystack I can't imagine. They offered to buy the hay, knowing that we wouldn't sell. You would have fired it then, but I met bluff with bluff: But, oh, what's the use! It's no use you running away. They'll get you without very much bother."

"They're going to have their work cut out," he said with quiet defiance. Then with sudden pleading:

"You love me, don't you, Mavie? Why drag me into it? They're bound to get you. Why not say that George treated you badly and that the night he came home he was drunk and attacked you? You could clear me if you like, you know."

"Love you! I don't love the thing you are. I thought I loved a man. Go on. Run away. But Bony will get you. He's a police tracker and more—he's a clever detective. They took off the regular ones and put him on."

"If they do get me I'll see that you hang."

And so they stood, each clearly revealed to the other in their evil beastliness. They shrank from each other, because the horror each saw in the other they each could see in themselves.

"No, they won't hang me," the woman said with a vicious laugh. "I have descended from the pioneers. You, you have risen from the gutter." She ran to the easel and from a grooved crosspiece of the frame snatched a small bottle. Facing him again, she cried: "You would run away with the money, eh? You would leave me to face it out, lie to protect you from what is coming to you, eh? I die that my death will convict you as my accomplice in the murder of my husband. Murder! A nice word. Craven! I go where you haven't the manhood to follow. But—you—will—be—sent—after—me—Mick. That is sure."

He watched her lift the uncorked bottle to her mouth. He watched her swallow the contents without making any action to prevent her. He ran out of the house, ran in the firelit glow towards the great rock, leaving the woman who had wrecked his soul with her allure and whose soul had been wrecked by his unclean beauty, left her writhing on the bed in the first awful sweat of lingering death by poisoning.

Chapter Twenty-Five

The Rabbit—And The Hunters

The sun, rushing upward from the bottom of the world, began to flood the sky above the Loftus farm. While the first beam of its light sank downward to the farm it painted with the whiteness of snow the squadrons of tiny puff clouds hanging without movement in the still air, so still that the smoke from the smouldering haystack rose in a straight column to within a few hundred feet of the clouds, where it mushroomed into a brilliant snowcap.

But this morning, there were no watchers of beautiful natural phenomena. Although so early, men were gathering together in parties, were converging on the wheat town in their motorcars and trucks, for all night Bony had been engaged in rousing the farmers in the district. Faced with much loss of time before police reinforcements could be hurried to the district, Bony had purposely released the essential facts, knowing that by so doing he would arouse the countryside to assist in the capture of Landon by cutting off all roads of escape.

A party of a dozen men stood in a group on the summit of the long granite rock west of the Loftus homestead, watching Bony walking slowly along the strip of soft moss-grown earth between the rock and the line of dense scrub. Each of them carried either a rifle or a shotgun. A little in front of them, keeping them back from the working half-caste, as it were, stood Detective-Sergeant John Muir.

The watchers saw Bony now in his hereditary element, far removed from a lady's bedroom. His hands were clasped behind his back; his head was thrust forward and his face downward. Presently he stopped, dug his heel into the spongy earth to make a mark, and then, looking up and at them, he crossed the short distance to the rock. He said:

"Gentlemen, as Sergeant Muir has told you, I have been engaged by the Western Australian Police Department to track down Mick Landon. I have no objection to you watching me at work. You may have the privilege of observing at work the finest tracker in Australia, for I have done much work for the Queensland police, if you leave behind you your weapons.

"Understand this. The Law requires the person of Mick Landon. At present I am the Law which demands the person of the supposed murderer of George Loftus that he stand his fair trial before a qualified judge and a jury of his peers. There"—Bony waved a hand to indicate all the vast extent of western bush—"there in that bush is Landon. I am going to get him for the Law. If you insist on bringing your firearms so that you may shoot him at sight, so that you may cheat the hangman of his fees, I shall refuse to make any effort—now. But, later, I shall start off on his tracks and get him today, tomorrow, or next week."

Several of the men murmured protestingly. Their mass temper was ugly, and Bony's only assistant was John Muir. The detective-sergeant would have spoken to them impulsively had not Bony, with most rare impulsiveness, stepped in front of him.

The crowd of angry men could not well be managed by the two policemen. They not only desired to take the law into their own hands, but in their eagerness to do so would constantly obstruct Bony and threaten to destroy the hunted man's tracks. All the policemen but one on the staff at Merredin were guarding important roads, searching motorcars and trucks, and the railway stations at which every train would stop. They, with parties of volunteers, were the nets set at the rabbit holes of a huge warren. In the bush ran the frantic rabbit.

"Please think," Bony urged the small crowd with forced calmness. "Let us look at your picture. Armed, you come on Landon. You riddle him with bullets and shot. In an instant his agony is over. He is dead. He is at peace. Now look at my picture. He knows how hopeless are his chances of escape, because he will guess I am on his tracks. He is taken alive. He stands in the dock fighting a losing battle for his life. Observe the sweat of terror on his face. He is condemned, and dies his first death. Cannot you see him dying a thousand times while he waits to hear the footsteps of the hangman? And you would be merciful to him. You would be merciful to one who stole Loftus's wife and murdered Loftus himself. You would be merciful to one who, although accidentally, shot Miss Jelly and then prevented me from going to her assistance. Come now! Which picture do you prefer?"

"What about it, sergeant? Will he hang?" demanded the Spirit of Australia in his powerful voice.

"I have never been more sure of a man being hanged," Muir replied grimly.

The crowd whispered among themselves. Then the old-young giant said:

"All right! We leave our guns behind. Ted can take 'em down to the constable guarding the house. But when we gets Landon we will see that he arrives safely at the Merredin lock-up."

Over Bony's sharp features flashed a whimsical smile, but his deep blue eyes continued to sparkle with emotion. There were those among the crowd with sufficient imagination to cause them to thank their lucky stars that they were not the rabbit.

"I am glad to find that you are men of perspicacity," he said in his grand manner. "At all times, please, keep behind me in as compact a body as possible. The sergeant will follow immediately behind me, in order to protect me should Landon be lying in ambush. Landon is armed. If he shoots me dead, if he shoots Mr Muir dead as well, even if he shoots half of you dead, then the survivors remember to take Landon alive to the hangman and not dead to the coroner."

Having known Bony for years, John Muir was astonished by the hatred in both the voice and the face of this otherwise calm and gentle-natured man. Hitherto Bony had revealed mental detachment in his placidly conducted, unhurried man-hunting. Muir did not understand Bony's friendship with the two Jelly girls and did not know of the remorse his friend suffered at having taken Lucy Jelly to the Loftus house, with its tragic result.

For the first dozen yards of the trail any one of those men could have tracked Landon, but when once Bony plunged into the thick-growing bogeta bush the ground became iron-hard and covered with the dead and blackened needle-pointed leaves. Yet, for Bony, the ends of broken branches and stripped twig tips blazed a trail easy to follow.

The thick-growing bush gave place abruptly to larger and more varied bush, with here and there comparatively open spaces where grew white gums and gimlet-trees. Here a short curve, as though drawn with a pencil, there a turned stone, now a newly broken dead twig, once a shining brass shell from Landon's revolver, all indicated the hunted man's mental condition. Until then he had not remembered to replace the discharged cartridges with live ones. Both Bony and Muir wondered how many live cartridges Landon did possess. For distances of several yards Bony, the tracker, saw nothing to aid him, but by now he knew that Landon took longer steps with his left leg and, therefore, was prone to circle always to the right. Save the empty cartridge shell, the following crowd saw Landon's tracks but five or six times in a mile. They could not see the little links of the long chain over which Bony almost ran, sure and faultless.

With John Muir close behind him, and behind the sergeant the crowd of eager men, Bony suddenly came on to a strip of clear mossy ground edging the gentle slope of a granite rock. Not having seen this "knob" during his walk from the great Burracoppin Rock to the Loftus homestead sometime previously, he turned to those who followed, saying:

"Can anyone tell me the area of this rock?"

"About forty acres," someone replied.

"Thank you! Landon stepped on to the rock at this place. Unless he is still on the rock in hiding, he must have stepped off it. I shall see where he left it. I suggest that you men walk over the rock to make sure he is not here whilst I walk round its edge to pick up his tracks, if he has gone farther on. Please don't move off the granite till I have picked up his tracks; otherwise you might destroy them."

"You won't slip away and leave us in the lurch?" queried the Spirit of Australia, his tall, straight figure a head above the others.

"I will not. You have my word."

"I'll back it, blokes," Hurley cried. "Come on! Let's give this knob an overhaul."

But five minutes later, before the area of granite could be thoroughly searched, they heard Bony's shout, and, running and leaping over the uneven surface, they rejoined the detective with the exuberance of schoolboys.

"Got 'em?" they shouted with exultation.

"Yes."

Pointing to the ground, Bony smiled in a way which made John Muir shiver. To the crowd there was revealed on the ground no scratch, no faintest impression.

The huge granite rock south of the original site of Burracoppin, when it was dependent on the passing traffic on the old York Road for existence from the custom of the prospectors to and from the new-found goldfields of Southern Cross and Coolgardie, must cover an area of four hundred acres. Towering above the original site of the Burracoppin Hotel, marked now by the fragments of thousands of bottles, the hill of granite appears like a great sea-washed rock; whilst from other points the imaginative observer may picture a miniature barren range cooling after one of the cataclysms which shook the world in its youth. It was on this huge rock that Bony once had sat and gazed on the valley of the wheat belt through which passes the Perth-Kalgoorlie railway.

Having taken every precaution not to be seen by chance searchers, having taken advantage of every crevice, every gully, every water runnel, Landon had reached a position on the highest peak whereon was built a surveyor's trig, like a beacon to warn England of Napoleon's invasion.

The man lay in a shallow declivity which, after rain, held gallons of water. There was now no water there, for the fierce sun long had sucked it into vapour. The hunted commanded a clear view of every side of that particular peak, and, being on the highest peak, even long-range rifle bullets could not reach him.

He had arrived there long before dawn, in time to witness the passing of the night-running mail-and-passenger trains at Burracoppin. He was convinced that the shadows converging upon him while he struggled with Bony were the figures of policemen, and he was sufficiently intelligent to know that all avenues of possible escape would have been closed to him before the attempted arrest had been made. Yet so sudden the final wrecking of that life of sensual abandon, when he had become lulled into security by the seeming apathy of the police, that it was not before he had reached the Burracoppin Rock that he realized the hopelessness of his case.

When standing near the trig, watching the lights of the passing trains, his mind had been swamped with despair. Time had returned to him a measure of calmness, and he had grimly decided that he would fight, and, if possible, kill many of his relentless enemies, before he turned the revolver upon himself. Before the dawn had come he had gone down to the old town water soak, filled the petrol-tin bucket attached to the windlass rope, and, having raided a solitary garden of all the vegetables he could carry, had returned to the trig, with water and food to last him many days.

The early sun began to heat the rock. There was no wind to keep down the temperature, and he lay in the long shadow cast by the trig, constantly peering round the carefully built cone of boulders. Now and then fits of helpless rage made him writhe. If only he had not been so supremely foolish as to have lingered near the Loftus homestead waiting a chance to get possession of the money hidden in the flock mattress, he might have boarded one of those trains before the cordon was properly drawn. On one of those trains, preferably that bound to Kalgoorlie, he could have travelled fifty or one hundred miles before dropping off at a wayside station to make a clean break for life.

Now, in broad daylight, he regretted his action remaining on the rock, in losing all that precious time during which he might have slipped through the cordon. It was too late now. Death had become a living entity, a stalking monster which sooner or later would reach him through his own stupidity; either by his own hand or by the hands of enraged men, or from the caress of the hangman's rope about his neck. There was no escaping death. Yesterday he lived without fear of it. Today he faced its creeping approach with so much horror that he could not clearly think. Then he saw the stalking death, and his teeth clenched fiercely to prevent his crying out at his loss of the remnants of his manhood.

With awful fascination Landon watched Bony and his followers cross a small clearing a quarter of a mile from the eastward edge of the great rock. He tried to count the number of men, but failed. They were bunched too closely together. Well, he would get many of them before they got him. Without doubt they were on his tracks, for he remembered crossing that clearing. Fool! Oh, fool! Why had he not kept on? Why had he stayed there to fight against inevitable death?

Better end this agony now, at once. He looked at the revolver, pointing the muzzle at his eye, imagined the leaping flame and the tearing, smashing bullet streaking through his brain like a comet—and hastily pointed the weapon from him. No, he couldn't pull the trigger. He excused himself on the plea that he might make a mistake, might only wound himself, and then tossed aside the revolver and clawed his face with his nails, so hateful was the realization of his cowardice.

When again he looked up and then down over the rock curves, he saw one of the pursuers. Now he was fighting for strength of mind, struggling to banish that devil of fear by conjuring mental pictures of dramatic scenes in which he was the hero. Probably, had not Bony appeared just when he did, on the edge of the scrub, which came almost to the east foot of the granite spurs, Landon might have regained self-control and died a brave if vile man

The appearance of the two detectives and the small crowd of followers dissolved Landon's morale as a snowflake in the hell of his imagination. He collapsed mentally. Physically he became governed by the subconscious imp of Fear which dwells deep in the mind of every man and woman.

With the swiftness and the snakelike glide of a goanna he ran down the western slope, carrying with him only the revolver, so great being his panic that he left behind him the small box of cartridges. Reaching the encircling spur, he raced away, anywhere, with no sense of direction, with no thought of direction, possessed by the one overwhelming desire to escape those human bloodhounds.

For fully half a mile he ran in a headlong rush, tearing his passage through belts of dense scrub which shredded his clothes and lashed his face, quickly bathed in perspiration, his magnificent chest coming to heave like that of a panting dog. He stopped only when he reached the summit of a quartz ridge, and then, looking backward, could see the peaks of the Burracoppin Rock through the tops of a line of white gums. Men were running about the rock like ants about a pebble.

On he went, senselessly wasting his strength by the rapidity of his progress. He came to the old York Road at the crossroad which led in a gentle fall to the Burracoppin railway station. A car was speeding up the road towards him. Himself concealed in the bush, he saw four men, other than the driver, and their gun barrels were pushed out over the car's sides. They were as sportsmen out for rabbits. *He was the rabbit.*

Utterly exhausted, he reached a smaller granite mass half a mile due south. There he flung himself down on the sun- heated rock, vainly trying to conquer the demon that rode him. Stupidly he looked at his empty hands, vainly tried to flog his mind to tell where he had dropped the revolver. Time! The passing of time made no impression on his mind. He could think of nothing but that carload of men who looked like sportsmen out for rabbits. His hands rubbed up and down his shredded trousers, the fingers working as the legs of caught crabs. The corners of his handsome mouth sagged. His face was grimed with sweat and dust. Every nerve in his body twitched.

And when he saw Bony step out of the scrub on to the rock at the exact place he had stepped on the rock, when he saw the crowd behind the two detectives, he sprang to his feet, waved his arms over his head, and shrieked.

He saw the crowd with Bony open out fanwise. Their sport sticks, cut to assist them through the bush, appeared to him like gun barrels.

"I give up—I give up!" was his wailing cry when he ran down the rock slope to the surprised tracker and his escort. They knew he was without a weapon because they had found the cartridges on the great rock and the revolver behind the bush where he had hidden from the "sportsmen" in the car.

"Save me! Help me! I give in—I give in!" Mick Landon sobbed when he fell at Bony's feet and wrapped his arms about the tracker's legs.

Chapter Twenty-Six

Finalizing A Case

So you see, John, your Burracoppin case was after all very simple and very sordid, requiring only one qualification in the personality of the investigator to achieve success."

Bony was smiling into the alert military type of face of John Muir while he and the detective-sergeant lounged in the shade of a big salmon gum on the side of the Goomarin Road a mile out of Merredin. A week had passed, and the magistrate at Perth had remanded Mick Landon for trial on the capital charge.

"What is that necessary qualification? How did you know that George Loftus's body was in the haystack? How did Jelly happen to become mixed up in the affair?"

With a face indicative of extreme pain Bony sighed. With slow significance he said:

"The qualification necessary in such a case is one which I possess to an acute degree and which in you, so far, I find lacking. You and our two chiefs are all lacking in patience. It is probable that you will eventually rise to the Western Australian Commissionership because you have organizing ability and an excellent address, but you will never make an outstanding detective. Colonel Spender is an excellent head of a police department, but he would be unequal to solving the mystery of a lost collar stud. In many respects Colonel Spender and you are akin."

"Don't rub it in too hard," Muir urged with heightened colour. "You have answered my first question in a most offensive way; now please answer the remaining two."

"Very well. How did I know that Loftus was buried in the haystack? Remember this significant point. It is undoubted that my investigations would have been greatly delayed if at Burracoppin I had announced myself as Detective-Inspector Napoleon Bonaparte. To have done so would have caused everyone to shrink into their little shells, as the customers at the hotel did when you appeared that evening. As a detective you are too distinguished. And your picture has appeared too often in the press.

"If Landon had known what I was he never would have invited me to examine the Loftus homestead the Sunday following the dance at the Jilbadgie Hall. He took me for precisely what I was supposed to be, and during my investigation of the homestead he became nervous only when we halted at the south end of the haystack. He thought then that the prowler of the night before suspected his secret and had been probing into it, and he simply had to know the truth about it. I pointed out tracks of the prowler which were not there, but I was interested less in deceiving him than in the abnormal number of blowflies buzzing and crawling deep in the hay.

"At this time I strongly suspected that Loftus had been murdered, for you will remember that I had evidence, which afterwards became definite proof, that Landon had recently slept in Mrs Loftus's bed and that Mrs Loftus had settled a garage account with new treasury notes of the same serial as that to which belonged the notes paid by the bank to her husband.

"The blowflies in the hay recalled the incident of Hurley's dog which, when with me one day, caught several rabbits. One of these dead rabbits I kicked into a posthole, and, filling in the hole, I rammed down the earth. Yet days afterwards the blowflies smelled the dead rabbit fifteen inches below the surface of the ground. It is the keen-scented blowfly that will hang Mick Landon.

"At the time George Loftus reached home from Perth, Landon, acting on his instructions, had started to cart hay to build the stack.

"He had laid the foundations of the stack, which that night was some three feet high. He was an alert young man, clever, as his social activities in Burracoppin proved, and his idea of burying the corpse near one end of the haystack, and proceeding to build over it, was original, you must admit.

"However, it does seem impossible for a murderer not to make at least one foolish mistake. The very act of homicide provides a shock sufficient to upset the balance, temporarily, of the human mind. Immediately the crime is committed the one thought excluding all others is how to hide the evidence of the crime. Having killed Loftus, the body had to be concealed somehow, anyhow. Like the man who realizes he is bushed, the murderer cannot sit down and calmly reason. Even though Landon had the cold Mrs Loftus at his back, he could not perceive that if the body was not buried deep below the ground surface the blowflies would be attracted. He reasoned that if the body was buried beneath tons of hay it would be out of sight, and, secondly, the hay in the stack, settling downwards, would become pressed into a solid mass around and above the corpse. He was fearful that if he buried the body the fresh-turned earth would attract attention, as it has done in many cases.

"The idea of burying a body deep in a haystack is good, but to conceal a body effectually he should have burrowed down through the foundations of the stack and dug a grave in the earth. With the stack above the grave the blowflies would not have been attracted, and the stack eventually could have been sold or cut into chaff. All that was lacking, John, was calmness at a critical moment, and, fortunately for humanity, the necessary calmness of mind is, usually, impossible in a murderer.

"Landon having broken down and confessed everything, we know that he and his paramour were in George Loftus's bed when the returning farmer knocked at the door. According to Landon, he only desired the woman for her sex attraction, but she was madly infatuated with him. A few minutes before Loftus knocked, the restless dogs had awakened them, and during those minutes when they sleepily debated why the dogs barked they did not hear a car pass along the main road. Therefore, when Loftus did demand admittance, they could have inferred that he walked home, that he had not driven his own car or had been brought home in any other.

"It does appear, and, having studied Mrs Loftus, it is more than credible, that what followed was a re-enactment of Macbeth. The woman urged; the man resisted the suggestion. But the woman's personality was the stronger, and the man obeyed her will. When she had lit the lamp in the kitchen Landon took a position where he would be behind the door when Mrs Loftus opened it. George Loftus stepped inside and Landon shot him through the head.

"They stripped the body. Landon dealt with it, and Mrs Loftus dealt with the clothes and articles they contained, cutting off the buttons, and, with the cigar case, silver match- box, watch and chain, buried them under the hearth in the japanned box. The collar pin, found among the notes in the woman's mattress, and which Wallace swears Loftus was wearing when they returned from Perth, is, perhaps, the most damning evidence against them after the proof that the bullet found in the dead man's skull was fired by the revolver I picked up near the road crossing the old York Road, and which Landon admits is his.

"And now, John, for your last question. Mr Jelly's part in the mystery concerning the disappearance of George Loftus is easily explained. He thought, as many people did, that the police had given up or deferred their inquiries. Believing that Loftus had not voluntarily disappeared, being suspicious that Mrs Loftus and Landon were lovers, he determined to do a little investigating himself. The first time he visited the homestead he was shot, and had, himself, to disappear till the slight wound he had received had healed sufficiently to enable him to conceal it. The second time he went to the farm he arrived after his daughter and myself, taking advantage of the farmers' meeting as I did; and, not being satisfied with feeding the dogs and thrashing one, he regrettably poisoned them. I do not agree with that act. The poor dogs were only loyal to their master. That is all, John. Even had Landon not confessed, you would have had more than enough evidence with which to hang him."

"Jelly must be an amateur detective," Muir said in his rapid manner. "Strange bird, Jelly! Did you know—— But when are you going back to Brisbane? Old Spender will be almost a lunatic by this time."

"Colonel Spender is a man of quick temper. He will not live as long as I will. The burning of life is hastened by violent emotion. I shall return to Queensland when I have finished a little private work totally unconnected with the police." Bony rose to his feet, and then added, when they began the townward walk: "This case should help you, John. Take all the credit you can. Never fail to blow your own trumpet, for worldly success depends upon one's ability to do that. Think of our alleged statesman: how they gab, gab, gab about themselves. Great fellows! Blue blood in them, John. Copy them, and you will rise high. Fail to do so, and you will remain hidden as are the scientific researchers—as I am."

John Muir gripped Bony affectionately by the arm, saying: "Bony, old man, thanks very much! You're a damned decent sort."

With well-controlled gravity Bony said, in order to hide how much he was touched by the other's act and words:

"When you are Commissioner you will give me far less worry regarding your career than you now do as a detective. The quicker I push you into the gilded chair, the sooner my worry will be removed."

Several days passed before Bony received the long- expected summons from the Merredin postmaster. In that official's office he was shown a telegram addressed to "Jelly— South Burracoppin." The message read: "Come Adelaide." On the reverse side of the form were written in a scrawl the words: "Sunflower Jelly—South Burracoppin."

"The clerk who received this telegram this morning remembered your previous inquiry and took special note of the sender," the official explained. "I am, therefore, able to tell you that the sender is a Mrs Chandler, who lives at 18 Mark Street, of this town.

"I am very much obliged to you," Bony said earnestly. "Do you know anything about this Mrs Chandler?"

"Next to nothing. She is, however, Mrs Westbury's sister."

"Indeed! Well, I'll go along and interview her. Again, I thank you very much. Good-bye!"

The woman who answered his knock on the door of 18 Mark Street was matronly and pleasant.

"Madam, you dispatched this morning a telegram to a Mr Jelly, of South Burracoppin," Bony stated sternly.

At once Mrs Chandler froze.

"I don't know what you mean," she said. "Who are you?"

"I am a detective employed by the Telegraph Department," he lied. "I am looking into the matter of a false declaration made on the back of a telegraph form. The counter clerk— —"

"I can say nothing about it," the woman cut in. "You had better see my brother-in-law, Sergeant Westbury, at the police station."

"Oh! Thank you. I will call on the sergeant," Bony said less frigidly, and, after raising his hat politely, walked off to the police station, hoping against hope that his long-growing suspicions about Mr Jelly were not proved truth and fact by the genial sergeant.

"Good day, sir!" exclaimed Sergeant Westbury, heaving himself to his feet when Bony entered the station office. The Burracoppin case being finalized, Westbury could find no further excuse for not paying due respect to his superior in rank. "Sit down, sir. Glad to see you—glad to see you, sir."

"Can you tell me, sergeant," Bony began when he was making a cigarette, "can you tell me why your sister-in-law sent a telegram to Mr Jelly, of South Burracoppin, this morning, in which she said: 'Come Adelaide'?"

"Eh! Well, yes, I can—I can." Sergeant Westbury became red of face and neck. "Mr Muir could have told you."

"Not wishing to put such a question to Muir, I refrained. I would not have put it to you, only I am pressed for time and must take the shortest cut, via yourself."

Sergeant Westbury came round his desk, drew close to Bony, stooped, and whispered into his ear.

"So that's it," Bony said softly. "I have been afraid it was. If I hadn't been so overruled by vanity when detailing my investigations to Muir, I would have sought his assistance. What you tell me explains Mr Jelly's morbid interest in criminology, and the roundabout way arranged for those telegrams to be sent him, and the success with which his extraordinary business was kept secret." Standing up, he held out his hand, adding: "I shall be leaving for Brisbane by tonight's express. Good-bye, sergeant! I have been much pleased with your valuable collaboration, and I have remembered you in my report."

"The pleasure is mine, sir—mine, sir—mine, sir," stuttered the delighted Westbury.

Slowly Bony sauntered to the Merredin Hospital.

Eric Hurley had given his blood to his sweetheart and now was recuperating in the Merredin Hotel as the guest of Mr Jelly. This afternoon Bony found Lucy much brighter and stronger in her bed in an isolated corner of a veranda ward of the hospital. When he had taken the chair at the head of the bed he looked down to find her regarding him shyly.

"I am afraid that being kind to me has delayed you returning to your home," she said. "Sunflower was here this morning, and she brought the table centre I wished to give to your wife. It was fortunate that I finished it before— before — —"

When she hesitated to refer to that night of terror Bony said swiftly:

"You are kindness itself. I shall never forget you or Sunflower. Sunflower promises to write to me sometimes. She is coming with your father and Eric at five o'clock. They are bringing afternoon tea, and I have induced the sister to lend us her teapot and permit us to boil water. We will have a kind of family tea, because I leave for Brisbane tonight on the express. As your father has business in Adelaide, we will travel together as far as that city."

"Has—has he had another telegram?"

"Yes, but you need not worry about it," he assured her with much earnestness. "As I promised you, I have found out what is his business, and it is really nothing of which he might be ashamed, although its nature is highly secretive. I am going to ask you to refrain from asking me questions about it, to be satisfied with what I tell you, and to believe me when I repeat that Mr Jelly is doing nothing of which he might be ashamed. Excepting the State of Queensland, your father's extensive knowledge of criminology is constantly in demand by the law officers of the Australian States; if Mr Jelly ever had to come to Queensland on his particular business, I should have known what I know about him today."

"You make me so happy," she cried softly. "I have been so afraid. I shall not now mind his going away. If he had only told me, it would not have been so bad."

"Well, as he promised me, he is going to give it up. When he returns from Adelaide he will be called to Perth, and after that he will go away no more. He has given me his word: he will keep it." Bony broke off to laugh. "You know," he continued, "you know, it is always wise to counter an attack with an attack. Your father sternly demanded what I meant by taking you to the Loftus homestead. Instead of expressing my real and honestly heartfelt regret, I counter-attacked by pointing out to him that he was not following his duty as a father by sneaking off now and then without telling you why he went away and where he went to. I reminded him of his promise to me; I told him that his goings on were disgraceful, and finally I told him that if he did not give you and Sunflower more attention that he would hear further from me."

Lucy sighed. Her eyes were very bright.

"I am glad there is no need to worry any more," she murmured.

"There is none whatever. I solved another little mystery this morning. I found out that your father and Eric have just paid the deposit on that vacant farm south of your own home. Eric must be leaving the Rabbit Department. I remember the farm they have bought. There is a very nice little house on it, isn't there?"

"Oh, Bony! True?" she asked, the fingers of one hand now at her lips.

He nodded. "And I've another piece of information," he said.

"What is that?"

"Sunflower says that she will never marry anyone because she cannot marry me," Bony explained gravely, and then laughed in his low, attractive manner. The expected visitors appeared at the farther end of the ward.

Quickly Bony leaned over the patient. He said:

"Don't tell them that we know about that farm deal, will you?"

Again Lucy sighed, her soul strangely at peace.

Bony's twinkling eyes beamed upon Mr Jelly advancing towards them. The cigar-shaped figure and the halo of grey hair above the farmer's ears made of him a picture of benevolence. Hurley smiled and nodded at Bony before falling on his knees beside the bed. Little Sunflower drew close to Bony, took one of his brown hands, and squeezed it.

Chapter Twenty-Seven

Landon Answers The Riddle

Mick Landon had not slept well. He awoke when the last day was full come. He lay with his eyes open for a long time whilst his mind struggled to dispel the terrible nightmare during which he had tried to flee from the monster, unseen and beyond the power of his imagination to create.

Presently his eyes became focused on a blot of discoloration in the centre of the whitewashed ceiling above him, and this mark, no larger than a crown piece, first puzzled him and then brought, with ever-increasing swiftness, realization of his situation. Now the familiar mental lethargy swept over his brain once again. It was a struggle against physical lassitude to rise from his bed. Dully he stared at the uniformed Recording Angel seated beyond the door grille of his cell.

There was a table there, and a warder had sat at it day and night for nearly three weeks, writing down every word spoken by him and to him and describing every action. Three warders took up the duty in timed shifts, and these Landon now knew to the individual wrinkles on their stern faces. Landon opened his mouth to speak, knew that the man on duty there would not answer him, refrained, and dressed slowly.

The chaplain came. The grille was unlocked to admit him and immediately relocked. He spoke of "Our Lord" and "Christ", and of the "salvation of souls". He suggested prayer, and, like an automaton, Landon sank on his knees beside the minister. He heard not a word of the plea to Christ to intercede with the Father for mercy on his soul. Without knowing what he said, he muttered the words of the Lord's Prayer.

It was strange how he felt that he was sleepwalking while being fully conscious of it, as though his mind was living one life and his body living another, the two lives running parallel, inseparable. His mental entity thought how strange it was that the minister's face was so haggard, whilst his bodily entity pointed out that the chaplain wanted badly a long holiday. When the minister reached the grille, and the warder was about to open it, Landon touched him on the shoulder. He said with effort: "Is it—is it today?"

Shocked by the knowledge that his spiritual charge had failed to understand the purport of his recent prayers, the minister could only nod his head in a helpless gesture before quickly making his escape.

A few minutes later a warder appeared with a tray and was admitted. He set the tray on the small clamped table.

"Your breakfast, Landon," he said kindly when Landon looked at him almost stupidly. "Come and sit down to it. We managed to wangle some nice crisp bacon and an egg. And a pot of strong coffee."

Before he sat down on the stool clamped to the floor like the table the wretched man leaned over the table and touched the warder on the coat sleeve. He said: "Is it—is it today?"

As the minister had done, the warder nodded. Then Landon sat down and mechanically ate his last breakfast. He ate slowly. He had utterly lost the sense of taste. Even the coffee was tasteless. The warder produced a carton of cigarettes, offered them to him, struck a match. Landon found, too, that he had lost his sense of smell. He saw the smoke which was expelled from his lungs but could not smell it. The warder withdrew, and Landon began to pace the cell.

His back was towards the grille when the doctor arrived. Hearing the lock click back, Landon swung round with suddenly flashing eyes, which quickly became lacklustre when he saw who was this visitor. "Well, Landon? How do you feel?" the medico inquired briskly.

"All right, doctor. Is it—is it today?"

With the ball of his index finger on Landon's pulse, the doctor nodded as the minister had done, as the warder had done. "You'll want a bracer," he said less briskly. "I've brought you one. It will make things easier."

When Landon had drunk the draught in the aluminium tumbler he said:

"What is the time, sir?" To which the doctor replied: "Don't know. My watch has gone bung. Don't worry."

When the doctor had gone Landon leaned against the grille, his fingers clenched round the bars. The recording warder looked stolidly at his book—or appeared to be so doing. "What's the time, warder?" Landon asked.

The warder made no reply. He was writing in his book.

Presently to Landon came the sound of quick steps of several men in the passage beyond his line of vision. The many footsteps were timed like those of a squad of soldiers. The warder stood up. The man's eyes appeared as though fixed, even though the lids almost obscured them. He did not look at the prisoner.

Beyond the grille two men appeared dressed in civilian clothes. Things they carried gleamed like polished steel. Behind them stood several warders, the chaplain wearing his surplice, the doctor, the governor.

Whilst the two civilians passed into the cell Landon's gaze was fixed on the weatherbeaten face of the taller, who walked forward towards him. With the coming of this man, whose face he remembered so well, every weight hanging to his muscles was lifted. He became buoyant with life. The lethargy vanished. He wondered why the tall man regarded him with frozen features. The other man slipped behind him. The tall man gripped Landon's wrists. He said: "It is a time for courage."

Then Mick Landon knew. He was not a friend, this tall, powerful man with the halo of grey hair resting on his ears. He was —! He was —! Landon screamed.

"Mr Jelly! Mr Jelly! I won't go! I tell you, I won't go, Mr Jelly!"

CPSIA information can be obtained
at www.ICGtesting.com
Printed in the USA
BVHW04s2047100618
518684BV00033B/208/P